One Body   One Spirit
One Hope   One Baptism
One Faith   One Father
One God
One Lord   **one**

One day at a time

The Regional Church of Lancaster County
www.theregionalchurch.com

West Cocalico
East Cocalico
Clay
Elizabeth
Penn
Ephrata   East Lampeter
Warwick   West Lampeter
Manheim   Lancaster
West Earl   Strasburg
Earl   Paradise
East Earl   Sadsbury
Brecknock   Bart
Caernarvon   Colerain
Salisbury   Little Britain
Leacock   Fulton
Upper Leacock   Drumore
                                East Drumore
                                Providence
                                Eden
                                Martic
                                Conestoga
                                Pequea
ONE Devotional   Manor
                                West Hempfield
© 2005 by The Regional Church of Lancaster County   East Hempfield
Lancaster, Pennsylvania, USA   East Donegal
www.regionalchurch.com   West Donegal
                                                     Conoy
Mount Joy
                                                     Rapho
ISBN: 1-9760387-0-6

Printed in the United States of America

Dedication

This book is dedicated to the people of
Lancaster County, Pennsylvania.

Acknowledgments

Thank you to the many contributing authors who made this book possible.
Edited by Mark Ammerman, Karen Boyd, Joanne Stauffer, Becky Toews and Keith Yoder.
House To House Publications Team: Lesley Johnson, Karen Ruiz, Sarah Sauder and Carolyn Sprague.

Thanks also goes to the photographers and organizations who allowed their work to be used in this project:
Don and Amy Barley
Leslie Bistline, Sullivan Studios
Habitat for Humanity
1719 Hans Herr House
In the Light Ministries
Beth Karpel
Lancaster Bible College
Landis Valley Museum
Michelle Long
Audrey Martin
Voni Metzler
Martin's Studio of Photography
Sight and Sound Theatres
Susan's Photography
Susquehanna Valley Pregnancy Services
TrueLight Communications: JeremyHess
Mark and Donna Van Scyoc
Water Street Rescue Mission
Willow Valley Resort and Conference Center

Fraktur by Ceci Good

Introduction

Welcome to ONE—a devotional experience to enrich your relationship with God. ONE is also an invitation to fellowship with over 200 authors and thousands of readers from Lancaster County.

We who trust in Jesus Christ alone for our salvation share in common one body, one Spirit, one hope, one Lord, one faith, one baptism, one God, and one Father (Ephesians 4:4–6).

Drawing from this common faith, the devotions in this book inspire in three ways:

1. The meditations nurture and challenge our spiritual growth.
2. Getting acquainted with authors throughout the County enlarges our appreciation for the Body of Christ.
3. The realization that thousands of fellow Lancaster Countians are agreeing in prayer daily is one way we "endeavor to keep the unity of the Spirit in the bond of peace (Ephesians 4:3 KJV)."

In one sense, ONE is an opportunity for us to participate in the fulfillment of Jesus' prayer in John 17:21 (NKJV) "that they all may be one, as You, Father, are in Me, and I in You; that they also may be one in Us, that the world may believe that You sent Me."

Many of the New Testament authors penned their inspired letters to the Body of Christ in a certain city or region (for example, the book of Ephesians was written to the "saints who are at Ephesus."). In a similar way today, the church in our region may be called the *regional church of Lancaster County.*

ONE is sponsored by the Regional Church of Lancaster County, a network of Christian leaders in relational partnerships that serve the church in our region. Through united prayer, witness unto Christ, strengthening the well-being of the church, and loving service, we trust the Lord to transform our region for His purposes. (See page 383.)

Through ONE, we can partner with the Lord to transform our region—one day at a time.

Keith E. Yoder, chair of the Regional Council of the Regional Church of Lancaster County.

Supporting life in
Lancaster County

January

Revival

[Ezra] "prayed: 'O my God, I am too ashamed and disgraced to lift up my face to you, my God, because our sins are higher than our heads and our guilt has reached to the heavens. From the days of our forefathers until now, our guilt has been great. Because of our sins, we and our kings and our priests have been subjected to the sword and captivity, to pillage and humiliation at the hand of foreign kings, as it is today.

Pray!
for Lancaster County

'But now, for a brief moment, the LORD our God has been gracious in leaving us a remnant and giving us a firm place in his sanctuary, and so our God gives light to our eyes and a little relief in our bondage. Though we are slaves, our God has not deserted us in our bondage. He has shown us kindness in the sight of the kings of Persia: He has granted us new life to rebuild the house of our God and repair its ruins, and he has given us a wall of protection in Judah and Jerusalem.'"

Ezra 9:6–9

In order for revival to happen in our region, we need the Lord to stir His people to pray! We are a part of the rebuilding of the "house of our God", as our hearts break with repentance over our sins and the sins of the generations before us. Let us ask God for increased dependence upon Him, recognizing and declaring Him our only hope, as we cry out for revival and spiritual breakthrough in our county!

Lord, forgive me for my self-reliance. Reduce me to desperation and dependence upon You. Help me to find others this week and join with them to agree in prayer for revival in Lancaster county. But first let it begin in me.

Today's devotional was edited from the 2003–2004 *Throne Of Grace Prayer Guide*, a weekly guide of Lancaster County prayer concerns gathered from regional intercessors and area prayer groups.

January 2

Clean Out The Attic

"...since you have taken off your old self with its practices and have put on the new self, which is being renewed in knowledge in the image of its Creator. Therefore, as God's chosen people, holy and dearly loved, clothe yourselves with compassion, kindness, humility, gentleness and patience."
Colossians 3:9–10,12

One day while cleaning out the attic of an apartment building, I went digging through boxes left by tenants long gone. Buried under other relics I came across some old, quite out-dated suits. It reminded me of a story my friend George told me.

One summer George found himself teaching a group of high school students with many bad attitudes. Before class, he purposefully dug out an old, outdated suit at home. He later walked into his classroom wearing the outfit. He told his students their attitudes were just like a cheap suit—ugly and poorly fitting. He quickly tossed off the old clothes to display a championship sweatshirt underneath.

What old things are in the attic of your heart? As we begin this new year, what better time to look around and see what's really there. Are we wearing some "cheap suit" attitudes? Would we look better to the world in a different set of attitudes?

What better season to get rid of old baggage. Clean up the clutter to make room in your heart for new plans and ideas. Maybe there are a few treasured items that need to be dusted off and put to good use again. Leave past failures at the foot of the cross. Be ready for doors of opportunity this coming year that God will open just for you, God's dearly loved child.

Lord, thank You for giving us life today. Help us to see Your goodness in each and every day. Refresh and renew our thinking as we embrace the gift of time that You have given us. May our thoughts and actions reflect You today and this coming year.

Sarah Sauder is the director of House to House Publications.

At Home

"...that Christ may dwell in your hearts through faith...."
Ephesians 3:17

This prayer was offered for the church at Ephesus, for those who were already believers in Jesus Christ and who therefore knew what it was to have Christ living in them. This raises a question as to why Paul would pray that Christ may "dwell" in their hearts when Jesus Christ was already present there.

The answer is found in the word "dwell." The Greek word translated "dwell" has in it the thought of "settling down and being at home." Quite some years ago a small booklet was written by Dr. Robert B. Munger entitled "My Heart Christ's Home." This booklet explains what Paul meant when he employed the word "dwell." It includes the following thoughts:

1) Every area of our lives will be accessible to Christ.
2) All that takes place in our lives will be acceptable to Him.
3) And every part of us will be available for His will and purpose.

What an appropriate prayer for us today, just as it was for the saints at Ephesus. May the Lord have total access to every area of our lives. May all that we permit in our lives be totally acceptable to Him. And may every part of our lives be totally available to Him for His will and service.

In that lovely hymn entitled "Channels Only" one stanza concludes with the words "Thou who boughtest to possess us, in Thy fullness, Lord come in." That is an invitation to Jesus Christ to "dwell" and thus to be "at home" in us.

O, Lord, may You so dwell in us in your fullness that You may be able to "settle down and be totally at home" in our hearts and lives. For Your dear name's sake. Amen.

Rev. Dr. Eric G. Crichton, Pastor Emeritus at Calvary Church, Lancaster.

January 4

Strategic Discernment Vs. Strategic Planning

"Your eyes saw my unformed body. All the days ordained for me were written in your book before one of them came to be."
Psalm 139:16

Years ago while preparing for our annual Senior Leadership Retreat I was laboring over our strategic plan. Struggling for inspiration, I picked up the Bible to see what God says about strategic planning. I searched the scripture and found Psalms 139:16 and Ephesians 1:11. It suddenly became clear. If God ordained all my days for me, if God works everything in conformity with the purpose of His will, why am I laboring over our strategic plan? Shouldn't I try to discern His will for my business? I knew that God had a specific purpose for me. I now realized His plan included my business.

How do we seek God's will for our organization? God speaks through His word (Psalms 119:105; 2 Timothy 3:16). God speaks to our hearts (Proverbs 16:9 and 21:1). God speaks through control of circumstances (Proverbs 20:24, Ephesians 11:1). God speaks through others (Proverbs 11:14, 15:22, 20:18, 24:6).

Are you discerning God's will for your organization or pursuing your own strategic plans? Through what circumstances has God been speaking? Have you sought Godly counsel? Have you spent time, quiet before the Lord in prayer and the word, allowing Him to direct your thoughts? When you do, God will reveal His plan in His timing. Be patient and surrender your will in lieu of His. Realize there is no greater calling, no greater source of satisfaction, than to fulfill His will. The burden of defining strategy and setting direction can be overwhelming. Instead surrender your burden and discern God's perfect will for your organization. Experience the freedom of relying on Him!

Father, give me the desire to surrender my agenda and discern Your will. Grant me discipline to listen for Your voice. Grant me courage to execute Your plan for my life for Your glory. Amen.

Kent Martin is the president/CEO of Signature Custom Cabinetry, Inc.

January 5

Ropes And Rags

"Ebed-Melech the Cushite said to Jeremiah, 'Put these old rags and worn-out clothes under your arms to pad the ropes....'" *Jeremiah 38:12*

E bed-Melech's job was to get Jeremiah out of the cistern. Ropes would have been enough to get the job done. Because Jeremiah had been stuck in the deep, thick mud of that cistern many days, he was very weak and frail. While the ropes would have been enough to get Jeremiah out of the well, they would have literally torn his body apart. Ebed-Melech realized that if he was going to actually rescue Jeremiah, he would have to do it gently.

Sometimes the job seems obvious: a word of correction to a brother or sister, a class lesson to be taught, a new ministry started, an outreach to be initiated. We have the means, the methods and the materials. But ministry is not just a job to accomplish. It is also the process and attitude by which the job is done. We must pray, not only for God to show us what to do and help us to get it done, but also that God will put us and keep us in a proper heart-attitude. When we try to minister to someone and we begin to get frustrated because "they just aren't getting it," that's a signal that we need to confess to God a wrong heart and ask Him for His heart.

In calling us into His work, God intends to give us both His ropes and His rags. Many times, in His ministry to the needy, we're told that Jesus "had compassion on them" (Matthew 9:36, 14:14, 20:34; Mark 6:34). If we will meditate on Jesus, we'll see not only the ropes God uses but also His very own rags.

Thank you, Lord, that You have rescued me out of the pit. Jesus, let Your heart beat within me, that I might rescue others with the same compassion with which You have rescued me.

Jim Gambini pastors the Mount Pleasant Brethren in Christ Church in Mount Joy.

January 6

Tree Climber

"He wanted desperately to see Jesus, but the crowd was in his way..." *Luke 19:3 (The Message)*

Zacchaeus was desperate to see Jesus, but he was small. His disadvantage did not become his excuse. He did not allow it to keep him from seeing Jesus. Instead, he was absolutely committed to seeing Jesus more clearly.

Zacchaeus' commitment lead to creativity. Instead of saying, "I'm too small to see Jesus," he said, "Because I'm small, I need to find another way to see Him." Then he saw a tree. He could have seen the tree as another hindrance blocking his view. Instead, he climbed it.

Jesus is always attracted to spiritual "tree climbers", those who are committed to seeing Him more clearly. Jesus saw Zacchaeus' hunger, and rewarded him. The crowd however, was very upset at Jesus for befriending a tax collector.

This story challenges me in two ways. First, am I desperate to see Jesus impact my life? What am I doing to position myself so I can better see Him and know Him? Do I allow handicaps and limitations to stop me from seeing Him or do I press through the distractions of this world? Am I a spiritual "tree climber", willing to take a risk? Or, am I a "tree hugger", holding on to excuses and never leaving the ground to get a better view? Let's commit to "tree climbing" because the view is always worth the climb.

The second challenge is in the area of association. Jesus was willing to get cozy with crooks. Jesus knew His purpose. He came to seek and save the lost, which required associating with them. Can there be a revelation of Jesus without association? The value of one lost man was worth the risk of association to Jesus. Let's determine to associate with lost people with the intent to influence them with the Good News.

Father, increase our passion for You, resulting in a greater passion for the lost. Help us to be willing to pay the price.

Merrill Smucker, pastor of Gap Community Church.

January 7

Burning Our Plow

"So Elisha left him and went back. He took his yoke of oxen and slaughtered them. He burned the plowing equipment to cook the meat and gave it to the people, and they ate. Then he set out to follow Elijah and became his attendant."
1 Kings 19:21

The writer of 1 Kings 19 records how Elisha was chosen to be Elijah's successor. We know that Elisha was a farmer since it is recorded that he was plowing with twelve yoke of oxen at the time of his calling. We could even speculate that he enjoyed his work and was good at it. Yet, when God's call came, Elisha was willing to put it all behind him and accept the call. He even decided to have an impromptu feast. He destroyed his plowing equipment to roast the oxen. Never again would he plow with this pair of oxen.

There could come a time in our lives when God asks us to "burn our plow". He may ask us to leave a job we love and in which we feel very secure to go do something completely new. Sometimes God has to help us "burn our plow". This can happen when we are reluctant to leave what we're comfortable with to take on His new assignment. He may allow our job to be eliminated or our business to fail so He can take us in a new direction.

Regardless of how God sends us in a new direction, if we are willing to be obedient, we can expect Him to fulfill His plan and purpose for our life. Elisha was obedient to God's call and was empowered to carry on the work that Elijah began. God will do the same for us.

Dear Lord, I know that You have a plan and purpose for my life. Guide each step I take so it will conform to what You have planned for me. In the Mighty Name of Jesus I pray, Amen!

Steve Shull, member of the Executive Committee of Connecting Business Men to Christ of Lancaster.

Father, Forgive Us

"'Now, O Lord our God, who brought your people out of Egypt with a mighty hand and who made for yourself a name that endures to this day, we have sinned, we have done wrong. O Lord, in keeping with all your righteous acts, turn away your anger and your wrath from Jerusalem, your city, your holy hill. Our sins and the iniquities of our fathers have made Jerusalem and your people an object of scorn to all those around us. 'Now, our God, hear the prayers and petitions of your servant...We do not make requests of you because we are righteous, but because of your great mercy. O Lord, listen! O Lord, forgive! O Lord, hear and act! For your sake, O my God, do not delay, because your city and your people bear your Name.'" *Daniel 9:15–19*

Pray! for Lancaster County

D aniel interceded to the Lord on behalf of his people. Because corporate sins brought the wrath of God on the city, Daniel confessed on behalf of his people. We too have the opportunity to intercede for our generation and petition God for forgiveness for the innocent blood on the land that has been shed through abortion.

Father God, I ask You to give Christ's bride a voice of righteous thunder to speak the truth of his word, birthing LIFE in our region and across our nation. I pray for the many Christian ministries in our region working on behalf of the unborn and their mothers. I ask You to provide them with workers and financial provision. I ask You to bless them and give them favor in their communities and with the men and women they seek to serve. Show me how I might partner with one of these ministries through prayer, volunteering, or financial help.

Today's devotional was edited from the 2003–2004 *Throne Of Grace Prayer Guide*, a weekly guide of Lancaster County prayer concerns gathered from regional intercessors and area prayer groups.

January 9

Every Part

"The body has many parts...and each one of you is...a part of it." *1 Corinthians 12:14,27 (Living Bible)*

Did you ever walk through the mall and see a man in a wheelchair? Or a lady tip-tapping along with a red-tipped, white cane? Did you ever hear someone trying desperately to get the words out to a sales clerk and being asked over and over, "What did you say?"

"Too bad," you thought. And you walked on.

But the man in the wheelchair is still in his chair, the lady with the cane still needs it to "see", and cerebral palsy's distorted speech is still unintelligible. These people live with their disabilities, day after day, month after month, and year after year—their entire lives.

Most people with disabilities travel this world alone. Family members don't understand; friends have deserted them. In a world of "normal" people, they do not belong. That world includes the church. Nine out of ten people with severe disabilities never attend church; they feel ashamed, afraid, and unwelcome.

But God has a different idea. To Him, a church full of "normal" people is not a complete body. He knew every person with a disability before birth (Psalm 139). He allows disabilities (Exodus 4:11) so that He can show his works through those with disabilities (John 9:2–3).

Every part of the body of Christ serves a vital role in its function (1 Corinthians 12). Everyone in the church should go out into the streets and bring people with disabilities in, so that His house may be full (Luke 14:23).

Look around your own church. Is the body there complete? Or is it time for you to go into the streets and bring others in?

Lord, forgive my blindness in not seeing that every part of the body of Christ is vital. Give me the wisdom and compassion to go out and bring all in so that the body may be whole. Amen.

Bob Weaver is the area director of Joni and Friends, the Disability Outreach of Joni Eareckson Tada.

Words To Live By

"The LORD is my shepherd; I shall not be in want..." *Psalm 23*

During days of grief this beloved psalm is often requested for memorial services. Millions have found comfort in these immortal words, and rightly so. However, these are also words to live by. Imagine that this is King David's testimony. His words reflect his choice. "The Lord is my shepherd."

Picture David in your mind, as an old man, a blank scroll unrolled before him. He reflects. His mind wanders back over the years, a smile flickers, and he is again a shepherd boy wandering the hills and valleys of ancient Judah with his father's sheep. He leads them to pasture and quiet waters. The next moment he is a young teenager with a sling and a few small stones. He is a hero. The smile darkens to a scowl as he finds himself in the palace gazing out over the rooftops of his kingdom. His body shudders at the recollection of his sin and its horrible consequences. Then his countenance becomes peaceful, as if a storm has subsided, replaced by sunshine and calm.

King David shakes his head as if to clear away the cobwebs of his reverie. He picks up the quill, dips it in the ink well, and begins to write. "The Lord is my shepherd....He leads me...He restores my soul...He guides me...Even though I walk through the valley of the shadow of death, I will fear no evil, You are with me...comfort me...I will dwell in the house of the Lord forever."

Dear Jesus, I choose You as my Shepherd. My life is full of hills and valleys, and I need You to lead me to pastures, to water, to righteousness. Forgive me for my sins and be my Savior as well as my Shepherd. In Jesus' name, Amen.

Harry Dow serves as senior pastor at Trinity ECC in Lititz.

Teach Us To Pray

"This, then, is how you should pray: 'Our Father in heaven, hallowed be your name. your kingdom come, your will be done, on earth as it is in heaven.'" *Matthew 6:9–10*

Charlie Peacock, our family's favorite musician-author wrote a lovely song with these lyrics: "Lord teach me to pray, not what to say/Not how to get what I want/Lord You understand what I am asking I know that You do..." This song mirrors the request of the disciples in the Matthew passage. We understand that this is how we should pray. And as God's adopted children we desire to approach Him as He directs. Yet deep down inside, I often wish Jesus had said, "Pray like this: 'Abracadabra, gimme gimme gimme. Amen.'" Too many of my prayers default into that form. I know what I want and I know what is best, don't I? But if we were to step back and look at our lives, we'd all agree with C.S. Lewis when he wrote, "If God had granted all the silly prayers I've made in my life, where should I be now?" We don't know what is best for us, but the sovereign God who chose to love us before time began knows. And what a comfort that is. Certainly we should lay our requests before Him, but above all we should pray, "Your kingdom come, your will be done, because when His will is done," it will be for our good in the end.

Our Father in heaven, hallowed be Your name. Your kingdom come, Your will be done, on earth as it is in heaven. Give us this day our daily bread, and forgive us our debts, as we also have forgiven our debtors. And lead us not into temptation, but deliver us from evil. For Yours is the kingdom and the power and the glory forever and ever. Amen.

Ned Bustard plans worship for Wheatland Presbyterian Church. He also works in Lancaster as an illustrator/graphic designer and creative director.

January 12

The Reward Of Righteousness

"He who pursues righteousness and love finds life, prosperity and honor." *Proverbs 21:21*

Righteousness is the ability to do right in every circumstance. It's the ability to conform to the highest standards of justice and do what is morally right. Why is it that our world has so many problems? We have more people in jail now than any other time in history. Crime rates are staggering, and "worldly things" have seemed to take over people's lives. Our Lord has taught us that as the end times come, we will see a moral decay such as the world has never seen. He warns all Christians to be aware that even the "elect" can be deceived. You don't have to look too far to see that this is happening. Even in our own families, this can be found to be happiness.

Personally, I have seen this decay. I have been challenged many times to do the right thing when opportunities have presented themselves. It's not easy being righteous in today's world. However, the Lord demands it of all of us and blesses us for being righteous. It is a battle we must fight everyday. The book of Matthew tells us, "Blessed are those who hunger and thirst for righteousness… (Matthew 5:6)."

I pray each day that I never take my eyes off of the Lord, and that I do what He wants me to do, not what I would like to do. I pray that all people see the might of the Lord, and they would see that being a righteous person is pleasant in the sight of the Lord. I pray that we all can be beacons of light for our Lord Jesus Christ and that we live our lives to reflect His glory so that we may find life, prosperity and honor, as He has promised.

Rich Garipoli is chief of police for Warwick Township, and a board member of Liberty Character Institute.

One

Set A Fire Under Us

"...His word is in my heart like a fire, a fire shut up in my bones. I am weary of holding it in; indeed, I cannot." *Jeremiah 20:9*

Sometimes I feel like I need to set a fire under my children to get them to have any passion or enthusiasm for obeying. Again and again I can make a simple request, such as, "Grace, put your shoes on." A few minutes later she's engrossed in a book, shoes nowhere to be seen. Again I say, "Grace, put your shoes on, please!" Next time I look, there's one shoe on the wrong foot and the other in her mouth as she connects trains together on the floor. To any parent, this lack of response can be frustrating.

Unfortunately, we can have the same type of slow obedience with our heavenly Father. Perhaps you've felt a tugging from the Lord to reach out to a neighbor, picket an abortion clinic, or to get involved in an upcoming election, but for one reason or another have not followed through. Just as we are blessed when our children quickly obey, God is honored when we are expedient in our obedience to Him.

Oh God, give me a passion to quickly obey Your words to me. I pray I'd be "weary of holding it in," that I could be more effective in standing for righteousness and building Your kingdom.

Sarah Erk, wife and mother of three children, serves on the Deaconate Team at New Covenant Christian Church in Washington Boro.

January 14

Now Faith

"Now faith…" *Hebrews 11:1*

Although we typically look at the first verse of Hebrews 11 as the classic definition of faith, I have recently been struck by the first two words: now faith…NOW FAITH…**NOW FAITH**. When is the time for faith? Now. If you have been wrestling in prayer for days, months, or even years, for a specific burden, now is not the time to give up. Now is the time for faith.

It seems that God is always presenting us with dreams we cannot fulfill by ourselves. That's because He wants us to learn how to rely on Him. Not an easy task in this self-sufficient age. But we have the *author and finisher of our faith* to teach us how. Remember in Mark, chapter 5, how Jesus was confronted with three seemingly hopeless situations: a man with a *legion* of demons, a woman who had been suffering from a wasting disease for *twelve years,* and a ruler whose daughter had just died? Each situation appeared impossible. But *now faith* in God produced sanity, healing, and life. And that's only one chapter!

All too often we believe we've heard from God. But invariably the exact opposite of what we expected seems to happen. This is where our faith meets the test it must if it is to develop. Abraham is promised that he will be the father of multitudes, yet Sarah remains barren. Joseph is given a dream that his brothers will bow down to him, but is sold as a slave in Egypt. Paul receives the call to be a light to the Gentiles, yet meets imprisonment, floggings, and shipwreck. People of faith are those who have learned to *call forth what is not as if it were.* And God, in His grace, gives us ample opportunity to embrace the lesson.

Father, please give us strength today to persevere in faith, calling forth the promises You have given us that Your Kingdom may be advanced.

Becky Toews leads the Women's Ministry at New Covenant Christian Church, where her husband pastors.

One

January 15

Let Us Be ONE That All May Be WON!

Pray!

for Lancaster County

"How good and pleasant it is when brothers live together in unity! It is like precious oil poured on the head, running down on the beard, running down on Aaron's beard, down upon the collar of his robes. It is as if the dew of Hermon were falling on Mount Zion. For there the LORD bestows his blessing, even life forevermore." *Psalm 133:1–3*

"Here there is no Greek or Jew, circumcised or uncircumcised, barbarian, Scythian, slave or free, but Christ is all, and is in all." *Colossians 3:11*

"Do not let any unwholesome talk come out of your mouths, but only what is helpful for building others up according to their needs, that it may benefit those who listen. And do not grieve the Holy Spirit of God, with whom you were sealed for the day of redemption." *Ephesians 4:29–30*

Have we tolerated racism and allowed gender, cultural, and generational differences to divide us in the body of Christ and in our communities? Have we spoken gossip, slander and unrighteous judgments against others? Let us repent and ask God to forgive us and let us work together to love one another

Lord, help me to embrace those who seem different than me. Show me someone this week, whom I can take the time to get to know better. By Your grace, I will love them with Your love.

Today's devotional was edited from the 2003–2004 *Throne Of Grace Prayer Guide*, a weekly guide of Lancaster County prayer concerns gathered from regional intercessors and area prayer groups.

January 16

Walk With God

"He has shown you, O man, what is good. And what does the Lord require of you? To act justly and love mercy and to walk humbly with your God." *Micah 6:8*

God is telling us how to come into His presence and what is acceptable to Him. As we walk with God each day, He wants us to be servant leaders, honoring Him in everything we do. Our decisions need to be based on what is right in God's eyes, following the examples of his son, Jesus. We should be asking "what would God have us do in each situation."

God wants us to have a heart of compassion for others, treating others as Jesus did. Our focus needs to be on God's great love for us and the expectation that we share His love with others, in all we do. Peter wrote, "Each one should use whatever gift he has received to serve others, faithfully administering God's grace in its various forms (1 Peter 4:10)."

God wants us to walk each day with Him in an intimate relationship that would guide our thoughts and actions. Our faith should grow stronger through the knowledge and experiences that we gain through our daily walk with Him. It is important to do all these things with a humble heart, thanking God each day for His love, mercy, and grace.

Dear God, thank You for loving us and being someone who walks with us each day. Help us to do what is right and focus on the needs of others. Be near to us, dear Lord, and guide our thoughts and actions. Help us to have a heart of compassion and humility, so that we honor You in all we do.

William Worley, superintendent of schools, Cocalico School District; chairperson, board of trustees, Evangelical School of Theology; ministry council president, St. Paul's Evangelical Congregational Church.

Prepare To Stand

"Therefore put on God's complete armor, that you may be able to resist and stand your ground on the evil day, and having done all the crisis demands, to stand firmly in your place. Stand therefore, having tightened the belt of truth around your loins and having put on the breastplate of integrity and of moral rectitude and right standing with God, and having shod your feet in preparation to face the enemy with the firm-footed stability, the promptness, and the readiness produced by the good news of the gospel of peace. Lift up over all the shield of saving faith upon which you can quench all the flaming missiles of the wicked one and take the helmet of salvation, and the sword that the spirit wields, which is the Word of God." *Ephesians 6:13-17 (Amplified Version)*

As we "Prepare to Stand" let's put on the armor of God. Let truth, God's truth, be our standard which "covers" us as a loincloth. Let integrity, as a breastplate (based on right standing with God) protect our hearts, the place from which life proceeds. As we stay on the message, the gospel of peace, we will neither waver nor stumble. When we express our faith, it becomes a weapon which will quench the missiles (accusations, way of thinking) of the wicked one(s). We allow the helmet of salvation to protect our thinking, to keep us from deception. Let's use the sword of the Spirit, the Word of God, to defend our position.

In our times, it is imperative that we prepare in this way to stand. We will be tested. Only the Word of God will stand the test. Our opinions or emotional arguments (arguments based on feelings, not truth) will fail.

Father God, enable us to "put on" Your armor, to prepare through our spiritual disciplines for the tests that will come. Let us base our preparation on the only true and stable foundation, Your Word. Amen.

Bruce Warner is distribution foreman at Caterpillar, Inc. and a prophetic intercessor.

January 18

What Is It That Troubles You?

"He asked them, 'What are you discussing together as you walk along?'...One of them . . . asked him, 'Are you only a visitor...and do not know the things that have happened these days?' 'What things?' he asked..." *Luke 24:17–19*

S ometimes we experience disappointments, frustrations and help-lessness. We find a friend and we talk about the things that have happened. Our "faces are downcast." We see only the things that caused the frustration and disappointments.

We forget that, as believers, Jesus is walking beside us. And in our preoccupation with our troubles, we are not aware of His presence. He asks, "What is it that troubles you?"

We say, "Don't you know all the things that have happened to me?" He asks "What things?" Jesus wants us to be specific. He tells us to talk to Him in prayer, to bring our burdens to Him and He will give us rest (Matthew 11:28–30). He takes us to the Scriptures. It is there that we find the heart of Jesus and His care for us. It is there that we find the fatherly discipline of His love (Hebrews 12:5–11). It is there that we find that the things that have happened to us are to strengthen us as His servants (Philippians 2:12).

When I invite Jesus into my life and share with Him and He with me, I find rest (Luke 24:29 and Revelation 3:20). I find renewed energy to live life in the power of His resurrection (Luke 24:33–34).

"Dear God, deliver me from the prison of my situation and circumstance. Help me to be aware always of Your presence and Your desire to have me share life's happenings with You. I desire Your involvement in my life and I open up it up to You. I want the power of Jesus' resurrection to motivate me to declare the good news to those around me. In the name of Jesus, Amen.

H. Howard Witmer, retired bishop and administrator in the Lancaster Conference of the Mennonite Church.

January 19

Always Pray

"I thank my God every time I remember you. In all my prayers for all of you, I always pray with joy because of your partnership in the gospel from the first day until now, being confident of this, that he who began a good work in you will carry it on to completion until the day of Jesus Christ." *Philippians 1:3–6*

In today's world the church needs the best thinkers and prayers. We call this intercession. Every time Paul remembered the Philippian believers, he prayed for them. He prayed what was in God's heart for them, that the good work started in them would go on and on and never stop until Jesus came for them. This is communion with God at any time and any place.

Persistence is the part of intercession where we pray until we hear God telling us that He hears and He will take over. Hannah persisted and got her wish and her son blessed many (1 Samuel 1:11). Daniel prayed daily regardless of the consequences (Daniel 3). The woman who touched the hem of Jesus garment experienced healing (Matthew 9:20,21). Intercessors always have their ears open for prayer needs. We say "flash" prayers, asking God to wake people to a new beginning.

There is great joy in praying and being in communion with God. Solomon said, "...There is no God like you in heaven or on earth (2 Chronicles 6:14)." He gives strength and hope each day if we keep turning toward him.

Lord, keep my mind clear and fresh each day with the thoughts You want me to have. Do not let me fall into the sin that so easily besets us as human beings. I give myself to You today. Direct my day as I give myself to You. In the name of Jesus. Amen.

Miriam M. Witmer, wife, mother and volunteer at Landis Homes Retirement Community and Mennonite Central Committee.

January 20

Temple Maintenance

"Do you not know that your body is a temple of the Holy Spirit, who is in you, whom you have received from God? You are not your own; you were bought with a price" *1 Corinthians 6:19–20*

You are a temple—perhaps a little different than the edifice built by Solomon, but the dwelling place of the Holy Spirit of God nonetheless. There was a whole team of Levites to take care of Solomon's temple but how carefully do you take care of your temple of the Spirit? Is it time for some temple maintenance? Desecration of the stone temple was carefully avoided—who was allowed to enter it was carefully monitored, and what took place there was strictly controlled. Are you that cautious with what goes into your body? Are you careful about what food goes in, what pictures you see, drugs (including cigarettes and alcohol) that enter?

What are you doing about regular exercise? (If you don't use it, you lose it!).

When was the last time you had a checkup, or appropriate screening tests? How can you know that the temple needs work without checking? You get your car inspected because the state requires it, and hopefully you change the oil occasionally—Your Holy Spirit residence deserves at least as much!

Remember, when you abuse your body, you are mistreating the Spirit's house, and when you take care of your health, you are making a nicer abode for the Holy Spirit.

Is there something you need to do today to take care of the physical part of your being? Just do it!

Dear Heavenly Father, Help me to be wise in caring for the body that You gave me and which now is the resting place of Your Spirit. Fill me with Your Spirit so that I can live for You. Amen.

Chip Mershon is a family physician at Cornerstone Family Health in Lititz is chairman of the board of the Water Street Rescue Mission Medical Clinic and is active at Lancaster Evangelical Free Church.

January 21

Seek First His Kingdom

"Are you so foolish? After beginning with the Spirit, are you now trying to attain your goal by human effort?" *Galatians 3:3*

Goals, ambitions, and aspirations—we all have them. I think of the Christian who has wholeheartedly submitted to God's will and trusts the Spirit of God to move in his life. Does he ever default to attaining these goals through his own human efforts?

Paul asks the Galatian believers some important questions that we should ask ourselves (Galatians 3:1–5). But the question in particular that gripped my attention is the one mentioned above.

Over time, is it our tendency to more easily and quickly rely on our efforts to attain goals? Personally, the answer is yes; I have found this to be true in my life. Often, I find myself making a decision based on something I have heard or read, or by trusting my judgment from past experiences. I neglect to seek first the Spirit for wisdom and direction. Perhaps we all run ahead of God more than we realize.

I find this interesting. When we first come to faith in Jesus Christ, our view of self changes. Our weaknesses show us how much we need the Lord. We realize how dependent on Him we really are. Yet, over time we fall away from that reliance on God. How tempting it is to try and attain goals for Christ using our own skills alone.

As we serve the Lord today, may we not be unwise and attempt to live the Christian life in our own power. Let us seek first His Kingdom and His righteousness (Matthew 6:33).

Dear Lord Jesus, I exalt your Holy name. I confess that often I'm attempting to accomplish great things for You by using my own power. I am thankful that You have given me the gift of your Holy Spirit. This day, grant me the grace I need to walk, not by my own power but by Your Spirit. Amen.

Wesley Siegrist pastors Erb Mennonite Church

January 22

The Father Seeks Worshipers

Pray!
for Lancaster County

"Shout for joy to the LORD, all the earth. Worship the LORD with gladness; come before him with joyful songs. Know that the LORD is God. It is he who made us, and we are his; we are his people, the sheep of his pasture. Enter his gates with thanksgiving and his courts with praise; give thanks to him and praise his name. For the LORD is good and his love endures forever; his faithfulness continues through all generations." *Psalm 100*

"Yet a time is coming and has now come when the true worshipers will worship the Father in spirit and truth, for they are the kind of worshipers the Father seeks." *John 4:23*

Every man, woman, and child who lives in Lancaster County, or any other place in the world, has the wonderful opportunity to worship the Creator. We all have the privilege of coming before Him with gladness and joy to celebrate His goodness, enduring love, and continuing faithfulness. Let us pray that the believers in Lancaster County would be "true worshipers". Let us pray that "today" would be the day we worship the Father in Spirit and Truth.

Lord, I will seek to worship You from my heart, wherever I am, with thankfulness, praise and the joyous attitude of an adopted child of a loving and everlasting Father.

Today's devotional was edited from the 2003–2004 *Throne Of Grace Prayer Guide*, a weekly guide of Lancaster County prayer concerns gathered from regional intercessors and area prayer groups.

January 23

Behind Enemy Lines

"But I say to you, love your enemies, bless those who curse you, do good to those who hate you, and pray for those who spitefully use you and persecute you." *Matthew 5:44 (New King James Version)*

One of Christ's most challenging demonstrations of love is found in the account of His arrest. Judas had just arrived to betray the Lord. We pick up the narrative from Luke 22:49–51: "When those around Him saw what was going to happen, they said to Him, "Lord, shall we strike with the sword?" And one of them struck the servant of the high priest and cut off his right ear. But Jesus answered and said, "Permit even this." And He touched his ear and healed him." What tremendous love!

Late in the winter of 1569, Dirk Willems of Holland was discovered to be an Anabaptist, this being illegal at the time, a "thief catcher" was dispatched to arrest him. Running for his life, Dirk came to a body of water still coated with ice. After making his way across in great peril, he realized his pursuer had fallen through into the freezing water.

Turning back, Dirk ran to the struggling man and dragged him safely to shore. The thief catcher wanted to release Dirk, but a burgomaster— having appeared on the scene—reminded the man he was under oath to deliver criminals to justice. Dirk was bound off to prison, interrogated, tortured and eventually put to death.[1]

Are there those in your life who curse you, who hate you? Who, when they have the opportunity, spitefully use you and persecute you? How may Christ be asking you to demonstrate the fruit of His kindness and love to that person today?

Oh Lord, May the fruit of Your love be dispensed indiscriminately upon all that I meet today.

Dave Myer is lead pastor of New Covenant Mennonite Fellowship, New Holland.

[1] From a 1660 Anabaptist martyrology compiled by Thieleman J. Van Bracht, translated as *Martyrs Mirror* (Scottdale: Herald Press, 1950), 741–742.

January 24
Taken For Granted?

"This is how God showed his love among us: He sent his one and only Son into the world that we might live through him. This is love: not that we loved God, but that He loved us and sent his Son as an atoning sacrifice for our sins….We love because He first loved us." *1 John 4:9–10,19*

The words "I love you" are sometimes taken for granted. Do you ever hear the words and simply respond without thinking, "I love you, too," or is your response a meaningful representation of what is within your heart?

God has blessed me with a wonderful family including two beautiful granddaughters. Kaeleigh, who is the oldest at two and one-half years of age, loves to sing. One of her favorite songs is "Tomorrow" from *Annie*. When she finishes singing her rendition of this familiar song, I always tell her, "I love YOU tomorrow and I also love YOU today." When she responds with her endearing smile and tells me "I love you, too, Grandma," I am reminded that the love we share for one another is only possible because God first loved us.

While it is amazing that a two and one-half year old can comprehend the meaning of love, it is even more amazing to try to comprehend God's own love for us. As I consider how very special His love is, I begin to realize how very loved I am. Please don't ever let me take His love for granted!

Dear Heavenly Father, I love You Lord, and I am grateful that You loved me first. I know that I do not deserve Your love, but You have given it to me anyway. I also do not deserve Your forgiveness for all of my sins, but You have given me forgiveness through Your only Son, my Lord and Savior, Jesus Christ. Thank you for first loving me. Amen.

Anne Worley is a wife, mother, grandmother, and teacher at Cocalico Middle School.

January 25

The Comfort Of His Love

"Whom have I in heaven but You? And there is none upon earth that I desire besides you." *Psalm 73:25 (New King James Version)*

In Psalm 73, King David penned these words lamenting the fact that he was surrounded by those who seemed to prosper in spite of their wickedness. At the end of his lament he finally comes to the place where he declares that even though everything seems to be going wrong around him, he will choose to desire a relationship with God.

Personally, I can relate to David and his frustration with his world. All around me I see sin and evil flourishing, and as David says in verse 3, I am envious of the boastful when I see the prosperity of the wicked. Sometimes I question the fairness of God when the wicked seem to flourish.

But God keeps bringing me back to the place where He brought David, to that place of comfort deep inside his heart of love. And I have to recognize that indeed there isn't anyone in all of heaven or earth that I'd rather be in love with than God.

It's in this place where God brings peace and contentment into my soul. I realize again that, although the world may literally be going to hell, God desires that I focus completely upon Him. I need to unhook my focus from all the distractions of an evil world and set my focus squarely upon Him and His heart of love for me. When I get it right, there's no better place to be.

Dear God, I acknowledge Your love for me today. Help me to focus solely upon Your presence in my life today. Continue to draw me into your heart of love. You alone are the strength of my heart and my inheritance forever. Amen.

Dale Weaver is senior pastor of Sandy Hill Mennonite Church in Coatesville, and is part of the Lancaster Transformation Network of Christians.

The Battle Is The Lord's

"…This is what the Lord says to you: "Do not be afraid or discouraged because of this vast army. For the battle is not yours but God's." *2 Chronicles 20:15*

I find this an instructive passage for those times in my life when I am faced with the fear of what seems like an insurmountable challenge. Jehoshaphat was facing possible annihilation by the enemy. He and the nation were in serious trouble. What could he possibly do?

First Jehoshaphat called all the people together for fasting and prayer. Then he prayed. In his prayer he proclaimed the sovereignty of God, acknowledged the power of God, rehearsed the purpose of God (for His people), claimed the promise of God, and confessed his need of God as he said, "We do not know what to do, but our eyes are on You."

Following Jehoshaphat's admission that the problem was too large for him, the word came from the Lord, "…the battle is not yours but God's." When did it become God's battle? When Jehoshaphat confessed his need and gave the problem over to God.

Why do I so often feel that if only I had more time, a better strategy, more energy, more education, or more cooperation from others, I could fix the problem? Why am I so reluctant to confess my need and allow God to take my problems and bring His victory, while delivering me from almost certain defeat?

Jehoshophat started at the temple with petition and ended there with praise. How often do I ask God for help and then forget to thank Him for the help He gives?

Almighty God, forgive me for the arrogance of self-sufficiency. Give me the humility to admit my need and to seek Your help. Fill my heart with gratitude and praise for all that You do for me.

Elvin J. Ressler is the bishop of the Millwood District of the Lancaster Mennonite Conference.

January 27

Time To Change?

"And he answered and spake unto those that stood before him, saying, 'Take away the filthy garments from him.' And unto him he said, 'Behold, I have caused thine iniquity to pass from thee, and I will clothe thee with change of raiment.'"
Zechariah 3:4 (King James Version)

Positive change is an element of the Christian life. Change in our lives is often frightening and usually difficult. Following are five areas that probably need to change if growth is to occur.

We need to alter our **attitudes**. We must not only admit that personal change is necessary, but also believe that we can change. (Philippians 4:13)

We need to change our **actions**. We need to start doing new things: helping instead of hurting, commending instead of criticizing, giving instead of taking. (Ephesians 4:26–32)

We may need to change our **associations**. We might need to start being around different people, people with better habits and goals. The Bible says, "Do not be mislead: bad company corrupts good character… (1 Corinthians 15:33)."

We may need to change our **affections**. Many people love money, work and pleasure more than anything else. Jesus once said, "For what profit is it to a man if he gains the whole world, and loses his own soul…. (Matthew 16:26 NKJV)."

We may need to change our **abodes**: the places we go, and the places where we spend our time. Your spouse, your kids, your parents, your brothers and sisters in the body need you. Spend your time with those who are most important to you. Nurture the relationships that count the most. (1 Peter 4:3)

Jesus, teach me Your way to change. Let me yield with Your grace. I ask Lord that You will guide me through my necessary changes. Thank You for establishing Your priorities in my life. Because I so believe in You and trust in You, I can also believe in me. Amen.

Diana Oliphant is a small group minister, missionary and servant/leader from The Worship Center.

January 28

The Eternal Hope

"But in your hearts set apart Christ as Lord. Always be prepared to give an answer to everyone who asks you to give the reason for the hope that you have. But do this with gentleness and respect." *1 Peter 3:15*

Making Christ our Lord happens in meaningful ways in our hearts, not with the words of our lips or even with the thoughts of our minds. Christ is ultimately made Lord when our hearts are uniquely "set apart". The ongoing nature of having a heart set apart is expressed by Peter's admonition to "always be prepared". We need to continually and consistently check our focus to be sure that our focus is on Christ and that our heart is set in the way and direction of Christ.

Because our hearts are set on Christ, we are able to have hope even in the middle of the worst situations of life. This passage reminds us of our call to give witness to the hope of Christ which is greater than all the tumult and trials of life we may experience.

This hope is greater because hope in Christ is about eternity and not limited to this world and this life. Christians are able to have hope at all times and in all things because our hope is in Christ and in eternity.

Christians should "always be prepared" to tell people why our outlook and perspective is ultimately one of hope and possibility. Truly, our hope does spring eternal! This eternal hope is shared respectfully and gently while boldly affirming that the ultimate hope is in Jesus the Christ!

Dear God, My hope is in You today and in eternity. Give me a bold, gentle, and respectful spirit to share that hope through my life. Help me to be prepared to share the hope I have in Jesus Christ, my Savior in my words, my thoughts, and my actions. Amen.

Kevin Readman is pastor of Ranck's United Methodist Church in New Holland.

January 29

No Condemnation

"Therefore, there is now no condemnation for those who are in Christ Jesus." *Romans 8:1*

When I was growing up, it was a common practice to try to obtain the autographs of famous Christians. Adults and kids alike would try and get their Bibles autographed by whoever was a fairly "big name." I obtained the autograph of Dave Wickersheim, a Christian pitcher with the Detroit Tigers. One man in our church had the autograph of Roy Rogers, the famous singing cowboy. And another man had the autograph of none other than Billy Graham. I noticed, even as a boy, that these various famous Christians would generally sign their name with a Bible reference below their autograph. I was told it represented their "life verse." And so, even as a young boy, I began to wonder, "What is my life verse?"

Now, many decades later, I can speak of various "life verses" that have been mine through the years: different verses for different periods of my life. But for many years, no verse was as important to me as Romans 8:1.

The notion that there was and would be absolutely no condemnation of me was a wonderfully overwhelming idea. I knew the wickedness of my heart. And though Jesus was, without question, my Savior, my heart…my thoughts…oh, I felt, so often, condemned by these! But here Paul tells us that there would be no condemnation of me! Jesus didn't bear in His body just SOME of my sin; Jesus bore ALL of my sin!

Do you feel condemned? Don't…at least not if you know our Savior. You've been made perfect! Enjoy the assurance that the day of judgment for you will be a great day indeed.

Lord, thank You for Jesus! Thank You that He not only took upon Himself my sin, but He gave me His perfection. Thank You that I need not go through life condemned or even feeling condemned.

Doug Winne is the senior pastor of Lancaster Evangelical Free Church in Lititz.

Stinging Truth

"For everyone born of God overcomes the world. This is the victory that has overcome the world, even our faith." *1 John 5:4*

Witness 2004 was a celebration weekend where 60,000 Christians came together to praise the name of Jesus. Christian musicians and speakers from around the nation came to lead in this annual event. One of the organizers told me that before the celebration someone said to him: "Oh, you Christians will put your hands in the air and be all religious, and then the next day you'll sin just like the rest of us."

The stinging truth in her statement discouraged my friend. I replied, "Yes, but that is who we are… we are all sinners because we are born of a sinful nature." Yes, we will sin, not because we want too, but because we are sinners.

I once had an alcoholic tell me that he was more religious than I was. At first I was offended and said, "No, you're not!" His comment burned a hole in my faith. Then I realized that what he said was true. Every time he went into a bar and started to drink, he was ready to die for his god, alcohol. He gave control of his life to the demon in that bottle. I finally had to admit, I was not as religious as that alcoholic. But I praise God for opening my eyes. Being religious never saved anyone. Religious leaders religiously sent Jesus to the cross. They didn't accept Him as the Messiah and died lost.

The difference between believers and non-believers is the reason why we put our hands in the air and praise our Savior. We claim the victory of our Savior in our lives. We praise Him, not because of what we've done, but because of what He's done for us.

Stand firmly on the joy of Jesus' victory and overcome the enemy's attempts to discourage your faith.

Loving Savior, thank You for dying to save me from sin's penalty.

Larry Rineer is interim pastor of Saint Paul's Church, Quarryville.

January 31

God Can

"...'Not by might nor by power, but by my Spirit,' says the LORD Almighty." *Zechariah 4:6*

Y ou can do it!" This is a statement you often hear as someone is encouraging another person to stretch himself to accomplish some goal, such as competing in an athletic game or graduating from high school or college. "You can do it!" may be good advice on certain occasions, but in the face of life's biggest challenges, it is incomplete and inadequate. We need help from outside ourselves; we need power from God Himself.

This was the message of God through the prophet Zechariah to the Jewish people who had returned from the Babylonian captivity to rebuild their once-beautiful capital city of Jerusalem. It was also a word of encouragement to Zerubbabel, the governor of the Jewish colony. He and the people had laid the foundation for the temple, but because of opposition from enemies the temple work was abandoned for eighteen years. Some of the Jews despaired of ever completing the temple. Then God sent a series of visions to Zechariah to encourage the people and their leader. "Not by human might or by earthly power, but by my Spirit," God said. What looks like a mountain of opposition will become level ground. "The hands of Zerubbabel have laid the foundation of this temple; his hands will also complete it... (Zechariah 4:9)."

We are in a similar situation today. The things we long for most— revival in the churches of Lancaster County, a nationwide turning to God, and worldwide evangelization—cannot be done by us in our own strength. But God graciously says, "What you cannot do, I can. Trust Me and My promises. By My Spirit I will do it."

Almighty God, in our weakness we look to You. Purify us from all sin; fill us with Your Spirit. We are trusting You to revive the churches and bring glory to Your name, through Christ our Lord.

John Hawbaker is senior pastor of Manor Brethren in Christ Church, south of Mountville.

February

February 1

One Body

"...that all of them may be one, Father, just as you are in me and I am in you. May they also be in us so that the world may believe that you have sent me." *John 17:21*

Pray! for Lancaster County

"There is one body and one Spirit—just as you were called to one hope when you were called—one Lord, one faith, one baptism; one God and Father of all, who is over all and through all and in all." *Ephesians 4:4–6*

The world is watching us. Do they see the unity in the Father that causes them to believe in Jesus? Do they see us loving one another? Do they see the Body of Christ coming together and joining in prayer and cooperative efforts to powerfully affect our region for Jesus Christ? As we build relational connectivity with each other among others in the region, God will reveal how each individual and ministry fits into the Holy Spirit's greater move across our county. And we can rejoice in how our one God, our Father over all, makes us all one.

Lord, let this "oneness" begin with me. Help me to step outside my own "camp" this week. Show me how to build relationships with other Christians in our region.

Today's devotional was edited from the 2003–2004 *Throne Of Grace Prayer Guide*, a weekly guide of Lancaster County prayer concerns gathered from regional intercessors and area prayer groups.

Stop, Listen And Love

"...I have loved you with an everlasting love; I have drawn you with loving-kindness." *Jeremiah 31:3*

A s our society moves at an ever increasing pace, how often have I missed a visitation of God's presence because I was too busy? In my busyness, I lose sight of what Jesus told Martha was "the most important part"—time sitting at His feet—time hearing Him speak.

Do we stop and let God convey the height, width, breadth, and depth of His love for us? God, our Father, the Creator of heaven and earth, the One through whom we live and move and have our being—LOVES us! Not only does He love us, He desires intimacy with us. The Psalmist declared, "As the deer pants for streams of water, so I long for You." Is our cry one of such longing?

Today, stop and sit before God. Tell Him your desire to know Him better, to see Him, to hear His voice. Because of His love for you, He will respond. As you spend time with Him and learn His character, you'll understand His unconditional love for you. In this intimacy we are "transformed into His likeness...(2 Corinthians 3:16-18)." We are changed by His love for us, and our capacity to love others grows. As we experience God in this secret place, we will find Him more and more in our life experience. Love becomes the motivation of all we do. Our spiritual wells, filled with His living water, will then overflow to our hurting and needy world.

Father, quiet my heart and give me grace to silence the cacophony of the world and hear Your voice. My desire is to draw closer in relationship with You—to know You intimately as my Friend and lover of my soul. And as you fill me with Your love, allow me to touch others with that same unconditional love.

Karen Hugo serves as an elder in The Taproot, part of the Lancaster County Micro-church Network.

February 3

The Good Life

"Then the angel showed me the river of the water of life, as clear as crystal, flowing from the throne of God and of the Lamb..." Revelation 22:1

We are all faced with the desire for a better life. Advertisers daily try to sell us products that will enhance or lengthen our life. Our culture lies when it tells us that life is better with an abundance of things, or that happiness is found in a vacation or pleasure. From time to time I have bought into these lies and each time found the good life to be short lived and disappointing. The writer of Ecclesiastes must have experienced this same frustration when he wrote "All man's efforts are for his mouth, yet his appetite is never satisfied (Ecclesiastes 6:7)."

The truth is that God wants us to experience a good life and has provided for it. Revelation pictures life flowing from the throne of God. In Deuteronomy 6, God promised the Children of Israel that it would go well with them and they would enjoy long life if they followed His commands. Jesus said in John 10:10 "The thief comes only to steal and kill and destroy; I have come that they may have life, and have it to the full." God is not just a God of life but of abundant life.

We can all experience this life, but we must go to the right source. May we all drink deeply from the River of Life. As we do, our region will see us living and experiencing the abundant life of Christ, and then they also will want to take a drink.

Dear God, forgive me for the times I have looked for life in things other than You. Help me to come to Your river to drink. May my life cause others to be thirsty for You. Amen.

Kevin Horning serves as the pastor of New Life Fellowship in Ephrata.

Your Heritage

"Ask of me and I will make the nations your inheritance."
Psalm 2:8

A s Christians, the truth of the Word of God clearly teaches that our God keeps covenant with those who keep covenant. When the Word says He will do X if we do Y, God is promising—by His own authority of being God—to keep His promise. He can invoke no higher authority than Himself to assure that He will fulfill His Word— for none exists. What He says He will do, He will do.

Psalm 2:8 says if we ask Him, He will give us the nations. After 2000 years, approximately 40% of the world still has not heard the Gospel, does not know of Christ's sacrifice, and has not been offered the grace of God as the solution for their sins. The Good News of Jesus Christ has been given to His believers to preach and the eternal destiny of others is entrusted to His church as we respond to His call. We must be obedient to ask, to send, and to go.

He will keep His part. We must do our part today, and every day until all have heard the Good News of Jesus Christ, our Savior.

Father, I repent for the hardness of heart that has allowed millions to be condemned for eternity without knowing You. Father I ask for the nations, that the Gospel would be preached to every tribe, people and nation, that Your Son may be glorified and His name be known by all mankind. I pledge to continue asking as long as I live or until all have heard. I am in covenant with You according to Your written word in Psalm 2:8. Amen.

Wayne Kaufman, pastors Gates of Praise Ministries in the Gates of Praise House Church Network. He serves on the boards of Harvest Net, The Regional Church of Lancaster County, and Lancaster House of Prayer.

February 5

Life To The Fullest

"The thief comes only to steal and kill and destroy; I have come that they may have life, and have it to the full." *John 10:10*

How many of us can truly say that we live life to the full? When we think of that statement, we often think of what the world wants—partying, spending money, sex, vacations, and basically living for ourselves. We know that this is not of God, but of the flesh. Ultimately living this life-style will make us empty and miserable.

Jesus said that He has come to give us life to the fullest! What does that mean for us today? Freedom! Absolute freedom! We can be filled with such joy that we don't desire the things of this world. When we are filled with the presence of Jesus, nothing in this world can ever take its place.

When we have the mind of Jesus, soon the things that used to bother us will dwindle away. We will care more about what God thinks of us than what men think. We will desire the things of God and this will make our joy complete. We will learn to be content in any circumstance.

So today stand firm! Know who you are in Jesus and remember the freedom and life that He has given you. Say to this world and to the enemy: "You can't steal or kill my joy! I have been set free!"

Dear Jesus, thank You for setting me free and giving me new life. I pray that I would walk in that freedom and new life. Let me have the mindset that is of Jesus and not of this world. Let me desire the things of God more than the things of men. Keep me safe from the evil one who tries to steal my joy and kill my life. I praise You, Jesus, for Your awesome love, forgiveness, and life. In Your precious and Holy name I pray. Amen.

Mike Wenger is the director of TNT Youth Ministry and youth evangelist for the Ephrata Area.

Hand Over The Keys

"We know that whoever is born of God does not sin; but he who has been born of God keeps himself, and the wicked one does not touch him." *1 John 5:18 (New King James Version)*

Picture this: you and Jesus are out for a drive in your car. As you travel you notice that you are making all of the lights on green and missing all of the potholes. Your eyes shift from the road ahead to meet His. As you have imagined this scenario, who is behind the wheel? Is Jesus the one who is driving?

Today's verse presents a wonderful promise and a qualifying condition. The promise, "that the wicked one doesn't touch him", is for those who have experienced the new birth Jesus described to Nicodemus (John 3). The condition is found in the words "keeps himself". So, we say to ourselves, "I have been born again and I definitely want to achieve this promise; let me craft a game plan to accomplish this. I will make up a list of my vulnerabilities and post yellow squares around my home, car and work place to remind me to 'toe the line' in those areas."

Jesus would say to you as he did to Martha—"You are worried and upset about so many things—only one thing is needed. Choose what Mary chose—sit at my feet (Luke 10:41–42)." How do I keep myself? By surrendering, submitting, abiding under His wing, laying my burden down and taking His yoke upon me—by letting Him drive.

Lord Jesus, I know what I must do in my head, but I am so geared to strive and solve and control. I am weary of hitting the potholes that are ever before me in this dark world. Establish this truth in my heart so I can stop striving and break the sin-repent-repeat cycle that results when I command the affairs of my life. Here, Lord—take my keys. I want to ride with You.

John Hughes serves as a worship leader in the Gates of Praise House Church Network.

Joy Maker

"Always be full of joy in the Lord; I say it again, rejoice!"
Philippians 4:4 (Living Bible)

I confess I do not always feel full of joy in difficult circumstances. Sometimes it occurs, however, when we least expect it, coming unbidden in our weariness. When these moments of joy do occur, we have to recognize them as a gift from the Lord.

I discovered joy on the day I was having my second miscarriage in four months. As I nursed my tired and grieving body, my little boy's face peered up at mine, begging me to pull him up on the couch with me. There is no rest with a toddler, so I scooped him up and laid him on my lap. He gently took my hair and started to pet me as he does when he means to be gentle. He pushed my hair over my face, and I proceeded to blow it out of my eyes. This act of blowing was extremely funny to him, and he began to giggle and laugh and laugh. Touched in the unsteady part of my soul, I began to weep. He kept gently pushing my hair in my face, and I kept blowing, he laughing and I crying. I felt a deep sense of gratitude for my dear little boy who could evoke this raw emotion and draw out the grief trapped inside of me. As he laughed, I wept. As he played, I healed. Joy?

Dear God, help us to recognize the moments of joy You give us in our pain. May we sense Your presence as You minister to us in very special ways.

The author of these words has requested anonymity. She and her husband are in ministry leadership in a local congregation.

February 8

Wholehearted Love

"One thing I ask of the LORD,
this is what I seek:
that I may dwell in the house of the LORD
all the days of my life,
to gaze upon the beauty of the LORD
and to seek him in his temple." *Psalm 27*

for Lancaster County

Is this my request? Is this my desire? What would happen if the church in our region awakened to a wholehearted love for the Son of God? We would have a deeper knowledge of God and we would live the first commandment: "…love the Lord your God with all your heart and with all your soul and with all your mind. (Matthew 22:37–38)"

Lord, show me where I do not love You with all my heart or soul or mind. Help me to lay aside every thing that diminishes my love for You in my heart, mind, soul, or strength.

Today's devotional was edited from the 2003–2004 *Throne Of Grace Prayer Guide*, a weekly guide of Lancaster County prayer concerns gathered from regional intercessors and area prayer groups.

February 9

Ash Wednesday

"Rend your heart and not your garments. Return to the LORD your God, for he is gracious and compassionate, slow to anger and abounding in love, and he relents from sending calamity."
Joel 2:13

On Ash Wednesday, priests in the Old Testament, and through the centuries in certain Christian traditions, have sprinkled ashes from burnt sacrifices over the believers. Sometimes the ashes are used to draw a cross on the forehead of the kneeling parishioner. As we examine history we find the ashes used on Ash Wednesday were meant to symbolize the need for humility, sorrow, repentance and a change of heart.

What does it mean to "rend our hearts"? The ashes on Ash Wednesday came from a desire to create an outward witness to what is taking place inwardly in the heart. This is what Joel was talking about. What is going on in your heart? Is it soft and pliable, responding quickly to the promptings of the Holy Spirit, or has it become hard and rigid from the pounding of life's experiences and spiritual laziness?

Father, I know that You are gracious and compassionate, slow to anger and abounding in love... I am sorry where I have offended You in any way by my actions. Please show me specific things that have come between You and me, so that I can repent, remove them and press ahead. In Jesus' name, Amen.

Brian Sauder leads D.O.V.E. Christian Fellowship International's leadership training school and serves on D.O.V.E.'s Apostolic Council.

February 10

My Words Today

Then the Lord answered Job out of the whirlwind, and said: "Who is this that darkens counsel by words without knowledge?" *Job 38:1–2 (New King James Version)*

Jesus declared that our love for one another would speak loudly enough to convince an unbelieving world that we are Christ's disciples and that the Father sent the Son (John 13:35; 17:20–23). Why then is the world not believing? Can it be that, even in the church where we claim to speak for God, our own words "darken" the counsel of the Holy Spirit to those whose ears Jesus died to open?

Perhaps we've forgotten that Solomon said that "he who has knowledge spares his words (Proverbs 17:27)", and that sin is almost always present where words are many (Proverbs 10:19). Instead of clearly proclaiming the gospel, we may be "hiding" the face of Jesus through communication that is "without knowledge": words that are judgmental, picky, religious, vain, foolish, hasty, prideful, and just plain inconsiderate of the real needs among us and around us?

I find myself speaking cleverly, but not compassionately, about the issues of life. I joke. I quip. I bandy the popular phrases of the contemporary church and culture. I use words to hide my own needs, to cover up my own lack of commitment to the needs of others. Instead, should I not simply come alongside someone to love them with the love of Jesus, to give a compassionate word of clear counsel concerning God's heart and God's grace? When did I last share a "word that fits" another's need, as Solomon counseled in Proverbs 25:11?

Dear God, may the words of my mouth and the thoughts of my heart be acceptable to You. May I use my tongue to bless, to praise, to pray and to preach only those things which unveil Your glory and declare Your goodness in Christ Jesus. Amen.

Mark Ammerman is the communications director of the Regional Church of Lancaster County, is an author, artist and elder at In The Light Ministries, Lancaster.

February 11

Makin' A List...Checkin' It Twice

"Commit to the Lord whatever you do, and your plans will succeed." *Proverbs 16:3*

Another translation says, "Roll your works upon the Lord and so shall your plans be established and succeed (AMP)." How well I remember when the reality of this verse of scripture first reached my heart. I had so much to accomplish on that particular day that I made a list to be sure I got everything done. It was good to have a goal, but the list was too long for one day, especially considering that I also needed to attend to my seven children!

I soon became irritable and anxious. Why did everything have to erupt on this day? I know the Lord was attentive to my dilemma. Quickly, I began to realize that I needed His help! Soon He came to my aid with the suggestion, "Why not start over and prioritize the list, starting with the most important at the top?" I began to feel the pressure lifting and before the day was over, I had completed it all with time to spare!

Some years later, I was sitting with a younger mom, and she shared this same struggle with me. I pulled out this verse in Proverbs 16:3 and we read it together. Now she also had the opportunity to put it into practice. It gave her light for her path and a fresh hold on a new truth for herself.

Heavenly Father, You have so much to teach us. Thank You for Your precious Holy Spirit to guide us to Your word, lead us into Your truth, and give us the power to follow and do what is shown to us. Give us the desire to love and revere Your direction and to not lean on our own understanding and miss Your very best for us. Remind us that we are here for Your purposes, not our own. Thank You for Your patience with us. In Jesus' name, Amen.

Naomi Sensenig and her husband, LaMarr, serve at D.O.V.E. Fellowship Westgate Celebration as intercessors and spiritual parents.

February 12

Abraham Lincoln's Birthday

"A man's wisdom gives him patience; it is to his glory to over-look an offense." *Proverbs 19:11*

E ach looked for an easier triumph and a result less fundamental and astounding. Both read the same Bible and pray to the same God, and each invokes His aid against the other. It may seem strange that any man should dare to ask a just God's assistance in wringing their bread from the sweat of other men's faces, but let us not judge, that we be not judged. The prayers of both could not be answered. That of neither has been answered fully. The Almighty has His own purposes. 'Woe unto the world because of offenses; for it must needs be that offense come, but woe to that man by whom the offense cometh....'"[1]

Father, I pray that You would train my heart not to hold an offense, but that my heart will hold dear the spirit of forgiveness. May forgiveness be such a part of my spiritual armor that I will not stumble over an offense. May the grace of Jesus be ever before me. Amen.

Jeff Burkholder is the chairman of the board of supervisors, Elizabeth Township.

[1] From the second inagural address by President Abraham Lincoln

February 13

Your Kingdom Come

"This, then, is how you should pray: 'Our Father in heaven, hallowed be Your name, Your kingdom come, Your will be done on earth as it is in heaven.' " *Matthew 6:9–10*

The prayer Jesus taught His disciples has begun to grip my heart. His invitation for His church to pray that His kingdom come on earth as it is in heaven stretches me. From the very start of His ministry, Jesus said, "...Repent for the kingdom of heaven is near (Matthew 4:17)." One day in Nazareth when He was handed the scroll, He read a passage from Isaiah that spoke of how the Spirit's anointing would help to bring the kingdom of heaven to earth by meeting people's needs (Luke 4:16-19). And that is what Jesus modeled while on earth.

The other day as I stood in a crowded mall I wondered what it would look like if God's kingdom would be here now as it is in heaven? How would people know? Then it struck me, the same Holy Spirit anointing that Jesus spoke about is here to anoint us and walk with us. As each Christian lives with that power, we will be able to point people to Christ. Burdens that held people in bondage will be broken and people will experience freedom. Jesus made a difference in lives of those He touched. He did not touch every one, but he did complete His Father's work (John 17:4). Today each of us has a sphere of influence. Are we so walking in that sphere to bring His kingdom on earth as it is in heaven?

Dear God, may I so live my life in deepening relationship with You that my life will point people to Your son, Jesus. May all I do help to bring Your kingdom here on earth as it is in heaven.

Fred Garber is the senior pastor at Bossler Mennonite Church. He is part of a local pastors' prayer group and a board member of Lancaster Love INC.

February 14
You Are Loved
"Love never fails..." 1 Corinthians 13:8

I had known her since childhood, and we were close friends. Over the years, although separated geographically, we kept in touch as we navigated early adulthood, marriage, and children. Then came the troubling news that her marriage was in trouble. In the following months she was sent reeling from a blow that seemed the end of life itself. She learned firsthand that human love is imperfect. It sometimes fails.

Many times I called just to tell her I cared. (No one ever gets tired of hearing, "I love you.") It didn't keep her marriage from falling apart, but she said later that my expressions of love and friendship, along with a listening ear, helped get her through.

On this earth, the Lord gives genuine friendship, also called "agape" love, to help us in our times of need. Agape love focuses on how we can meet another person's needs. Genuine friendship loves for love's sake, not just for what it can get in return. Jesus offers a perfect model of this kind of friendship and unconditional love. He spent intentional time with a handful of people, the twelve disciples, not only to train them, but for loving companionship as well.

However, even the best of human love—the love you have for your spouse, parents, children or friends—fails. Human love may fail, but God *is* Love and His Love will never fail. God's infinite love is a mystery—inexplicable and incomprehensible. He has loved you with an everlasting love (Jeremiah 31:3). Jesus calls you His friend (John 15:15), and He is your greatest Friend who will "stick closer than a brother (Proverbs 18:24)."

In Jesus, you see and can experience love that is complete and fully extended—the fullness of love. You are passionately loved today.

Thank You for loving me, Jesus. Help me to listen, love, and care for others with Your agape love—a heart made sensitive by You.

Karen Ruiz is the editor of House to House Publications, Lititz.

Grace And Truth

"He replied, 'Isaiah was right when he prophesied about you hypocrites; as it is written: "These people honor me with their lips, but their hearts are far from me. They worship me in vain; their teachings are but rules taught by men." You have let go of the commands of God and are holding on to the traditions of men.'" *Mark 7:6–8*

Pray!
for Lancaster County

"For it is by grace you have been saved, through faith—and this not from yourselves, it is the gift of God—not by works, so that no one can boast." *Ephesians 2:8–9*

Praise God today that it is by grace we have been saved! It is through faith, a gift of God—not by works! As we hold steadfastly to the commandments of God, we can let go of the traditions of men. We can release those things that keep our hearts from the Lord. And as we let go of the traditions of men, we are letting go of many of the things that divide us as humans and as Christians.

Lord, show me any undue dependence upon religious traditions. If any of these have sidetracked or replaced my trust in You and in Your sacrifice for my sins, forgive me. I will look again to the cross and rejoice in the death and resurrection of my savior Jesus Christ.

Today's devotional was edited from the 2003–2004 *Throne Of Grace Prayer Guide*, a weekly guide of Lancaster County prayer concerns gathered from regional intercessors and area prayer groups.

"All" Means "All"

"I have given you authority to trample on snakes and scorpions and to overcome all the power of the enemy; nothing will harm you." *Luke10:19*

Webster defines "all" as "wholly, entirely, completely." When Jesus declares, "I have given you authority over all the power of the enemy," He does not leave anything out. When the enemy comes against us in any way, we have the authority to overcome him.

I own a small business and there are many ways the enemy comes to rob, kill and destroy there. He comes against finances, personnel, attitudes and even equipment. But Jesus has given me the authority to stand against the enemy, to be an overcomer. I can stand with Jesus and declare the enemy has no place in my business and in the authority of Jesus' name, he must go.

He has given each of us that authority. The understanding of our authority comes as the Holy Spirit reveals who we are as children of God. We walk in that authority by grace and faith. When everything in the natural appears to be failing, when it seems like a downhill slide and even when debits are greater then credits, we must stand on God's word. We stand declaring in faith that we are overcomers and that no weapon formed against us will prosper.

Lord, may my first response to negative situations be to agree with You and declare that You alone are God. May I declare that all things are in Your hands and that I am in Your hands. May I believe and declare that by the authority You have placed in me, I will overcome ALL the work of the enemy because of the finished work of the cross.

Keith Charles serves in marketplace ministry at his lumber manufacturing business and, along with his wife, serves as director of the Healing Rooms of Lancaster.

February 17

Don't Look For The Exit Sign

"...In repentance and rest is your salvation, in quietness and trust is your strength, but you would have none of it. You said, 'No, we will flee on horses.' Therefore you will flee! You said, 'We will ride off on swift horses.' Therefore your pursuers will be swift! Yet the LORD longs to be gracious to you; He rises to show you compassion. For the LORD is a God of justice. Blessed are all who wait for him!" *Isaiah 30:15,16,18*

It is difficult to persevere, confident of God's timing and faithfulness, when circumstances scream at us to find the nearest exit door from the place of testing. One lesson we must learn is that God's process for maturing us usually runs directly through the wilderness of testing and opposition. We walk through the valley of the shadow of death to learn about our shepherd's rod and staff. Only after the lessons of that valley are *walked through* does He prepare a table for us in the presence of what opposed us and *then* the anointing pours over us and the cup of blessing overflows (see Psalm 23).

God desires to pour out the full measure of blessing, but not before the desert place has tested our hearts and proven His. When we try to "run on swift horses" to escape the process designed to teach us repentance, rest, quietness, and trust, God is obligated to send the process swiftly to the next place we run until we finally embrace it and learn His heart.

Remember, God is gracious and *longs* to show compassion, but He cannot do so if we constantly run for the nearest exit from the place He has determined we will discover it.

Lord, teach me to view my circumstances through Your eyes. Help me to rest in You and not run from what I must walk through in order to receive Your anointing and blessing.

Paul D. Blank is the pastor of Immanuel Christian Fellowship in Manheim.

February 18

The Strength Of Quiet Trust

"...in quietness and trust is your strength, but you would have none of it. Yet the LORD longs to be gracious to you; He rises to show you compassion. For the LORD is a God of justice. Blessed are all who wait for Him." *Isaiah 30:15,18*

We are surrounded by a culture that demands quick action. Whenever problems arise, this mentality can quickly leech over into our walk with God. The Word promises that our salvation comes through repenting and resting, yet we strive to be acceptable to God on the basis of our works. When difficulties arise God promises that quieting ourselves before Him and trusting is our source of strength. Yet we quickly react to the urgent in our lives and spring to action before finding the place of peace and quiet before God where our trust in Him gives us strength.

I believe God wants His people to be a witness of His truth in how we live out our salvation. We're to be resting in faith and responding to difficulty in a quiet trust that testifies to the strength of God in us. When we take the time to be still before God, we will find that His answers for us are much different than the instinctive reactions we first had. We also learn that waiting on God in quiet trust results in fruit far beyond what our natural responses could have accomplished. God longs to be compassionate and gracious to us, but He requires our trust and yielding to do so.

Dear Father, help me to learn that my strength is in being still before You and receiving Your provision and heart. Help me not to react to my circumstances, but instead to find a place of peace in You and to be moved by Your Holy Spirit. In Jesus' precious name, Amen.

Paul D. Blank is the pastor of Immanuel Christian Fellowship in Manheim.

February 19

A Kinder, Gentler Church

"But in your hearts set apart Christ as Lord. Always be prepared to give an answer to everyone who asks you to give the reason for the hope that you have. But do this with gentleness and respect." *1 Peter 3:15*

A recent Barna poll asked individuals who would not consider themselves Christians to rank various social groups from most favorable to least favorable, such as military officers, ministers, evangelicals, Democrats, Republicans, real-estate agents, TV performers, lawyers, lesbians, and prostitutes. Out of the eleven groups specified in the poll, evangelicals ranked tenth behind lawyers, lesbians, and Republicans, but finished ahead of prostitutes. Only 22% of the respondents gave evangelicals a favorable rating.

I heard this and I began to wonder what was wrong with this picture. Why do evangelical Christians leave such a bad taste in people's mouths? Is it deserved? Well, I definitely believe that there are many Christians who are in the background serving the poor, taking care of the needy and loving people in Christ's name. But there are also many who are filled with anger, hatred, prejudice, and pride. Some people's view of Christians is tainted by their experience. Maybe they were used by a church, maybe they were hurt by a Christian, or maybe they saw people in the media who claimed to represent Christ yet didn't portray a Christ-like love and compassion.

But if we are honest, we have to point out that we are also to blame. We haven't taken Peter's advice in 1 Peter 3:15 to share Christ with others in gentleness and respect. When we seek to share Christ with people, I pray that we will seek to be people of gentleness and respect, following the way Christ interacted with people. May we be filled with love and compassion for people.

Father God, may we be people known for our gentleness and respect. May we share with people about You in the spirit of Christ.

Ryan Braught is the pastor of youth ministries and nurture at Hempfield Church of the Brethren.

February 20
One In Christ

"I in them and you in me. May they be brought to complete unity to let the world know that you sent me and have loved them even as you have loved me" *John 17:23*

Shortly after the close of the Civil War, in a fashionable church in Richmond, Virginia members of the congregation were invited to come to the altar rail to receive Holy Communion.

Several rows of worshipers had come and knelt to receive communion side by side, when a black man walked down the aisle toward the altar. A tense silence gripped everyone. No one else got up to come down to receive the bread and wine, although many had not yet received communion. The black man started to kneel alone.

A tall, graying man with a military bearing quietly rose from his pew and strode down the aisle to the black man's side. Together, they knelt.

Before the pastor could continue, people recognized that the person kneeling beside the black man—without showing any distinction—was General Robert E. Lee. Although Lee said nothing, everyone realized he had shown his faith through his act of joining that lonely black worshiper at the altar.

Lee's example then is an example for us all today. ***We must not be content with any system that divides us as fellow Christians.*** We must seek to demonstrate our essential unity. Only then can we say truly: "We are one in Christ."

Look for ways that you can demonstrate the unity that we have in Christ. Pray for congregations in your neighborhood. Attend a community worship service and worship with those from various denominations and backgrounds. Scripture promises us the world will see the reality of Jesus Christ as they see His Church in unity.

Father, I thank You for the Body of Christ. I pray that You would bring us to a place of complete unity. Lord may You be at work in my heart to make me an instrument of unity. Show me practical ways that I can demonstrate the reality that we are one in Christ.

Kevin Eshleman is the executive pastor of Ephrata Community Church.

February 21

Don't Be Hindered

"Look at the nations and watch and be utterly amazed. For I am going to do something in your days that you would not believe, even if you were told." Habakkuk 1:5

This verse was fulfilled in and through George Washington's life. If at twelve years old someone would have told George that the Lord declares that He has chosen you to raise up a nation and to lead it. What would be your response? How many of us have aborted God's dreams and plans for our lives because the task seemed so big, so impossible! The impossibilities never seemed to hinder George Washington because he lived his life for others. In his own heart he had already died to himself. Humility, sacrifice and a profound love for prayer were the hallmarks of his life.

In delivering his Farewell Address to the American people as President of the United States of America, George Washington closed with prayer for his beloved country. Let us pray it together today:

"Almighty God, We make our earnest prayer that Thou wilt keep the United States in Thy holy protection... and finally that Thou wilt most graciously be pleased to disposed us all to do justice, to love mercy, and to demean ourselves with charity, humility and pacific temper of mind... without a humble imitation of whose example in these things we can never hope to be a happy nation... through Jesus Christ our Lord. Amen."[1]

Jeff Burkholder, chairman of the board of supervisors, Elizabeth Township

[1] written at Newburg, June 8, 1783

February 22

A Heart Of Flesh

"The sacrifices of God are a broken
spirit; a broken and contrite heart, O God,
you will not despise." *Psalm 51:17*

"I will sprinkle clean water on you, and you will
be clean; I will cleanse you from all your impurities
and from all your idols. I will give you a new heart
and put a new spirit in you; I will remove from you your heart of
stone and give you a heart of flesh. And I will put my Spirit in
you and move you to follow my decrees and be careful to keep
my laws." *Ezekiel 36:25–27*

"I am the vine; you are the branches. If a man remains in me
and I in him, he will bear much fruit; apart from me you can do
nothing. If anyone does not remain in me, he is like a branch
that is thrown away and withers; such branches are picked up,
thrown into the fire and burned. If you remain in me and my
words remain in you, ask whatever you wish, and it will be
given you. This is to my Father's glory, that you bear much
fruit, showing yourselves to be my disciples." *John 15:5–8*

No matter how hard a man or woman tries to change, in our
strength it is hopeless. No matter how hard a group of Christians tries to change their world, it is hopeless. Our hope is in
God who alone can take out our impure and stony hearts and give us
hearts of flesh. Only hearts of flesh can break in repentance. And then
we can trust God to make us into disciples of Jesus and bring forth the
fruit we desperately desire—all to His glory.

*Lord, I need You. Every minute, every hour, every day. Apart from You,
I can do nothing. Through You, I can do all things that You command
me.*

Today's devotional was edited from the 2003–2004 *Throne Of Grace
Prayer Guide*, a weekly guide of Lancaster County prayer concerns
gathered from regional intercessors and area prayer groups.

February 23

Thanks To God

"This is the day which the Lord has made; let us rejoice and be glad in it." *Psalm 118:24*

I believe that living a life of gratitude is tantamount to victorious Christian living. It is impossible not to live victoriously when one's heart is filled with gratitude, not only for our Lord Himself, but for all that He has done on our behalf.

Paul wrote, "He that spared not His own Son, but delivered Him up for us all, how shall He not with Him freely give us all things?" Could a believer be any more sure of victory in his daily life? It is a matter of knowing and appropriating the Word of God so that the "all things" become sanctified in one's walk with the Lord.

Perhaps reasons for gratitude have never been more clearly delineated than in the hymn "THANKS TO GOD."

Thanks to God for my redeemer,
Thanks for all Thou dost provide!
Thanks for times now but a mem'ry,
Thanks for Jesus by my side!
Thanks for pleasant, balmy springtime,
Thanks for dark and dreary fall!
Thanks for tears by now forgotten,
Thanks for peace within my soul!

Thanks for prayers that Thou
    hast answered,
Thanks for what Thou dost deny!
Thanks for storms that
    I have weathered,
Thanks for all Thou dost supply!

Thanks for pain and thanks for pleasure,
Thanks for comfort in despair!
Thanks for grace that none can measure,
Thanks for love beyond compare!

Thanks for roses by the wayside,
Thanks for thorns their stems contain!
Thanks for home and thanks for fireside,
Thanks for hope, that sweet refrain!
Thanks for joy and thanks for sorrow,
Thanks for heav'nly peace with Thee!
Thanks for hope in the tomorrow,
Thanks thro' all eternity!
—August Ludvig Storm, 1891

Dear Father, thank You for the capacity to take joy in You today. Help us to rest and rejoice in the good gift of Your grace. In Jesus' name, Amen.

Dr. Peter W. Teague is the president of Lancaster Bible College and Graduate School in Lancaster.

February 24

Let Us Rejoice And Be Glad

"This is the day which the Lord has made; Let us rejoice and be glad in it." *Psalm 118:24*

As a boy I enjoyed singing the chorus, "This is the day that the Lord has made, We will rejoice and be glad in it." The challenging word is "will."

The human will has great power. In *The Christian's Secret of a Happy Life,* Hannah Whitall Smith wrote:

"By the will, I do not mean the wish of the man, or even his purpose, but the deliberate choice, the deciding power, the king, to which all that is in the man must yield obedience." She then quotes Fenelon, "Pure religion resides in the will alone."

It is refreshing and beautiful when a believer refuses to yield the joy of the Lord, which is his strength, to circumstances in his life. In 1968, after the accidental death of his son, Dr. P. B. Fitzwater, teacher of Bible doctrine at Moody Bible Institute said:

"More than thirty years ago I heard Dr. James Gray preach … on 'The Providence of God,' using as his text Romans 8:28. I then consciously and deliberately took my stand upon the truth proclaimed, and now desire to testify, even with tear-dimmed eyes, that it is true; that through the years my hopes have been again and again crushed, my way has been frequently shrouded in darkness, but when I got far enough to obtain a right perspective, I found that my severest disappointments were His most gracious appointments."

Through an act of his will, this dear servant "consciously and deliberately" claimed every day to be the day that the Lord has made in which he would rejoice and be glad! While the cross remains, we can never doubt the love and sovereignty of our God.

Dear Father, thank You for the capacity to take joy in You today. Help us to rest and rejoice in the good gift of Your grace. In Jesus' name, Amen.

Dr. Peter W. Teague is the president of Lancaster Bible College and Graduate School in Lancaster.

February 25

The "Judas" In Me

"Even my close friend, whom I trusted, he who shared my bread, has lifted up his heel against me." *Psalm 41:9*

If someone is called a "Judas," that person is a traitor. Do you ever feel a bit sorry for Judas? I do. He was a very zealous, committed, nationalistic child of Israel and of Israel's God. He was a man who had his own idea of what a Messiah should do—based on his best hopes for deliverance and victory; a desire for the enemies of God and the enemies of the people of God to be totally destroyed. Judas was hoping for a Messiah who would topple governments and rogue nations—to do away with terrorists and all those who participated in Rome's axis of evil.

Judas thought that if Jesus was forced to face death, that crisis would be the catalyst to bring about the revolution Judas longed for. He arranged for Jesus' betrayal and took things into his own hands to accomplish his own agenda.

But Jesus didn't bite. His training in the desert with fasting and prayer, at the beginning of His earthly ministry, strengthened him to resist the devil's temptations to be another kind of Messiah at the end of His earthly ministry. Jesus' refusal to be Judas' idea of Messiah undid Judas. He realized what he had done in betraying Jesus. However, Judas' change of mind and sorrow did not lead him to salvation, but rather to despair and suicide. I always think of Judas and Peter when I hear, "Godly sorrow brings repentance that leads to salvation and leaves no regret, but worldly sorrow brings death (2 Corinthians 7:9)."

Judas took things into his own hands. This led to his death. How often do you and I do the same? We take things into our own hands. Does this not lead to *despair*?

Lord Jesus Christ, Son of God, have mercy on me, a Judas.

Ray Reitz is the pastor at Mountville Mennonite Church.

February 26

Walk With God

"But the word is very near you, in your mouth and in your heart, that you may do it." *Deuteronomy 30:14 (New King James Version)*

God knows our lame excuses: "I didn't know what I was supposed to do. How was I to know?" He told Israel, "My will is not mysterious or hidden."

As our children grew, we taught them to not only obey our rules, but to listen to their hearts when there were no declared rules. Even when we had not given exact instructions or rules for a specific situation, they knew the thing to do because of their day-to-day experience with us. It was in their heart—through our relationship. It was in their mouth. They could say it for us. Later, by God's faithful grace, each of them transferred this knowing to God.

God is saying to us, "Walk with Me day-by-day and you will always know My will." He says that the knowing of His will is *very near* with 'muchness', force, and abundance. It is easy to see how distance in relationship with God diminishes our ability to know His will. On the other hand, those who delight to do His will also delight in daily communion and fellowship with Him and have "an exceedingly near" ability to accomplish and produce His will. They can confidently know and say His will because they know Him. The shortest route to knowing His will is the single step of drawing near to Him and choosing to know Him.

Dear Father, let me walk with You today for I delight to do Your will. Oh God, let my mouth declare and my heart acknowledge Your will so that I may accomplish all that You plan and desire for me. In the name of Jesus Christ, Who came to earth so that He could do Your will. Amen.

Ruth Ann Stauffer is the coordinator of Teaching The Word Ministries' intercessors. She serves the Body of Christ in intercession, teaching, counseling, and prophetic ministry.

One

February 27
Stand Still And Hold Your Peace

"The LORD will fight for you, and you have only to be still."
Exodus 14:14 (Revised Standard Version)

Imagine yourself part of a ragtag band of people, tired from a day's journey and standing on the shoreline of the Red Sea. An army, whose destructive power is renowned around the world, is about to overtake you. Their grief over the death of their first born has turned to anger and revenge. Adding insult to injury, you carried off the gold from Egypt. As darkness sets over the landscape, you begin to realize the hopelessness and fear rising in your heart. On this sleepless night you sit by the water's edge, wondering about your future.

How many sleepless nights have you spent wondering about your future, about bills, marriage, or some other personal problem? You thought that by leaving Egypt (the world's way) and becoming a Christian, life would become smooth sailing. You never thought that you would have to come face to face with the strength of the enemy, who kept you in bondage before you accepted Christ. We fail to realize that the Lord brings us to this point so that our confidence in Him will rise.

Exodus 14 shows how God's hidden nature is always a part the situation. In verse 8, God is controlling the situation for His purposes. In verse 14, we are commanded to stand still. In other translations, this verse is interpreted as "hold your peace." Isn't fear the opposite of peace? Fear is an effective weapon that the devil uses to pull us away from God. God gives us inner-peace (John14: 27). Look at verse 22 in Exodus 14: God's way is not found where you expect it. That is why it is so important to stand still, hold your peace, and let Him show you. As the Lord answered the Israelites by making a way, He will answer you. Remember that the Lord is the same yesterday, today and forever.

Lord, teach us how to stand still when we don't see Your hand.

Bill Willis is a layman at New Covenant Christian Church.

February 28

A Different Kind Of Wisdom

"Who is wise and understanding among you? Let him show it by his good life, by deeds done in the humility that comes from wisdom." *James 3:13*

Occasionally, each of us believes we are wise and have some understanding concerning a situation or happening in our lives. Maybe we do not think of ourselves as wise in general, but at times we are absolutely brilliant and have complete understanding of the present circumstances.

James points out that wise and understanding people should demonstrate their wisdom through the living of a good life and by deeds done in humility. This method of demonstrating wisdom and understanding is so different from what we experience in our daily lives that it may be difficult to even imagine.

This wisdom is different because it is not the same as being wise concerning things of life and of this world. James is encouraging and lifting up godly wisdom. The wisdom of God is not about academic knowledge or anything connected to education. God's wisdom comes from being so connected with God in prayer, study, and action that the person has an awareness of God's nature and the appropriate actions that would reflect God's nature.

James continues in verse 17 saying, "but the wisdom that comes from heaven is first of all pure, then peace loving, considerate, submissive, full of mercy and good fruit, impartial, and sincere."

WOW, that gives me much to think about and work on in my life of discipleship. Attaining wisdom is challenging because as you grow more wise, you also grow more aware of the areas in which you are unwise. The mark of discipleship is continuing the journey to become wiser.

God of wisdom and understanding, thank You for Your patience with me. Help me to recognize when I am unwise and help me to discern what is wise, so that I may become a more humble and more faithful disciple of Jesus Christ, my Lord. Amen.

Kevin Readman is the pastor of Ranck's United Methodist Church in New Holland.

March

Working together in the Lancaster marketplace

A Purified Church

"But who can endure the day of his coming? Who can stand when he appears? For he will be like a refiner's fire or a launderer's soap." *Malachi 3:2*

"John answered them all, 'I baptize you with water. But one more powerful than I will come, the thongs of whose sandals I am not worthy to untie. He will baptize you with the Holy Spirit and with fire. His winnowing fork is in his hand to clear his threshing floor and to gather the wheat into his barn, but he will burn up the chaff with unquenchable fire.'" *Luke 3:16–17*

"We demolish arguments and every pretension that sets itself up against the knowledge of God, and we take captive every thought to make it obedient to Christ." 2 Corinthians 10:5

"Put to death, therefore, whatever belongs to your earthly nature… Because of these, the wrath of God is coming… put on the new self, which is being renewed in knowledge in the image of its Creator." *Colossians 3:5–10*

Here we have our part to do. It is our choice to fight the battle in our mind, taking thoughts captive, and making them obedient to Christ. As we do this we are able to submit to Christ and His Lordship over our thought life, our words, and our actions. Let us ask God to let His fire fall, consuming everything in our lives that is not of Him.

Dear God, I present myself to You, as a living sacrifice. Upon Your altar I lay my life. Burn out my dross. Change me. Let my life be a witness to how good and acceptable and perfect Your ways are.

Today's devotional was edited from the 2003–2004 *Throne Of Grace Prayer Guide*, a weekly guide of Lancaster County prayer concerns gathered from regional intercessors and area prayer groups.

March 2

Think On These Things

"And now, dear brothers and sisters, let me say one more thing as I close this letter. Fix your thoughts on what is true, honorable, and right..." *Philippians 4:8 (New Living Translation)*

This is one of the most important verses in the Bible. What occupies your mind and what you think means more than anything else in your life. Your thought life will determine how much you earn, where you live, and what you become in life. Your life today is a result of your thinking yesterday; your life tomorrow will be determined by what you think today.

You can change your life by beginning to think different thoughts. Matthew 12:34 says we speak what we think in our heart. What we think about needs to change...needs to be transformed (Romans 12:2).

Also how you spend your time will greatly determine what you think about. No doubt about it—Satan will bring his greatest temptations to people who have time on their hands. It takes discipline of character and proper goals to handle correctly the extra hours given to an individual in our society. We need to fill our time with tools and things that help you think right.

You can change your life by changing your thinking. You can change your thinking by changing the use of your free time and by changing your environment. Use Philippians 4:8 as a guideline to be applied in your thought life.

Dear God, I understand that my life today is a result of choices and thoughts I had yesterday. I want You to help me to continue to transform the way I think and how I utilize my time. My desire is that from this day forward I want to accomplish everything You have given me "a mind" to accomplish. I will allow Philippians 4:8 to guide my thinking from this day forward and I ask this in Jesus' Name. Amen.

Duane Britton, M.A., has served in a leadership role for twelve years and the last nine years as senior elder/pastor of D.O.V.E. Christian Fellowship Westgate Celebration, Ephrata.

March 3

Here Am I

Then Mary said, "Here am I, the servant of the Lord; let it be with me according to your word..." *Luke 1:38 (New Revised Standard Version)*

A re there any words in scripture that convey the meaning of a life in Christ more fully than those of Mary, upon being told by Gabriel that she was to bear the Son of God? Her simple response is a model of the posture we should have before God at all times and yet it is so difficult to follow.

In today's culture, the word servant often carries a negative connotation. A servant is always in relationship to a master. I like to think I am my own master, but a servant is precisely what Christ says I must be. And more than that, I must "let it be with me" according to His word. In other words, I must submit, or *abandon*, my will to His—totally, without reserve, in all circumstances. The freedom that comes from allowing God to take utter control of my life is without comparison, but surrendering that control is a stumbling block for many, if not most, who would follow Christ.

I believe her willingness to be the Lord's servant in any and all circumstances was the core of Mary's blessedness and the reason she found favor with God. As difficult as it is, submitting ourselves to God's word for us is also the core of our relationship with Him. By surrendering ourselves to His will, and starting each day saying, "Here am I, Lord," we find perfect freedom, perfect peace.

Dear Lord, let me always remember that I am Your servant, abandoning my will to Yours for the sake of Your perfect plan, even when it is hard to do so. Help me rely on the power of Your precious Son, Jesus Christ, to live in Your will each and every day. Amen.

Kim Wittel is the director for ministry development with Love INC (Love In the Name of Christ) of Lancaster County and is a member of St. Peter's Lutheran Church.

God's Complete Knowledge

"O LORD, you have searched me and you know me."
Psalm 139:1

Are there facts about your life that you would be afraid to have appear on the evening news?

Knowledge is a powerful thing. It both draws us and frightens us at the same time. We all want to be known and understood by another human being, but at the same time there are things about us that we hope nobody ever finds out!

As a child, I remember being attracted to a swamp in my neighborhood that was off limits to me. It was full of amphibious life that a young boy considers high adventure, as well as sharp objects submerged in the mud. Wading in one summer morning, I stepped on a broken bottle and cut open my toe. I remember well the agony of trying to hide my injury from my mother as I secretly applied first aid to my gaping wound. I also remember the growing fear within me, as each day my toe became increasingly infected.

We all have things about us that we would like to hide. The fact is God says that he *is acquainted with **all** our ways* and even *before a word is on our tongue, He knows it completely. (Psalm 139:4)* God's complete knowledge of us both draws us to Him and strikes fear in us at the same time.

Finally, when my toe became so infected that my mother noticed me limping, she reproved me for my foolishness, she took me to the doctor for stitches, and she nursed me back to health.

The amazing truth about God is, that despite knowing everything about our predicament, He still sent His Son to forgive us and to save us. This kind of love should comfort us. It should be *too wonderful...to take it all in! (Psalm 139:6)*

Dear Lord, please search my heart today! Point out anything in me that offends You, and guide me along the path of everlasting life.

Bill Haughery is a pastor at CrossWay Church of Lancaster in Millersville.

Flooded With Light

"I pray that your hearts will be flooded with light so that you can understand the wonderful future he has promised to those he called. I want you to realize what a rich and glorious inheritance he has given to his people. I pray that you will begin to understand the incredible greatness of his power for us who believe him. This is the same mighty power that raised Christ from the dead and seated him in the place of honor at God's right hand in the heavenly realms." *Ephesians 1:18–20 (New Living Translation)*

What a picture our Heavenly Father provides for us through His servant, Paul. We are to pray that our heart is flooded with light. This illumination is to take over our senses and flood our mind. When we look at the outcome of this flood, it is not destructive but intoxicating. It transforms us from hopeless people to people of purpose, power, and love.

When I first began to study this prayer, it immediately dawned upon me that I needed to change positions. I need to look at this from God's perspective and not my own. Paul says these things are already reality. God has already given us a future, an inheritance, and His transforming power. We need to pray for the scales of unbelief to fall from our eyes. I need my heart flooded with light to see and understand things from His perspective.

Obviously, this prayer should be a regular part of our life. If we are to "begin to understand," we must continually ask that our understanding increase. We can see the power of God at work in the life of Jesus, however, what about you and me? Make this a personal, daily prayer!

Father, I want You to flood my heart with Your wonderful light and love. Overwhelm me! I want to understand the greatness of Your power. Help me to see things from Your perspective and forgive me when I doubt Your Word. Amen.

Michael Shelley is a pastor at Lititz Christian Church and a council member with the Regional Church of Lancaster County.

March 6

Seeing The Invisible

"For since the creation of the world God's invisible qualities—
his eternal power and divine nature— have been clearly seen,
being understood from what has been made, so that men are
without excuse." *Romans 1:20*

If God were real, why wouldn't He have given us more proof that He exists? This was the question of a close co-worker who is an atheist. I don't remember exactly what I said at that moment, but as I continued to ponder his question, God reminded me of a scripture that speaks directly to the question!

I'm referring to Romans 1:20, which at first glance seems to make no sense! This verse says, "God's invisible qualities—His eternal power and divine nature—have been clearly seen." How can something that is invisible be clearly seen? The clue follows: "being understood by what has been made."

When we examine what God has made, we can begin to understand His qualities that otherwise could be considered invisible. How could we see God's eternal power? Observe the routine movements of the earth around the sun or the changing of seasons. How could we observe God's divine nature? Notice the intricacies of the human eye or study the nervous system.

The verse ends with a challenge: God's creation leaves men without excuse when it comes to acknowledging His existence. A person who never set foot inside a church or laid eyes on a page of scripture is surrounded daily by evidence of a divine creator with eternal power!

The next time you marvel at the beauty of the autumn leaves, or gaze in awe at the petite perfection of a newborn, remember you're seeing God's invisible qualities right before your very eyes.

Father, all You've created is amazing, flawless, and beyond compre-
hension. Thank You for the way You reveal Yourself in the things that
surround me each day. Amen.

Ron Ressler, with his wife Molly, serves as an overseer/coach for cell group leaders at Living Hope Community Church, west of Lancaster City.

Holy

"...The Lord spoke, saying: 'By those who come near Me I must be regarded as holy...'" *Leviticus 10:3 (New King James Version)*

The Lord said this right after He sent fire to consume two priests who were irreverent in His presence. Hebrews 12:28–29 gives us the same warning. God is still "a consuming fire." But what does it really mean to regard God as "holy"?

The word "holy" means to be perfect in every way, totally beyond the created realm or comprehension or experience, and filled with supernatural, even fatal power.

According to John Bevere, Our sun is 93 million miles away. It would take a jetliner 21 years flying nonstop to get there, and a car 200 years. It only takes light 1.3 seconds! Light travels 670,615,200 miles per hour. The distance it covers in one year is called a light year. Scientists have measured our universe to be at least 13.2 billion LIGHT YEARS wide! How does God compare? God is so big that the entire universe fits between His thumb and pinky finger (Isaiah 40:12)! No wonder Mount Sinai shook when God came down. How could it possibly hold Him? Yet, God is so loving that He humbles Himself to look at this earth and care for each microscopic speck of dust called man (Psalm 113:5–6).

When I think of this I wonder, "What is man that You [God] are mindful of him (Psalm 8:3-4)?" How could I have so much boldness and pride to disrespect Him by disobeying even the smallest detail of His directions for even the briefest of moments? What am I thinking when I sin? Still, God promises to help me whenever I simply humble myself and live respectfully before Him (James 4:6).

Oh God, You are so holy—unsearchable, incomprehensible, incomparable, and absolutely perfect in every way. Please forgive me for any disrespect I have shown toward You, and help me regard You as holy in everything I think, say, and do today. Amen.

Dean Witmer recently completed his pastorate at Living Truth Fellowship, Christiana, and helped to form the Lancaster Transformation Network.

March 8

Children Of The King

"But when the time had fully come, God
sent his Son, born of a woman, born
under law, to redeem those under law, that
we might receive the full rights of sons. Because you are sons, God sent the Spirit of his
Son into our hearts, the Spirit who calls out, 'Abba,
Father.' So you are no longer a slave, but a son; and since you
are a son, God has made you also an heir." *Galatians 4:4–7*

Pray!
for Lancaster
County

"Praise be to the God and Father of our Lord Jesus Christ,
who has blessed us in the heavenly realms with every spiritual
blessing in Christ... In love he predestined us to be adopted as
his sons through Jesus Christ, in accordance with his pleasure
and will— to the praise of his glorious grace, ... In him we
were also chosen, having been predestined according to the
plan of him who works out everything in conformity with the
purpose of his will, in order that we, who were the first to hope
in Christ, might be for the praise of his glory. And you also
were included in Christ when you heard the word of truth, the
gospel of your salvation. Having believed, you were marked in
him with a seal, the promised Holy Spirit, who is a deposit
guaranteeing our inheritance until the redemption of those who
are God's possession—to the praise of his glory." *Ephesians
1:3–14*

What does it mean to be called sons and daughters of the
Most High God, belonging to Him and being complete in
Him? Let us pray that we and every one in our region would
receive a revelation of this truth—to the building up of the Body of
Christ and the salvation of the lost.

*Oh, Most High! I will call You, Abba Father. I will declare myself as
Your son or daughter. I will live to please You.*

Today's devotional was edited from the 2003–2004 *Throne Of Grace
Prayer Guide*, a weekly guide of Lancaster County prayer concerns
gathered from regional intercessors and area prayer groups.

March 9

Knowing God's Wisdom

"But the wisdom that is from above is first pure, then peaceable, gentle, willing to yield, full of mercy and good fruits, without partiality and without hypocrisy." *James 3:17 (New King James Version)*

Are you making an important decision? Are you seeking how to respond to a difficult situation? Are you facing a moral dilemma—what is the right choice?

How can we know God's will in such situations? God's wisdom, that is, God's viewpoint and His purpose in a situation, is knowable. James, in this passage, gives us eight characteristics of wisdom from above—that is, from God.

We can test our decisions, responses, and choices by comparing a course of action with each of the following characteristics. First, is it pure with no hint of wrong doing? If not, there is no need to consider the course of action any further; it is not God's wisdom. Then is it peaceable; does it lead to wholeness and well-being?

When we consider a course of action, is it gentle as compared to harsh and unfeeling? Am I willing to yield to reason as other truth is laid alongside my present understanding?

Is it full of mercy and compassion? Will it potentially be full of good fruits (results)? Does it show partiality toward anyone? Are the expectations the same for myself as others; is it without hypocrisy?

When we are able to clearly answer "yes" to each of the above questions, then we have confidence that our course of action is consistent with godly wisdom. If we cannot clearly answer "yes" to a particular question, then we may ask the Lord to show us how to adjust our action to do so.

Heavenly Father, with so many decisions to make in life it is good to know that Your wisdom is available and knowable. By Your Spirit, guide me to make choices in light of wisdom from above. Through Your Son who is Your wisdom to and in us. Amen.

Keith Yoder, Teaching The Word Ministries, member of Regional Council of Regional Church of Lancaster County.

March 10

Expectation

"In the morning, O Lord, you hear my voice, in the morning I lay my requests before you and wait in expectation" *Psalm 5:3*

What do you expect of the Lord? Do you expect Him to do good things or do you wallow in fear that He will bring disaster upon your life? Webster's dictionary defines the "expectation" as "the act of expecting or looking forward to a future event with at least some reason to believe the event will happen." Expectation differs from hope. Hope originates in desire, and may exist with little or no grounds for belief that the desired event will arrive. Expectation is founded on reasons, which render the event probable. Expectation is the prospect of good to come (Psalm 62:5).

I realize that when I pray for God to work in a person or situation, often I do not expect that He will do it. I wrestle with fear that He won't move and my prayer will go unanswered. Instead of making myself vulnerable by expecting God to do good things, I live with less passion, almost surprised when God does do something amazing. I wonder how many of my prayers are rendered less effective because of my lack of faith, my lack of expectancy.

Jesus commanded his disciples to pray with faith, believing that He would answer them (Matthew 21:22). I believe this is how we are to pray today as well. God will see the expectancy with which we pray and will be glorified by our faith in Him. This is also a great way to be a light to others.

Father, please help me to pray expecting You to work. I desire to look for the good things that You do to advance your kingdom and use me to bring You glory. Help me to pray in faith. I love You.Amen.

Mandi Wissler is a senior at Lancaster Bible College majoring in Women in Christian Ministries. She is enjoying her last year on campus being a resident assistant for nine girls.

His Power

"I pray that you will begin to understand how incredibly great is His power to help those who believe in him..." *Ephesians 1:19 (Living Bible)*

Can we say that we truly *believe* the words in this scripture? It's obvious in scripture that Paul understood this "power" that is available to us. Having experienced this astounding power first hand from the time of his conversion, Paul was able to challenge the believers in Ephesus in a deeply personal manner.

It seems that we so easily forget the fact that the power of God is practical for our everyday life. If God can raise Christ from the dead, surely He can get you through this day. Of course, He can heal you of your past and definitely He can set you free completely from your sin.

It's sad that because of our unbelief, and perhaps our inability to understand the truths of God's word, many of us have a difficult time living our lives in obedience to what is required in scripture. Perhaps, we would be more successful if we took our eyes off of our weak areas and focused instead on Jesus Christ, the Son of the all powerful God, who has made available the ability to live as one who is not bound in the grip of sin.

Every day, there are many people around us who are yearning for a spiritual experience and watching us to see if what we believe is real. It's exciting to think, that as we exemplify the ever living, life-changing, power of God to a hurting world, we will see our prayers answered for salvation to come to those in need!

Father, help me to open my heart in a fresh way to Your life changing power. Give me the grace and strength to live my life every day in a way that would bring honor and glory to Your son Jesus.

Mike Stoltzfus gives leadership to the Lancaster Micro Church Network. He also serves on the council of the Regional Church of Lancaster County.

March 12

Heavenly Vintage

"The fruit of the Spirit is love, joy, peace, patience, kindness, goodness, faithfulness, gentleness, and self-control..."
Galatians 5:22

Are you passionate about something or someone? Quite frankly, in my current role as a stay-at-home mom, I don't "feel" passionate about much—just plain tired! Although I thoroughly enjoy my family, I do long for more time to do other things that bring some measure of fulfillment (music, writing, studying Scripture, reading, and teaching). Since becoming a mom, though, I've found there isn't much time (or energy) left after I've met the daily demands of child-rearing.

A wise friend once reminded me that "passion" (in the truest sense of the word) has to do with suffering. When we speak of "The Passion of Jesus Christ" we refer to the suffering that Jesus went through on our behalf in order to reconcile us to God. To think of passion in terms of what I'm willing to suffer for has been a helpful angle. Truly, the calling for which I gladly lay down my life is motherhood. When all is said and done, there is nothing I want more than to help my kids discover the fullness of life that is in Jesus Christ.

I'm also passionate about being a mom because it has clearly been the "school" where God is refining me the most. Until I stayed at home all day with my kids, I hadn't experienced myself as impatient and demanding. It is in the confines of our home that our Lord is showing me the rough edges of my character and where He is slowly, day by day, transforming my sometimes prideful spirit. How thankful I am that as I parent my children, God is lovingly parenting me!

Gracious Jesus, thank You that "love, joy, peace, patience, kindness, goodness, faithfulness, gentleness, and self-control" can be displayed in our lives by the power of Your Spirit. Each day, may I yield to You so that I may become more like You. Amen.

Rila Hackett is a member of First Presbyterian Church on Orange Street, where her husband, Don, is an associate pastor.

Image Maker

"…but if we walk in the Light as He Himself is in the Light, we have fellowship with one another, and the blood of Jesus His Son cleanses us from all sin." *1 John 1:7 (New American Standard Bible)*

Many of us have created an enhanced image of ourselves—one that depicts what we believe others want us to be, what we wish we were, who we really are not. Predictably, we convince those around us to embrace a "me" that is more tolerable and less pathetic than what we know to be true. That image is presented to others to be loved. Our goal is simply this: to avoid rejection. And as a result we are never truly accepted. Evading the Light, we hide our hearts from the Father as well as from one another. Secretly fearing what lies deep within, we are determined to protect the reality we've created from ever discovering truth. Thus isolation produces loneliness.

And this is precisely the issue the "apostle of love" addresses in 1 John 1:7. When we as the Body of Christ walk in the Light, we are exposed for who and what we really are. With nothing to hide from God, we have nothing to hide from man. Free to be honest with both God and man, we are able to enter into true fellowship and God is able to purge us even further through relationships founded on intimate transparency.

Disconnecting our hearts from the truth, we attempt to give others shallow information about who we are—mere data concerning our condition. However, this only serves as a facade, which imitates transparency but lacks vulnerability. Yet the two are inseparable. True transparency insists on vulnerability.

Father, help us to understand the meaning of true transparency. Help us to expose our hearts completely to the Light and to maintain no false reality of one another.

Jonathan Jacobs is on the leadership team of the Lancaster House of Prayer, Consuming Fire Ministries, MorningStar Satellite School, and The Gemeinschaft.

March 14

Knowing His Secrets

"The secret of the Lord is with those who fear Him, and He will show them His covenant" *Psalm 25:14 (New King James Version)*

How exciting it is to share in a secret! What thrills we experience when a friend takes us into their confidence, and shares the intimate details of some tantalizing mystery. Our Heavenly Father wants to be that friend to us, if we would reverence Him and take time to come into His presence, allowing our hearts to be intimately entwined with His Spirit. He will share His great mysteries as He did with Paul the apostle, bringing hope, joy, peace and a sense of personal destiny into our hearts. When we accept Jesus Christ as our Savior, we must come to the understanding that we are no longer strangers and foreigners, but have become family, or members of the household of God. We are being built together with other believers, creating a dwelling place of God in the Spirit (Ephesians 2:19–22) so that God can dwell with us and walk among us (2 Corinthians 6:16).

In this spiritually enriched environment, through the leading of the Holy Spirit, God desires to show us, by allowing us to discover and discern the secrets of His word, how we will come to an understanding of His covenant and know the leading of His Spirit. This will cause us to rejoice, knowing that in Christ He has chosen and adopted us, making us accepted in the Beloved. He has redeemed us through His Blood and forgiven our sins according to the riches of His Grace. In Him we have also obtained an everlasting inheritance (Ephesians 1:3–14).

Dear Father God, as I reverently come into Your presence, I pray that Your spirit of wisdom and revelation be released into my life. Enlighten the eyes of my understanding, that I may know what is the hope of Your calling, the riches of Your inheritance, and the greatness of Your power towards us who believe. In the name of Jesus Christ, Amen.

Allan Chambers gives Apostolic Oversight to Global Covenant Ministries.

March 15

A Humble Church,
A Merciful Church

"He has showed you, O man, what is good.
And what does the LORD require of you?
To act justly and to love mercy
and to walk humbly with your God." *Micah 6:8*

Pray!
for Lancaster
County

"Submit yourselves, then, to God. Resist the devil, and he will
flee from you. Come near to God and he will come near to you.
Wash your hands, you sinners, and purify your hearts, you
double-minded. Grieve, mourn and wail. Change your laughter
to mourning and your joy to gloom. Humble yourselves before
the Lord, and he will lift you up." *James 4:7–10*

L et us confess and repent of any pride that the Lord reveals both
individually and in our region. Confession and repentance are
one way to resist the devil and cause him to flee. Let us to draw
near to God and pray that the Church would walk in humility, mercy
and justice.

*Lord, I humble myself under Your mighty hand. Help me to love mercy
and do justly. Show me the need around me and help me to meet that
need.*

Today's devotional was edited from the 2003–2004 *Throne Of Grace
Prayer Guide*, a weekly guide of Lancaster County prayer concerns
gathered from regional intercessors and area prayer groups.

March 16

Fresh Worship

"Then I saw a Lamb, looking as if it had been slain, standing in the center of the throne, encircled by the four living creatures and the elders....He came and took the scroll from the right hand of Him who sat on the throne. And when he had taken it, the four living creatures and the twenty-four elders fell down before the Lamb...." *Revelations 5:6–8*

When Christ reveals who He is and shows His power, we have a God-instilled response in our spirit to worship. When the Lamb appeared to open the scroll, that's when the multitudes appear in this heavenly scene. Though it's clear that worship is taking place in heaven prior to the entrance of the Lamb, heaven erupts in raucous jubilation when His power to open the scroll is revealed.

This concept is seen several times in the Gospels. The woman at the well actually entered into an argument with Jesus until He revealed Himself to be the Messiah; once that happened, she instantly worshiped Him. The men on the road to Emmaus did not worship Jesus (with whom they had traveled for nearly an entire day) until He revealed His power to them. After the Resurrection, Mary thought that Jesus was a gardener. She pled with Him to tell her where they had taken the body—but the moment Jesus revealed His identity to her, she worshiped.

Seeking a "newness" to our personal and congregational worship can be a waste of time if we only focus on the act of worship. Instead, fresh and powerful worship is the natural response as we fix our eyes on Jesus Christ, and fervently seek to uncover all that He wants to reveal to us.

Jesus, reveal Yourself to me in a fresh way today so that my worship of You can be ever-expanding. Thank You for all that You have shown—I long for more!

Diane Moore, a Lancaster United for Life board member, is active in politics, and plays keyboard for the music ministry at New Covenant Christian Church.

March 17

A Saint Patrick's Day Thought

"In the beginning was the Word, and the Word was with God, and the Word was God. He was in the beginning with God. All things come into being by Him, and apart from Him nothing came into being that has come into being. In Him was life, and the life was the light of men. And the light shines in the darkness, and the darkness did not comprehend." *John 1:1–5 (New American Standard Bible)*

My great grandparents came from Ireland and at this time of the year we are wearing a lot of green in my home as we dance around to reels and jigs. Today we all celebrate Ireland's Saint Patrick. In Patrick's famous writing, "Confession", he includes a reworking of John 1: "There is no other God, nor ever was, nor will be, than God the Father unbegotten, without beginning, from whom is all beginning, the Lord of the universe, as we have been taught; and His son Jesus Christ, whom we declare to have always been with the Father, spiritually and ineffably begotten by the Father before the beginning of the world, before all beginning; and by Him are made all things visible and invisible..." Today let us focus on the mystery of the Holy Three and meditate on the glory of Jesus Christ—the pre-existent Word—that holds everything together and is the light our dark world so desperately needs.

Then pray this prayer from the Book of Common Prayer:

Almighty God, in Your providence You chose your servant Patrick to be the apostle of the Irish people, to bring those who were wandering in darkness and error to the true light and knowledge of You: Grant us so to walk in that light that we may come at last to the light of everlasting life; through Jesus Christ our Lord, who lives and reigns with You and the Holy Spirit, one God, for ever and ever. Amen.

Ned Bustard plans worship for Wheatland Presbyterian Church. He also works in Lancaster as an illustrator/graphic designer and creative director.

March 18

Doing Justice In The Market Place

"...What does the Lord require of you but to do justice [do what is right], to love kindness [mercy], and to walk humbly with your God." Micah 6:8 (New American Standard Bible)

Over 400 times the Scripture speaks of justice and righteousness. This is obviously extremely important to God. The market place is a practical place to live out these principles. We show it in the way we use the time and resources entrusted to us—like our expense account and office supplies. Are we on time? Are we loyal to our employers and employees? Do we find ways to encourage, or do we criticize?

Loving mercy is not just superficially being polite in a professionally correct manner; it is seeking ways to reach out to those in need when you have the authority to make a difference. Do you have the courage to make a difference in the lives of the helpless? In local government, I see countless examples of people's lives simply falling apart. When we fail to love mercy, we fail to be Christ-like.

Humility is an attitude. It is coming to a full understanding of dependence on God, and God alone. When we experience God working through us to make a difference in people's lives in the work place, it is humbling. I have found that I can only walk humbly if I stay in His Word daily. I need to spend time in the morning before leaving for work in personal devotion and prayer with God. I also find it important to meet with my accountability partner once a week.

As you enter your place of work today, see it as a place God has called you to. Pray that He will use you to honor Him today.

Dear God, open my eyes and ears in the market place. Give me Your strength to live justly, and fill my heart with the burden to show mercy. Use me to make a difference in the lives that I touch each day.

Dick Shellenberger serves as County Commissioner in Lancaster County.

God Put On Skin

"All this took place to fulfill what the Lord had said through the prophet: 'The virgin will be with child and will give birth to a son, and they will call him Immanuel'—which means, 'God with us.'" *Matthew 1:22,23*

Alittle boy, so the story goes, was afraid one night when thunder and lightning boomed and flashed outside his bedroom window. He cried out, and his father came and crawled in beside him in the little boy's bed. The father told his son he need not be afraid, because God is with him. "Yes, I know," the boy answered, "but I want someone to be with me who has skin on." God "put skin on" to come and be with us in his Son Jesus. Immanuel, meaning "God with us," is one of the most precious names of our Lord Jesus.

John wrote, "The Word became flesh and made His dwelling among us (John 1:14)." The eternal, almighty Lord came and lived among His creation in the form of a man. This Messiah, fully God and fully human, walked among us, teaching the multitudes, healing the sick, feeding the hungry, and delivering the oppressed. Then He died for us, arose for us, and now lives within us by His Spirit as we trust in Him.

God does not promise we will never go through difficult times or face intense temptation, but He does promise always to be with us and never to forsake us. He has said, "When you pass through the waters, I will be with you… When you walk through the fire, you will not be burned…. For I am the Lord your God…(Isaiah 43:2–3)." Believers face adversity, sometimes even martyrdom, but God will be with us, always, the whole way into eternity! What more do we need?

Almighty Father, thank You for coming to be with us and to be our Savior. Thank You for promising to be with me always. Take my fears as I rest in You.

Jim Leaman is the pastor of Groffdale Mennonite Church, Leola.

March 20
Fearfully And Wonderfully Made

"For you created my inmost being; you knit me together in my mother's womb. I praise you because I am fearfully and wonderfully made..." *Psalms 139:13–14*

Many of us struggle with perfectionism. It carries through in our daily lives, seen in an attention to detail and being the best at everything. This pursuit shifts us out of a life of joy and into a stressful churning of the soul as we try to supercede our humanity in order to silence the shout of insecurity. This drive affects us on a spiritual level—it is the belief that we must live up to our own expectations in order to be good enough for God to use our lives to maximum potential. God created us; He knows our flaws and our subtle shades of beauty. Furthermore, "wonderfully made" does not include a clause that adds "if you have a clean house, an influential career, a perfect body, and never lose your temper."

What if we believe that our core value is wonderful, that we are unique from birth and have a special place that no one else can fill? Many Christians give lip service to this belief while living in a pattern of trying to prove their worthiness of being adored by God. Will you spend today mapping out how to be a "perfect" Christian—or will you blindly decide to trust that maybe you are enough "as is?" While I still pursue excellence, I know that God loves me more than all of my accomplishments; thus, my only responsibility is to connect with Him regularly in order to live the life for which I am fearfully and wonderfully made.

Dear God, Please help me to relinquish my own expectations of what I should be. Heal my need to prove my worth by my success. Help me to listen to the whispers of the wonderful things You have created in me, so that I can serve You joyfully.

Tricia S. Groff, M.S. is a counselor at Crossroads Counseling Center, Lancaster, and a cognitive therapist at ACADIA, Lancaster.

Because Of His Compassions...

"Arise, cry out in the night, as the watches of the night begin; pour out your heart like water in the presence of the Lord. Lift up your hands to Him for the lives of your children, who faint from hunger at the head of every street." *Lamentations 2:19*

Jeremiah was seeing his people being taken into captivity, being scoffed, and mocked. He was watching children die on every corner of the street as a result of the disobedience of Israel to the Lord. So he exposed his feelings, and poured out his heart to God. He was interceding and inviting the people to do the same. But in the midst of his lamentation and his affliction he remembered the goodness of God and had hope. So he said, "Because of the Lord's great love we are not consumed, for his compassions never fail. They are new every morning; great is your faithfulness...(Lamentations 3:22, 23)."

Personally, when I read the newspaper, or hear the TV news, or minister in Lancaster prison, or in the streets of the city, I remember that once I was, myself, in Rikers Island jail in New York City. Then, I say to Him, "O Lord, you took up my case; You redeemed my life." I also know that many people were crying out and praying to the Lord for me, and that He heard their cries and saw my need of Him.

Dear Lord, we have sinned and rebelled against you as individuals, and as a nation. Please forgive us. Remember our sins no more, and have mercy on our children. You are our portion; therefore we will wait for You. Amen.

Marta Estrada is an author and church pioneer in Medellin, Colombia, South America. She is a member of Petra Christian Fellowship in New Holland, and founder of a program that helps to restore teenagers that are involved in prostitution.

March 22

Resurrection Life

"...Then he said to me, 'Prophesy to these bones and say to them, "Dry bones, hear the word of the LORD ! This is what the Sovereign LORD says to these bones: I will make breath enter you, and you will come to life...Then you will know that I am the LORD.'"

for Lancaster County

"So I prophesied as I was commanded. And as I was prophesying, there was a noise, a rattling sound, and the bones came together, bone to bone. I looked, and tendons and flesh appeared on them and skin covered them, but there was no breath in them.

"Then he said to me, 'Prophesy to the breath; ... "This is what the Sovereign LORD says: Come from the four winds, O breath, and breathe into these slain, that they may live.'" So I prophesied as he commanded me, and ... they came to life and stood up on their feet—a vast army." *Ezekiel 37:4–10*

"We were therefore buried with him through baptism into death in order that, just as Christ was raised from the dead through the glory of the Father, we too may live a new life. If we have been united with him like this in his death, we will certainly also be united with him in his resurrection. ...anyone who has died has been freed from sin. Now if we died with Christ, we believe that we will also live with him." *Romans 6:4–8*

We need God to breathe His resurrection life into us, causing the church of Lancaster County to arise as a mighty army for His glory! Praise God that as Christ was raised from the dead, so we may receive new life as well.

Lord Jesus, I will declare that You are risen indeed!

Today's devotional was edited from the 2003–2004 *Throne Of Grace Prayer Guide*, a weekly guide of Lancaster County prayer concerns gathered from regional intercessors and area prayer groups.

Give Him Everything

"So they pulled their boats up on shore, left everything and followed him." *Luke 5:11*

This reaction of Peter and the others to Jesus' call is where we want to find ourselves after hearing from the Lord. The prophet also came to this point in Isaiah 6:8 when the Lord asks, "Whom shall I send?" and Isaiah responds, "Here am I. Send me!" We too desire to be counted among the faithful who respond with confidence. But why do we hold back from the Lord? Why don't we give "everything?"

After a night of fruitless fishing, Peter first drops the nets out of obedience because Jesus "said so" (Luke 5:5). Maybe he thought "it's worth a try" and did as instructed. However, the next time Peter drops the nets is in verse 11 when Christ invites him to be a fisher of men. This time it was out of surrender. He hands it all over…his everything. He moves beyond just submission to one command and yields himself to the Commander. At that point he could have declined and still enjoyed the abundance of fish gained by his initial obedience. Because we know how the story ends, we understand how much Peter would have missed had he not surrendered.

In responding to Christ, we must completely surrender to what He asks of us. God doesn't excuse disobedience because we're waiting for certain feelings or situations to come in order to take action. He desires more than random compliance, but for us to allow Him complete access over all of the affairs of our lives…all of the time. It can be sort of scary, can't it? This letting go and trusting…this surrendering to the unknown. But here is where we'll find true freedom and abundance beyond measure.

Dear Lord, may my actions display an attitude of surrender to Your desires for my life. Today may I see Your will as supreme over mine.

Daniele Evans is a pastor's wife and mother of three. She serves on the leadership team of Christ the King Community Church, Lancaster.

March 24

Resurrection Hope

"Praise be to the God and Father of our Lord Jesus Christ! In his great mercy he has given us new birth into a living hope through the resurrection of Jesus Christ from the dead...."
1 Peter 1:3

There is a song that was popular a number of years ago called "Because He Lives." The chorus goes, "Because He lives I can face tomorrow; because He lives all fear is gone; because I know He holds the future, and life is worth the living just because He lives." Because of the resurrection we have a hope and a future. Life is worth living because He lives.

Because He lives there is hope—no person is beyond the reach of His love; no situation is too big for God to solve.

Because He lives there is hope—for our children in an uncertain world; for the backslidden child and wayward spouse.

Because He lives there is hope—for healing for the sick and hurting; for wholeness of those abused and addicted.

Because He lives there is hope—for broken relationships; for financial needs.

Because He lives there is hope—for a mighty move of God in our region; for our nation to turn back to God.

Because He lives there is hope—even in death for there is eternal life through Jesus Christ our Lord. *"We have this hope as an anchor for the soul, firm and secure... (Hebrews 6:19)."*

Pray the words of this wonderful hymn: *"My hope is built on nothing less than Jesus' blood and righteousness.... When darkness veils his lovely face, I rest on His unchanging grace. In every high and stormy gale, my anchor holds within the veil.... On Christ the solid rock I stand; all other ground is sinking sand."*

Lester Zimmerman is the senior pastor of Petra Christian Fellowship in New Holland.

March 25

Resurrection: Ability

"And what is the exceeding greatness of His power (*dunamis*) toward us who believe, according to the working of His mighty power." *Ephesians 1:19 (New King James Version)*

Feeling powerless? We've been there, and may be there today. The gradually increasing weariness has spent our energy. The huge challenge intimidates like an unmovable mountain. The future is in a fog, with no clear "next step".

The Apostle Paul, who longed to know the power of Christ's resurrection (Philippians 3:10), also prayed for believers in Ephesus that they may know the exceeding greatness of Christ's power. Paul placed four "power morals" in this passage—set like jewels in a crown—to give us...faith.

When the Father raised Jesus from the dead, the power (*dunamis*) was the *dynamic power of a miracle and supernatural ability.* The earth quaked, a huge stone rolled away, and a disfigured dead body was completely restored to life. That's power!

Paul came to rely solely upon this power in his service for the Lord. He chose to boast about his weakness so that Christ's power could more fully work in him and through him.

God's power gives us the *ability* to do what we cannot do alone, to overcome what we have failed to conquer, to face what seems insurmountable, to go beyond the limits of the possible. Just as Jesus trusted His Father to bring Him *through* death, we can also trust God to act in His ability to bring us through our powerlessness.

Lord, I need the same power by which You raised Jesus Christ from the dead in my life. I believe I am made able to do all things through Christ who strengthens me. Today, I am going to depend upon You to admit my weakness, face the challenges, and take the next step. Also, I receive Your ability today to help my neighbor, friend, or stranger in their powerlessness.

Keith Yoder, Teaching The Word Ministries, member of Regional Council of Regional Church of Lancaster County.

March 26

Resurrection: Energy

"And what is the exceeding greatness of His power toward us who believe, according to the working (energeia) of His mighty power." *Ephesians 1:19 (New King James Version)*

The explosive power of the resurrection has been distributed to the members of Christ's Body on the earth. It is working in us today. Paul called it a mystery—Christ in us.

Christ has given us measured portions of His great power to work through us in specific ways. Sometimes we call these workings of His power "spiritual gifts". It is His ability giving us the energy to love as He loves and to serve as He serves.

It is His energy motivating us to show mercy, to build understanding of the scriptures, to speak the impressions He puts in our hearts and minds. It is the passion of His Spirit moving us to witness for Christ or warn a brother or sister of spiritual danger.

Paul realized that it was Christ's energy working through him to help others to mature in Christ. It is the energy from Christ within each member that causes us each to do our part, work together, and supply life to one another so that the Body of Christ grows in love. Yes, most often the energy of Christ is released by speaking the truth in love.

Like a power line carrying electricity to make the appliances work in our homes, so the energy of Christ powers the working of all of the members of His Body.

Father, thank You for entrusting Your limitless power to work in us. I open my heart for You to energize me to express the life and work of Christ today. I also welcome Christ to work through the fellow believers that You intend to shape my life that we may grow together into His likeness. Today, continue Your work in each believer in our region that we may become more complete in Christ.

Keith Yoder, Teaching The Word Ministries, member of Regional Council of Regional Church of Lancaster County

Resurrection: Strength

"And what is the exceeding greatness of His power toward us who believe, according to the working of His **mighty** (ischus) power." *Ephesians 1:19 (New King James Version)*

Wrestling. Well-conditioned bodies with bulging muscles straining and pressing. He who is quickest and wisest in the use of his strength wins. That's the picture of "mighty" in Paul's prayer—muscle power.

War. Those who would defend their territory fight from fortifications. Whether tall towers and thick walls above ground or bunkers buried in the earth, the shelter is built to be strong.

We wrestle against powers in the spiritual realm. Our battles require strength to resist temptations and to overcome evil thoughts. Jesus wrestled with the evil one and prevailed. In the wilderness He overcame through declaring the Word of God. In Gethsemane He prevailed through yielding to the will of His Father—then an angel came and strengthened Him.

As we speak the Word of God and pray in agreement with the will of God, the mighty power of the resurrection is released. As we believe in the Word of God that we speak, evil thoughts are made subject to the power of Christ. (2 Corinthians 10:5).

The Lord is our fortress, our rock, our shield. His nature within strengthens us in the face of the pressure to serve self or to become discouraged.

His nature within also empowers us to love God with all of our heart, mind, and **strength**!

Father, I am more confident in resisting evil knowing that the mighty power of the resurrection is available to me. Today, I pray for fellow believers throughout our County to be strengthened with might in their hearts—to resist evil and love You.

Keith Yoder, Teaching The Word Ministries, member of Regional Council of Regional Church of Lancaster County

March 28

Resurrection: Dominion

"And what is the exceeding greatness of His power toward us who believe, according to the working of His mighty **power** (kratos)." *Ephesians 1:19 (New King James Version)*

When one nation conquers another in war there are various phases of engagement until dominion is complete. The victory may begin with "shock and awe" displays of *explosive power* that subdue the enemy. High-tech weaponry may be directed at selective targets with pinpoint accuracy and controlled *energy*. Superior *strength* breaks down fortifications and flushes out the enemy.

Finally, the conquering army goes throughout the territory, city by city, village by village, to restore order and to establish a new government. When the new government is established, *dominion* is assured.

It was with this understanding that Paul prayed for the church at Ephesus and at Colosse. He wanted them to know that the power of Christ's resurrection had delivered them from the dominion of darkness. They were transferred to the Kingdom of God's Beloved Son. (Colossians 1:13).

When we declare Christ Lord, the power of His Kingdom now governs our lives and gives us dominion over Satan and self.

I find this is a daily choice, so I begin many of my days asking Christ to fill me with His Spirit. I then ask the Holy Spirit to "establish the government of Jesus Christ in my heart today." As I am governed by the Holy Spirit, it will be evident in the fruit of self-control, or self-government.

Father, thank You for the power of the resurrection to free us from the dominion of sin and to place us in the Kingdom of Your dear Son. Establish the government of Christ in my life today. For those throughout our region who struggle under the domination of habits, addictions, and the emptiness of serving self, send messengers to them today with the good news of Your Kingdom.

Keith Yoder, Teaching The Word Ministries, member of Regional Council of Regional Church of Lancaster County

March 29

The Fragrance
Of Christ

"But thanks be to God, who always leads us
in triumphal procession in Christ and through
us spreads everywhere the fragrance of the
knowledge of him. For we are to God the aroma of
Christ among those who are being saved and those who are
perishing. To the one we are the smell of death; to the other,
the fragrance of life. And who is equal to such a task? Unlike
so many, we do not peddle the word of God for profit. On the
contrary, in Christ we speak before God with sincerity, like men
sent from God." *2 Corinthians 2:14–17*

Through us" God "spreads everywhere the fragrance of the
knowledge of Him": what a promise for our region! God uses
us to manifest the sweet aroma of the knowledge of Christ in
everyplace we live and go. This week, let us speak the truth about God
and Christ to those who know him and to those who don't.

*Lord, we pray that all that we do would give testimony of our being in
the presence of the King of Glory.*

Today's devotional was edited from the 2003–2004 *Throne Of Grace
Prayer Guide*, a weekly guide of Lancaster County prayer concerns
gathered from regional intercessors and area prayer groups.

March 30

The Final Proof

"And if Christ has not been raised, our preaching is useless and so is your faith." *1 Corinthians 15:14*

Today many people are in search of truth. How can they know for sure that Christianity is the one and only true religion? Why should they believe Jesus' claims above the claims of other leaders who claim divinity?

There was a Muslim in Africa who became a Christian. Some of His friends asked him, "Why have you become a Christian?"

He answered, "Well, it's like this. Suppose you were going down a road and suddenly the road forked in two directions, and you didn't know which way to go, and there at the fork in the road were two men, one dead and one alive—which one would you ask which way to go?"

Everything we believe hinges on the resurrection. If Jesus is not able to conquer death and defeat Satan then He is no different than any other prophet who gained a following and was buried and is now honored as a dead leader. He would only be a prophet among other dead prophets and religious leaders such as Mohammed or Buddha. The resurrection was the final proof of the claims of Christ. Because He rose from the dead we now have the confidence that He truly is the Son of God and that we have forgiveness of sin.

Lord Jesus, I thank You for Your victory on the cross. I thank You that You have given me the same power of the resurrection to live a victorious life and to also rise from the dead and live eternally with You.

Lester Zimmerman is the senior pastor of Petra Christian Fellowship in New Holland

March 31

Setting The Stage

"...Lazarus is dead..." *John 11:14*

You know the story well. The sick brother. The plea for help from his two sisters. Jesus' declaration that this sickness would not end in death. And the deliberate decision of Jesus to wait two additional days. Finally, Jesus declares plainly: "Lazarus is dead."

"Lazarus is dead." It seems rather harsh—cold or rude or uncaring...unless you remember Who is speaking. You must remember that He is the Resurrection and the Life. And when He Who is Life declares that something is dead, He is often setting the stage for the display of His glory and a resurrection. Jesus could have run to Lazarus' side immediately and brought healing. Instead He allowed the natural process of death to run its course, and then against that drab, hopeless backdrop, He painted the bold colors of resurrection.

What if it is at those times, when we feel the most helpless and empty and drab and hopeless—due to a lost dream, a failing relationship, or a tragic circumstance—that our God and King, the Resurrection and the Life, is setting the stage for the display of His glory in our lives? What if when it appears that He is most absent we would understand that He is most present—doing great works in our lives?

Just as Jesus brought life back into the lifeless body of His friend, He is also able to bring that same life into all areas of our life. Don't be distracted by the hopelessness of the backdrop, the Artist is preparing to paint a masterpiece on the canvas of your life!

Father, give me the faith to believe that You are constantly at work in my life, even when I think that You are not moving "on schedule." Your ways are perfect, and I trust You. In Jesus' name, AMEN.

Michael Evans is the lead pastor of Christ the King Community Church, Lancaster, and works with the Urban School Services Department of the Association of Christian Schools International.

April

April 1

Blessed Is He Who Comes In The Name Of The Lord!

for Lancaster County

"The crowds that went ahead of him and those that followed shouted, 'Hosanna to the Son of David! Blessed is he who comes in the name of the Lord! Hosanna in the highest!'" *Matthew 21:9*

L et us shout together: Hosanna in the highest! Blessed is he who comes in the name of the Lord! Jesus, we welcome You to our region. We declare You King! Stir our hearts by your presence. Open our mouths. Move our hands and feet. You are our head. We are your body.

Lord, I will sing You a new song. Your praise shall continually be on my lips.

Today's devotional was edited from the 2003–2004 *Throne Of Grace Prayer Guide*, a weekly guide of Lancaster County prayer concerns gathered from regional intercessors and area prayer groups.

April 2
Commitment Level

"My people come to you...and sit before you to listen to your words...but they do not put them into practice. With their mouths they express devotion, but their hearts are greedy for unjust gain. Indeed, you [as a prophet] are nothing more than one who sings love songs with a beautiful voice and plays an instrument well, for they hear your words but do not put them into practice." *Ezekiel 33:31–32*

Ezekiel lived in a day where people were willing to hear the word the prophet had to declare saying, "Come and hear the message of the Lord." The problem was that they viewed the word from God as an entertaining edict to consider, not as an emphatic mandate to obey. The spiritual barrenness that resulted from this practice coupled with the arrogant attitude that could easily dismiss God's clear directives, led the nation into decline, decay, and ultimate defeat.

21st century North Americans are given ample opportunity to hear the Word of God. The airwaves are filled with messengers of God declaring the truth. Conferences abound where Christians gather to hear renowned preachers declare messages from God's Word. Multiple-millions of dollars are spent for Christian concert tickets and worship celebrations. Millions of books are sold to eager buyers who want to read the most current popular author who has a message from God that will bless their lives. Faithful pastors labor to present a clear explanation of Word of God and deliver that message under the unction of the Holy Spirit. People are entertained by what they hear, read, and see in these opportunities. But are people responding in obedience to what they hear? Do people today do as they did in Ezekiel's day: "sit...to listen to your words, but they do not put them into practice?"

May the admonition that Jesus gave in his parable in Matthew 7:24–27 propel us beyond hearing the words of God and arrive at a commitment level that "puts them into practice."

Robert Reid is the senior pastor at Calvary Monument Bible Church.

April 3

Where Are You God?

"If you had been here, my brother would not have died."
John 11:21

John 11:21 echoes a prayer we all have uttered in a moment's discouragement, often brought on by our own acute sense of time. We find ourselves locked in time on this earth. It is at the core of our existence.

Here we are stuck in time trying to relate to a God who does not wear a watch. We find ourselves interacting with God who is the same yesterday, today, and forever, who exists in the eternal now of the "I Am That I Am."

When we cry out, "Where are you, God?" what we are often saying is from our own perspective, "You appear to be late God." It is in this season of lateness that our faith is tested and grown, and our need for patience is revealed. Mary and Martha thought Jesus was late and the opportunity for Him to meet their need had passed. Jesus' response was to call Lazarus back from eternity into the time of this earth that they would know the Father had sent Him (Jesus).

God is not late.

Father, I thank You for Your faithfulness toward me. Help me to rest in Your promises and to trust in Your timing. You are my Alpha and Omega. You are my peace. In Jesus' name, Amen.

Wayne Kaufman pastors Gates of Praise Ministries, Gates of Praise House Church Network and is a board member of Harvest Net, The Regional Church of Lancaster County and the Lancaster House of Prayer.

April 4

It Is Finished

"When he had received the drink, Jesus said, 'It is finished.'
With that, he bowed his head and gave up his spirit."
John 19:30

K nowing all was completed, Jesus cried out, "IT IS FIN-
ISHED!" These are words of triumph and victory. To many it
looked like Jesus was defeated. His disciples deserted Him
and ran away in fear. His crucifiers sighed in relief that it was finally
over. His friends came to bury His body and pay their last respects.

But Jesus didn't say, "I give up." He didn't say, "I am defeated."
He said, "IT IS FINISHED." He said, "MISSION ACCOMPLISHED."
"And having disarmed the powers and authorities, He made a public
spectacle of them, triumphing over them by the cross (Colossians 2:15)."

IT IS FINISHED MEANS:

* The payment or ransom for our sins was completed. There is nothing more we can do to earn our salvation. It is finished in Jesus!

* Guilt and condemnation which people had lived under for so long
  by trying to be good enough through good works was wiped away.

* Jesus triumphed over Satan, sin, sickness, death and hell. He took
  away the sting of death and broke the power of Satan.

* The broken relationship and alienation from God was mended. The
  restoration was now complete.

* The Old Covenant was fulfilled and a New Covenant based on
  better promises had begun.

The last Passover lamb was killed. Jesus became the Lamb of God.
His blood and death became the last sacrifice ever to be required by
God. It was finished! We are now more than conquerors through Christ
because IT IS FINISHED!

*Lord Jesus, Thank You for completing Your mission so that I can walk
in Your victory. Today I speak to every negative situation in my life and
declare, "It is finished!"*

Lester Zimmerman is the senior pastor of Petra Christian Fellowship
in New Holland.

April 5
Faith Hall Of Fame

"And without faith it is impossible to please God, because anyone who comes to him must believe that he exists and that he rewards those who earnestly seek him." *Hebrews 11:6*

This verse comes out of the "Faith Hall of Fame" (Hebrews 11). This chapter commends the people of the past who lived out their beliefs in God and his plans for them.

As I look at the "Faith Hall of Fame", I have to acknowledge that Abel was murdered, Noah wasn't encouraged by his neighbors while building the Ark, Abraham never lived to see the nations that were his offspring, Moses had to give up being royalty in Egypt, Daniel had to weather numerous changes of leadership and political scandals, etc.

Faith is not as easy or as self-gratifying as some might think. Nor is it reserved for the top 10% of society. Faith is an inward choice to seek and to continue seeking God no matter what happens.

For me, this is comforting. I am just a plain man living life in the minor leagues of humanity. Perhaps, someday, I will receive the opportunity to be one of those "super stars" that shines for God in the land of the living. But even then God's criteria will not change. He will be watching my heart for the persevering faith that enables me to receive the crown of righteousness that his Son Jesus bought for me.

I hold on to this truth. If I can persevere through this short life with the faith of the men and women of Hebrews 11, I will be acknowledged when it matters most, standing before Almighty God.

Lord, You made me, you have a purpose for me and your blessing will shine through in the end. I will trust you to carry out your plan as I walk with you in obedience. Amen.

Dan Neff is a small business owner and seeks to bring the knowledge and blessing of the kingdom of God into every area of life.

April 6

The Normal Christian Walk

"I know that when I come to you, I will come in the full measure of the blessing of Christ." *Romans 15:29*

We need to stop compartmentalizing the Church's experience. God is calling us to integrate into all our Christian theology and practice the expectation that the fullness of Christ is to be part of everyday life. Clearly, there is ebb and flow in any work of the Spirit. But we can constantly expect more and more of His "river of grace" and influence to be poured out on us wherever the work of the kingdom flows. We need to live in a faith that expects that normal Christianity will always reproduce effectively no matter what the moral challenges it faces. The Gospel is designed to reach the hardened and imprisoned. The Kingdom of God flourishes best when it faces impossible odds and the power of the Spirit must unexpectedly flow through unforeseen circumstances to blow away the opposition.

This type of approach to "normal Christianity" sets up the Church to live a life of "expectancy" in the most basic fashion and a life of "spiritual influence" at the most strategic level. The Church doesn't have to labor for long periods of time without the deep societal influence that comes through the Holy Spirit.

The outpouring of the Holy Spirit places things in motion that the church strategically needs. He brings tremendous amounts of leverage, influence, and opportunity to bear. And He does it all without being "program-centered." This is a very spontaneous work and yet a very deliberate and practical mission.

Lord, Your kingdom is not some borderline religion that is relegated to an off-in-the-corner existence. It is the centerpiece of working salvation in the earth. Help us live a normal walk of devotion and transformation that impacts the world for Your glory.

Don Lamb prays with leadership for revival and transformation in the region.

April 7

Appointed By God

"I appoint you over nations and kingdoms to uproot and tear down, to destroy and overthrow, to build and to plant."
Jeremiah 1:10

How awesome it is to know that God appoints me over nations and kingdoms in order to uproot and plant, to destroy and to build! Sounds preposterous, doesn't it? Yet we are all called and appointed by God for these very purposes.

To understand how this happens, read the first chapter of Jeremiah. We see in verses 7 and 9 that God puts His words in our mouths. When I turn to the Lord and trust Him, He places His words on my lips. These are the words that need to be spoken at a particular time and place, as directed by God.

Then we see in verse 12 that the Lord watches to see that His word is fulfilled. Whatever God wants accomplished, He watches to see that it happens. The words are His, and He makes sure they do what He wants.

Can anyone doubt that whatever God speaks will happen? Then I must not doubt that it will happen when He chooses to use me as the vessel through whom He speaks. All spiritual nations and kingdoms must obey the Lord and the words of the Lord, even when His words are spoken from our lips. He watches to see that it happens!

Let's draw near to the Lord so He will impart unto us His counsel, His wisdom, and His words. Then we can be strong in the Lord and in His mighty power (Ephesians 6:10).

Dear Lord, speak to me and direct me. I want to be where You want me to be and I want to say what You want said to those that I encounter. Place Your words upon my lips, to the glory and honor of Jesus Christ. Amen.

Jim Meador is the lead pastor at Willow Street Mennonite Church.

April 8

God's Heart

"LORD, I have heard of your fame;
I stand in awe of your deeds, O LORD.
Renew them in our day, in our time make
them known; in wrath remember mercy."
Habakkuk 3:2

for Lancaster
County

"'In a surge of anger I hid my face from you for a
moment, but with everlasting kindness I will have compassion
on you,' says the LORD your Redeemer." *Isaiah 54:8*

Although thousands of years have passed, our situation is the
same as it was in the days of these prophets. We have heard
of and experienced the awesome deeds of God. And now we
need them to be made known to every lost soul in our region. Let us ask
the Lord to reveal His heart to Lancaster County. We need the Holy
Spirit to touch hearts and convict souls, so that people would come to
know him personally. And let us declare the Lord's triumphs over judgment.

*Lord, I will pray for the lost. Show me someone that does not know
Jesus and I will reach out to them with Your heart.*

Today's devotional was edited from the 2003–2004 *Throne Of Grace
Prayer Guide*, a weekly guide of Lancaster County prayer concerns
gathered from regional intercessors and area prayer groups.

April 9

Spiritual Parents

"Even though you have ten thousand guardians in Christ, you do not have many fathers…" *1Corinthians 4:15*

Imagine a Christian more mature than yourself putting his arm around you and saying, "I see God's potential in you. I want to stand with you for the long haul and see God fulfill His destiny in your life." After the initial shock wore off, how would you react? Probably by giving a hug back and shouting "hallelujah!"

Most Christians find it takes more than another sermon on Christian living to scratch their spiritual itch. They need more of His Word, and a mature, compassionate spiritual "father" or "mother" to support them in their walks with Jesus.

God is raising up spiritual parents who are willing to nurture spiritual children and help them grow up in their Christian lives. This is a fulfillment of the Lord's promise to "turn the hearts of the fathers to their children, and to turn the hearts of the children to their fathers (Malachi 4:6)." Although this scripture has implications for our natural families, its significance for spiritual parenting in the church is profound.

Believers do not need to be super-spiritual giants in order to serve as spiritual parents and help others. No one is a finished product. We are all learning to live in recovery from sin and growing in amazing grace, and we can all start somewhere. Each of us must place our arms around someone who is younger in the Lord and help them in their journey with Christ. Maybe you never had a spiritual "father" or "mother." Ask the Lord where to begin, and experience the joy of becoming a spiritual parent to another. The rewards are eternal.

Dear God, Thank You that I don't need to be perfect, just faithful and obedient to help someone else grow spiritually. Help me to make a spiritual investment in another's life. In Jesus' Name, Amen.

Larry Kreider serves on the executive team of the Regional Church of Lancaster County and as international director of D.O.V.E. Christian Fellowship International.

One

Spiritual Adoption

"He predestined us to adoption as sons through Jesus Christ to Himself, according to the kind intention of His will, to the praise of the glory of His grace..." *Ephesians 1:5–6 (New American Standard Bible)*

I cherish my eldest son and his wife. They are special, not just because they have worked through infertility issues and have come out on the other side loving God and each other more, but because they now have responded to God's call for adoption of my first grandchildren.

This is exciting! Have you ever thought about adoption? Not physical or legal adoption of previously unwanted children, but spiritual adoption—like Paul wrote to the Roman and Ephesian Christians.

Adoption is a work of divine love, mercy and grace. It is according to the kind intentions of the Father, not the child. It is a permanent legal relationship. Adoption positions us for unspeakable benefits. We become heirs of promises now, and an eternal inheritance to come. It puts us into kinship with Jesus, but also a worldwide family of spiritual siblings where we share the same Father. Same life-style. Same rules. Same family name. Same mission. Same destiny. Same enemy. Adoption also calls us to a love relationship with other family members that must be observed by the world and expresses itself in unity as Jesus prayed in John 17:21-22.

When I look for the first time into the longing eyes of my son's two precious adopted Russian children, I expect a swell of tears and not just because they will give me a much coveted identity—*grandpa*, but because they will constantly remind me of my heavenly Father adopting me—selecting me from the orphanage of sin, the world.

O God, my dear heavenly Father, I worship You for Your love, mercy, and grace expressed in adopting me. Help me today to advance the family name in the midst of my spiritual siblings and those in the orphanage of sin. Amen.

Pastor Leon R. Shirk serves as the senior shepherd to the body of Christ at Bethany Grace Fellowship, East Earl.

Life Verse

"My life is worth nothing unless I use it for doing the work assigned me by the Lord Jesus—the work of telling others the Good News about God's wonderful kindness and love."
Acts 20:24 (New Living Bible)

A number of years ago I was challenged to choose and live by a life verse—a goal that is higher than any earthly goal or endeavor. This verse from Apostle Paul certainly fits that category and has been a challenge for me. Paul, who had many credentials, a good upbringing and the best schooling available declared these meant nothing when he met the living God.

People live for so many "things" today. They pursue—sometimes at any cost—wealth, power and pleasure. Some of their goals are worthy but many are empty and fleeting. What are you seeking today? What values and goals drive your life right now? I want to be about the work of living close to Jesus and have His anointing on my life. I desire to "have a good name that is more desirable than riches (Proverbs 22:1)." I want to tell others about the hope and healing that God offers.

Our world is needy. Our world is large. But opportunities to serve begin with our neighbors and extend to "around the world." I challenge you to share the message that "He (Jesus) has rescued us from the dominion of darkness and has brought us into the kingdom of the Son He loves, in whom we have redemption, the forgiveness of sins." Nothing is worth more than living in that reality.

Lord, may I use the natural talents and spiritual gifts that You have given me to do Your work today. May I be faithful in sharing the Good News with others. May You bless and empower me to be Your servant today. Thank You for Your abundant mercy and love. Amen.

Nelson W. Martin is the director of support for Prison Ministries and an overseer in a number of Mennonite Churches in the Lititz area.

April 12

Addictive Emotion

"Father, forgive them, for they know not what they are doing."
Luke 23:34

What powerful words from our crucified Lord—more often admired than imitated! We are quickly becoming a culture ensnared in revenge which is motivated by resentment. Even among those who say they are followers of Christ, the one who was wrongly accused, shamefully abused, and painfully accosted—and yet pleaded, "Father forgive them." How do we feel when we are slighted? How do we respond when another is in the honored place that we covet? How do we treat another who has mistreated us?

Max Lucado in his book *In the Eye of the Storm* writes, "Resentment is the cocaine of emotions. It causes our blood to pump and our energy level to rise. But, also like cocaine, it demands increasingly larger and more frequent dosages.... A person bent on revenge moves unknowingly further and further away from being able to forgive, for to be without the anger is to be without the source of energy. This explains why the bitter complain to any who will listen…that is why the resentful often appear unreasonable. They are addicted to their bitterness. They don't want to surrender their anger, for to do so would be to surrender their reason to live." The good news, as he points out, is that "mercy is the choice that can set them free."

What has been causing resentment in your life? Are you willing to see it as a sin that will destroy you? Or, do you cherish this destructive and addictive emotion as justified because of the particular set of circumstances you face?

What are we sowing by our lives—seeds of bitterness or seeds of mercy? A harvest is coming. May that harvest be one that reflects the character of our Savior who could say, "Father forgive them."

Heavenly Father, as You have been merciful and forgiving to me, may I be so to others. In Jesus' name, Amen.

Robert Reid, senior pastor of Calvary Monument Bible Church, Paradise.

April 13

Stand Together

"The body is a unit, though it is made up of many parts; and though all its parts are many, they form one body. So it is with Christ." *1 Corinthians 12:12*

Paul says that the body is a unit made up of many parts. Many times we think about our brothers and sisters in other parts of the world as the uncle no one talks about or the part that the body doesn't need.

As Christians, sometimes we think that we can complete the Great Commission with the parts we have, when what is really happening is that we are wasting a lot of time and energy trying to do everything with one foot or one hand.

The Lord calls us to stand together as a family—as one body. 1 Corinthians 12:26 says that when one part of the body suffers we all suffer, and when one part of the body is happy we are all happy. Is that happening in our churches today, or is it easier to forget the hand that's being tortured or the stomach that is going hungry? Is our church truly acting as one body, or as many body parts doing their own thing?

If we want to see the Word of God spread through the nations like a wild fire, we need to get back to the body, put our pride to the side, and say to our brothers and sisters around the world: "Let's do this together." Only then will we see the growth of the body of Christ like never seen before.

Lord Jesus, help us to work together with our brothers and sisters around the world. To see the nations reached and Your kingdom truly comes. Teach us to love and to give unselfishly to our family in Christ. Amen.

Chad Miller is a missionary/church planter serving in Fortaleza, Brazil.

One

April 14

The Riches Of His Glorious Inheritance

"I pray also that the eyes of your heart may be enlightened in order that you may know the hope to which he has called you, the riches of his glorious inheritance in the saints."
Ephesians 1:18

It is no small thing God accomplishes in bringing salvation to selfish hearts that are caught in a world of corruption. He made the physical world breathtaking to show us how much power He has available to rescue us. One of the reasons all the glories of creation are revealed is to lead us toward the conclusion that our situation requires His all-powerful touch to move us beyond our failures.

Most believers quickly lose their appreciation of the awesomeness of God's intervention in their lives. They take for granted having a heart that is captured, a spirit that is enlightened, and a soul that is delivered from judgment. They act like it is no problem for God to win a sinner back to Himself—transform a rebel into an obedient servant of God.

God exerted wondrous creativity and power to construct the universe. Through these glorious achievements, he was simply expressing His "omnipotence." But the power He released to create the universe and form super novas, galaxies, mountains, canyons, and oceans was nothing compared to the wondrous work of rescuing, winning, and transforming hardened hearts. Here God's astounding power was strategically released to orchestrate countless encounters of grace to invade man's world for the working out of his salvation.

Therefore, the wonder of it all is that God actually wins back His chosen few. This is not difficult for God, but it is unusual for man to allow God to do what He longs to accomplish, to actually respond to His amazing work of grace.

Lord, help us respond to the continuous overtures of Your grace on our behalf and yield to Your intentions to transform our lives.

Don Lamb prays with leadership for revival and transformation in the region.

April 15

Our Youth

"Then little children were brought to
Jesus for him to place his hands on them
and pray for them. But the disciples rebuked
those who brought them. Jesus said, 'Let the
little children come to me, and do not hinder
them, for the kingdom of heaven belongs to such as
these.' When he had placed his hands on them, he went on
from there." *Matthew 19:13–15*

Pray!
for Lancaster
County

"But you are a chosen people, a royal priesthood, a holy
nation, a people belonging to God, that you may declare the
praises of him who called you out of darkness into his wonderful light."
1 Peter 2:9

"But the Lord is faithful, and he will strengthen and protect you
from the evil one." *2 Thessalonians 3:3*

As people who carry the Lord in our hearts, we have the awesome privilege and responsibility to bring young people to
Jesus. We can show Jesus to them by a smile or an encouraging word. We can engage them in a caring conversation. And we can
serve in many ways such as the nursery, children's Sunday school, Vacation Bible School or youth ministry.

*Lord, we ask You to ignite the hearts of our youth with increased pas-
sion for You. Open doors for them to share the gospel with their friends.
Protect them as they make decisions and face daily pressures. We pray
that the little children of our region would be encouraged to come to
Jesus, and that the church would open its arms to receive them in Your
name.*

Today's devotional was edited from the 2003–2004 *Throne Of Grace
Prayer Guide*, a weekly guide of Lancaster County prayer concerns
gathered from regional intercessors and area prayer groups.

April 16

A Heart Of Flesh

"I will give you a new heart and put a new spirit in you: I will remove from you your heart of stone and give you a heart of flesh." Ezekiel 36:26

I read this verse at a time in my life when I was struggling with issues from the past. For many years I had ignored and suppressed the emotions that were attached to these memories and I began to feel dead inside. I had put a wall around my heart.

Not only did this affect my relationship with others, it affected my walk with the Lord. I loved the Lord and desired to follow Him but I didn't want Him to get too close. I was very safe and comfortable behind my walls. When I opened that part of my heart to the Lord, I found a joy and love that I hadn't experienced before. Life had been dull and dry, now it is an exciting adventure. The Lord has opened my heart to such a vast array of emotions, crying with those who weep, celebrating with those who are rejoicing. He has taken this heart of stone and turned it into a heart of flesh. I am able to receive His love more freely, without boundaries.

Are there any areas of your heart that you have been hiding from the Lord? Any areas that you have been trying to ignore because it is too painful or scary to bring it out into the open? God understands and He wants to bring you healing and freedom. He wants to remove those things that hinder you and shower you with His love.

Dear Lord, please bring to light those things that I have been holding onto. Help me to release them to You and receive Your love to the fullest.

Kristene Knerr, licensed social worker, serves as Director of Social Services at Faith Friendship Villa, a Christian non-profit ministry in Mountville. She attends and serves at Living Hope Community Church in Lancaster.

April 17

Receive His Lavish Embrace

"Listen, my lover is knocking… I have taken off my robe—must I put it on again?" *Song of Solomon 5:2–3*

The Lord is knocking at our bridal chamber, longing for a relationship with us. Will we be as the maiden in the Song of Solomon who put her pajamas on, crawled in bed and said, "Maybe later" in response to the bridegroom's knocking? When she finally opens the door, she discovers that he is gone and only his fragrance remains on the doorknob. Are we satisfied with only a fragrance, yesterday's manna or what worked last year or even last month? Or will we quickly respond to His knocking and open our hearts (even those little closed drawers in our heart) and welcome Him into every aspect of our lives?

Corrie Ten Boom once gave the illustration of a piece of embroidery placed between God and us with the right side up toward God. We see the loose frayed ends, but God sees the pattern. There are those days when I yell at the kids, get frustrated when my schedule gets interrupted, and experience disappointments. That's when the frayed loose ends of my life are magnified in my eyes. But when I sit in His presence and remind myself of His unconditional love for me, it is then that I feel His embrace and hear Him speak the truth that "You are loved, my daughter." Now is the time to refuse the lies we have listened to and allow His truth to speak to our hearts. I am challenged once again to be thankful, acknowledge the pain, receive His comfort and embrace His refining process.

Dear Lord, I receive Your grace today to respond to Your call to intimacy with You. Thank You for Your unconditional love expressed through Jesus Christ. Continue to refine me to be more like You. Amen.

LaVerne Kreider serves with her husband Larry giving oversight to D.O.V.E. Christian Fellowship International and serves on the leadership team of a micro-church near Lititz.

April 18

Show Us The Way

"Let every soul be subject to the governing authorities. For there is no authority except from God, and the authorities that exist are appointed by God." *Romans 13:1 (New King James Version)*

Who wants to hear about being submissive to authority? It's not a favorite topic, but the truth is we are all under authority in heaven and on earth. God commands us to respect all civil, secular, and church authority.

Jesus is the only perfect example of being in submission to the Father. He did nothing outside of the Father's will and he obeyed with a right heart. Sometimes we obey, but we are rebelling in our heart—this is not submission. In Numbers 12 we are given an example of Aaron and Miriam criticizing or challenging Moses position. God punished Miriam for her smug attitude toward Moses' authority and His own authority. God will deal with rebellion in our hearts as well.

I am guilty of criticizing and judging authority in my life, and I believe that each one of us can be convicted by James 4:11. The tongue is full of poison and it corrupts, but we are called to speak words characterized by the fruits of the Spirit.

What about when authority is wrong? Is it always our job to tell them? Perhaps God wants to test our character in submitting to the authority that He placed over us. Instead of being quick to react and to be offended, pray for them, let God judge and deal with them. We are called to love even those who hurt us (Matthew 5). God is able to show us the way if we will allow Him to work within us.

Jesus, I pray to become a believer who can learn to serve faithfully and uncritically under authority. May I be responsible in treating those under my authority with respect, love, and mercy. Help me to be a model that displays Your glory. Thank you Lord for Your mercy. Continue to prepare your Bride. Amen.

Marie J. Miller leads Banner Ministry at New Covenant Christian Church.

April 19

God's Protection

"But the Lord is faithful, and he will strengthen and protect you from the evil one." *2 Thessalonians 3:3*

I believe that invisible dog fences have a spiritual application! What is an invisible dog fence? This kind of fence emits a radio signal that travels along an underground wire. A lightweight receiver worn on a dog's collar picks up the radio signal and alerts him as he nears the underground boundary that is customized for his master's yard. If he continues toward the boundary, he will receive a mild correction, similar to a static shock. With a little simple training, a dog will quickly learn his boundaries.

As God's children, our "yard" is large, abundant, fulfilling and complete sphere of spiritual life. We have a conscience that shocks us when we approach a forbidden area. When we are young and rebellious, we will tiptoe to those boundaries and wish to cross over. God has set up those fences for our safety and welfare. One day in a fit of adventurous desire, we race to a destination not proper for us. We charge through that prick in our conviction and enter a dangerous zone of self-satisfaction. While on the outside, we may eventually come to our senses and turn around to head back to our place of peace and contentment.

When we have been disobedient and wish to return to obedience, we will have to contend with that feeling of a damaged relationship with our Master. Wandering back to God in false humility or self-condemnation will stretch out that time of healing. Probably the best way to lessen the shock is to run back through with the same vigor we used when we left.

Lord, help me not to give room for the devil by allowing rebellion in my heart. Cause me to run back quickly to You when my heart strays.

Carl Harper is the owner of Harper's Tree Service.

April 20

Fulfillment

"...Elizabeth was filled with the Holy Spirit. In a loud voice she proclaimed...Blessed is she who has believed that what the Lord has said to her will be accomplished." *Luke 1:41,45*

I asked the Lord to speak to me through Mary. Here is the imaginary dialogue between us:

"I envy you, Mary. What was it like to have the angel of the Lord come to you and say, *Greetings you who are highly favored? The Lord is with you!*"

"Cathryn, you surprise me. You should know. Hasn't the Lord said the same thing to you? *I have chosen you.*"

"You are right. I'd forgotten. But what about being the mother of Jesus, the Messiah? You must be someone special."

"That is what people thought in my day too, but I'm just an ordinary woman. It's believing God and obeying Him that matters. Every day the Father is looking for those who will bear the image of His Son. You have the chance to incarnate Jesus this very day."

"I can bear Jesus too? How can this happen to me?"

"I asked the same thing, *How can this be, since I am a virgin*? It was impossible, but I learned with God all things are possible. When each of us realizes it is impossible to bring Jesus into the world with our own strength, we understand our need for the power of the Holy Spirit, *The Holy Spirit will come upon you, and the power of the Most High will overshadow you.* God did it all. My part was to believe what the Lord said and to offer myself. His handmaid."

"Thanks, Mary."

Lord, help each of us to remember that there will be a fulfillment of what You speak.

Cathryn Clinton Hoellwarth, a writer and teacher, is ordained through Teaching The Word Ministries.

April 21
Only Connect

"...while I was among the exiles by the Kebar River, the heavens were opened and I saw visions of God." *Ezekiel 1:1*

When my husband, Gary, was diagnosed with a terminal liver disease, I became a modern exile. Banished from my comfortable, predictable suburban life by the medical news, I became withdrawn and scared. My security was being threatened on many levels. As my husband's health deteriorated over time, my inner loneliness and fear grew larger, but had to be disguised for the sake of Gary and my two girls. Few things or people could connect with me, and yet I longed for connection and security. I prayed. I grieved. I hoped.

One summer morning, as I read the Word of God in Ezekiel 1:1, I finally connected to a powerful realization. God is on His glorious throne, reigning and living and breathing and touching people. He spoke to Ezekiel. He touched Ezekiel with His Hand. God allowed Ezekiel to see visions of God's eternal glory. Somehow, I knew without a shadow of a doubt, that God Almighty wanted to show me His glory, to touch me with His hand and to speak to me with His voice. I connected with God, with Ezekiel's experience and with myself. After feeling so vulnerable for so long, the connection was electric and powerful. God is....and He reigns...and He cares.

Ezekiel's experiences after seeing visions of God's glory were difficult on a daily basis, something with which I can still identify. God did not explain His reasons for the difficulties in Ezekiel's life or in mine. However, yielding to the very Source of Life provides the answer to the question: "How can I cope?" Only connect.

Master and Savior, You lead me beside quiet waters, You restore my soul for Your name's sake. Fear is present, yet easily vanquished by breathing Your Name, Our Father. Please guide me to the rock that is higher than I am—and meet me there.

Professor Joanne T. Stauffer teaches at Lancaster Bible College.

April 22
Thy Kingdom Come
"your kingdom come, your will be done on earth as it is in heaven." *Matthew 6:10*

"If any of you lacks wisdom, he should ask God, who gives generously to all without finding fault, and it will be given to him." *James 1:5*

for Lancaster County

Let us pray for the National Day of Prayer in early May. It is a unique opportunity to demonstrate to our region and to the nation that Jesus reigns on the earth! Let us pray that its organizers would have wisdom and clarity in their final preparations. Let us encourage Christian friends to pray for Lancaster County and our surrounding region. And let us participate fully in the celebration of the National Day of Prayer.

Lord, I pray that Your Kingdom would come and that Your will would be done in our county.

Today's devotional was edited from the 2003–2004 *Throne Of Grace Prayer Guide*, a weekly guide of Lancaster County prayer concerns gathered from regional intercessors and area prayer groups.

April 23

Bread Upon the Waters

"Cast your bread upon the waters, for you will find it after many days." *Ecclesiastes 11:1 (New King James Version)*

Solomon is the writer of these scriptures and his wisdom for us is not to wait for some *perfect* time to give. There never is a *perfect* time. If giving is not part of our life-style, when rough times come, it will be put at the bottom of our list. Sometimes it won't even be put on the list. Some of us may say, "Well, I'll wait until I make more money, or get a raise or a better job." If that is what we want God to do for us, we have to give Him something to work with. Have we been planting seeds? Have we been casting our bread upon the water? When we plant and sow seeds of giving, we will open up the door for God to bless us. Many times we use this scripture in the context of finances, but it can also be applied to other areas of our lives. Jesus said the kingdom of God is compared to the principle of the sower and the seed.

We can apply this in any area of ministering to others. For example, we can apply this in using our giftings, talents, and the ministry God has given us. I believe God increases and develops our giftings in ministry as we are willing to step out and use what we have already been given.

Father, I come to You in Jesus' name. I thank You for all You have blessed me with.

Sam Smucker is the senior pastor of The Worship Center and serves on the Executive Team of the Regional Church of Lancaster County.

April 24

Humble Yourself

"So humble yourselves under the mighty power of God, and in his good time He will honor you." 1 Peter 5:6 (New Living Translation)

Someone once gave me this verse because they felt God wanted me to have it. At first I was extremely offended. I thought, "There must be a terrible mistake. I know I am humble." I finally came to recognize I was wrong.

What is humility? When I looked the word up in a dictionary, I came across two important descriptions: freedom from pride and arrogance, and a sense of one's own unworthiness through imperfection and sinfulness. Being free from pride and arrogance is important but having a sense of one's own unworthiness hits it right on the mark. We should not think, "I am so unworthy, O God pity me." This is not it at all. We are ALL unworthy because of our imperfections and sin, but through Christ we *are* worthy. In the eyes of God, we are extremely important, but we need to bring glory to Him who deserves it, not ourselves.

Do we do things for God only for show or to get credit for what we've done? What is the point in this? God has given us everything we have. For example, God has blessed everyone with special gifts. When we become absorbed in ourselves, we forget about the One who gave us this gift in the first place.

We need to say, "God, I humble myself before You and realize it is You *through* me, not me on my own." This is humility—coming to the realization that we need God in everything and knowing we are NOTHING without Him. When we come to understand and apply this to our own lives, God in His timing will bless and honor us.

Dear God, I am nothing without You. I pray that You show me true humility in my life so that You can receive all the glory and praise. Amen.

Leticia Kreider is a small group leader at D.O.V.E. Westgate and is a Junior at Warwick High School.

April 25
We're The Apple Of God's Eye
Psalm 17

How special are you to God? You are the apple of His eye! Zechariah 2:8 says, "He who touches you touches the apple of His eye."

The eyeball or globe of the eye, with its pupil at the center, is called "the apple" from its rounded shape. In Hebrew *apple* means "little man." We could read verse 8, "I will keep you as the little man of my eye."

I'd like to suggest four ways that God demonstrates that we are the apple of His eye.

1. **He hears us when we cry** (Psalm 17:1). There are numerous times I felt distressed, disappointed and even despairing, but what a consolation to know that God hears and truly cares. He sees every tear drop; "He bottles those tears and keeps them in his book."

2. **He helps us when we try** (Psalm 17:5). Have you ever felt you've done your best—yet it was not good enough? Remember, God will always do the rest. Our strength—however small it may be—plus God's help, can handle any situation for "we are laborers together with God."

3. **He hides us when we are shy** (Psalm 17:8). There are times I feel like I have let God down. I have betrayed His trust. I have failed to carry out His plan, and I feel ashamed. But even then, He invites me to His throne of grace and hides me under the shadow of His wings.

4. **He holds me when I die** (Psalm 17:15). What a blessed reality to know that God not only is with us here and now, but always will be with us. We are safe in the arms of Jesus because we are and shall always be the apple of His eye!

Thank You for the promise to hear, help, hide and hold me in every situation I face today. Help me to rely on Your grace and power for all I encounter tomorrow, in Christ's name.

Fred Heller is a pastor of Hammer Creek Mennonite Church, Lititz.

April 26

You Can Make A Difference

"Is not this the kind of fasting I have chosen: to loose the chains of injustice and untie the cords of the yoke...is it not to share your food with the hungry and to provide the poor wandered with shelter...if you spend yourselves in behalf of the hungry and satisfy the needs of the oppressed, then your light will rise in the darkness...." *Isaiah 58:6–10*

It was another hot day in a large city of northeast Brazil, and we were tired and thirsty as we walked back to our temporary housing in a school building. We were a group of students on a two month outreach working with Youth With A Mission, bringing food and love to the city's street children. On this particular day a group of children followed us, one of whom was a crippled boy. Our repeated warnings not to follow us did not deter them, and upon reaching the school we told them of the policy of not allowing children into the school.

However, they would not be denied. Finally we decided, policy or not, we would bring them in and care for them. I cannot forget the scene of the young boys feeling safe and secure as they lay sleeping for hours that afternoon on mats on the floor of a very noisy hallway.

As night approached, it broke our hearts to tell them they had to leave. The next morning our hearts were ripped again, the chaplain of the school found the crippled boy sleeping alone outside the school doors. The hard, cold and impersonal statistics of thousands of children sleeping unprotected on the streets of Brazil had become the face of a beautiful, intelligent crippled boy we now knew by name. Touched by the child's persistence, the chaplain took him into his own home until he could find a home for him. One boy found a home, but millions still sleep on pieces of cardboard in the streets of the cities around the world.

Lord Jesus, may the passions which grip Your heart, grip ours. May our ears hear the cries of your children around the world, sleeping alone, cold and hungry. Forgive my selfishness. Help me to have the faith of a child...to knock and keep on knocking...to believe I can make a difference. Use me.

Jane Fasnacht works with D.O.V.E. Missions International, Lititz.

Resentment

"Get rid of all bitterness, rage and anger, brawling and slander, along with every form of malice. Be kind and compassionate to one another, forgiving each other, just as in Christ God forgave you." *Ephesians 4:31–32*

Have you ever accidentally thrown a lit ember onto a pile of trash? Before long the smoldering charcoal catches the debris on fire. Soon a raging blaze develops and destroys the pile.

Resentment is a lot like the glowing ember. Outwardly its potential for great destruction isn't obvious at first. But resentment held inside soon destroys the person who clutches it! As resentment takes root in our heart, it corrupts us little by little as we cling to it. We retain the false belief that it will give us some kind of revenge toward the one who has slighted us, accused us, or inflicted pain upon us.

Think of the conversations you've heard others speak about their past. "My Daddy left me when I was three … My Mother was drunk all the time … Mom always favored my older sister … I couldn't do anything right" … and on and on. We've all been hurt. We've all been tempted to withdraw from others so we won't be hurt again. And we've all known the fleeting pleasure of resentment and its promise of retaliation.

Yet resentment allowed to endure brings bitterness. Bitterness hurts no one but the one who hangs on to it. As Job says, "Resentment kills the fool." S.I. McMillen said that, "The moment I start hating a man, I become his slave."

Only Jesus knows how badly we've been hurt. He was hurt too. And only He can help us as we forgive and refuse to allow resentment to evolve into bitterness, ultimately destroying our very lives.

Dear God, show me how to let go of resentment and love those who have hurt me.

Steve Brubaker is the Director of Residential Programs for the Water Street Rescue Mission in Lancaster.

April 28

The Name Of The Lord

"The name of the LORD is a strong tower; the righteous run to it and are safe." *Proverbs 18:10*

Say this passage out loud several times, each time putting emphasis on a different word. This little exercise can get you thinking about different aspects of this verse (or any verse).

"The NAME of the Lord…" In the Hebrew culture, names were very significant. They were often a reflection of the person's character. God the Father has many names:

Yahweh (the Lord); Jehovah (Self-existent One); Elohim (God who is mighty and strong); El Elyon (Sovereign Ruler); El Roi (the God who sees); El Shaddai (God Almighty); Adonai (Lord and Master). He also has compound names, such as Jehovah-Jireh (the Lord will provide—Genesis 22:1–19) and Jehovah-Rapha (the Lord who heals—Exodus 15:22–27). These are just two of His many compound names that people, long ago, gave God when He met a need in their lives. Did you know that you can give God a compound name? What is an area of great need in your life? You can cry out to God and when He answers you will be able to say, "The Lord who _____ " (you fill in the blank). Meditate on the names of God and praise Him that He will meet you in your point of need.

Dear God, I praise Your name, Your many names which reveal your character. Thank You that I can trust in Your name. I know that You are my Strong Tower and my Deliverer.

Steve Douglass, with his wife and children, serve God with New Covenant Christian Church.

April 29

Offended

"A man's wisdom gives him patience, it is to his glory to over-look an offense." *Proverbs 19:11*

We often cry, "I am offended!" But, have we really been sinned against as stated in Matthew 18? Too quickly, we can jump to this conclusion and in so doing abdicate our responsibility to walk in grace, forgiveness and mercy. We also then shift responsibility to the other person to reach out to us. We want them to pursue us to be reconciled.

What is being "sinned against?" Is it not an "evil" intent directed specifically at "me"? Whatever it is, it's definitely bigger than a simple benign misunderstanding.

Our first responsibility when we think we've been offended is to forgive (Matthew 6:14–15). It is also in our interest to overlook an offense (Proverbs 19:11). Take the opportunity to sow seeds of grace and mercy. Who knows when you might need that "fruit" handed back to you.

Lord, help me to be discerning and see situations and people through Your eyes. Let me be quick to sow mercy, grace and forgiveness and slow to jump to a conclusion. Bless those in my family and those I may come in contact with today. May my glory to You increase Jesus! Amen.

Janet Sauder is the mother of five children and the wife of Brian Sauder who is a member of the apostolic council for D.O.V.E. Christian Fellowship International.

April 30

Full Of Light

"The lamp of the body is Your eye; when your eye is clear your whole body also is full of light; but when it is bad, your body is also is full of darkness. Then watch out that the light in you may not be darkness." *Luke 11:34–35*

The challenge for all of us is often not the destination, but the journey. Our society bombards us daily with pictures, images, and input that we'd rather not be exposed to. It was perhaps easier for our grandfathers and great-grandfathers who lived without TV advertisements and the media at large.

What our society calls "dysfunction" or "addiction", the Bible calls "bondage". The symptoms are the same—a place where our will is surrendered and something else has control over us, where we are bound and not free. Other names for these bondages are alcoholism, drug use, pornography, smoking, anger, eating—and the list goes on.

Pray that innocence would be restored and increased in you and your family. Submit to the Lordship of Christ and His Word. Ask the Lord to use you as a vessel of honor, to stand for righteousness and to be a beacon of hope and deliverance to others held captive.

Don't stand in the cave of darkness, bondage and death, trying to fight alone. Call a trusted friend or pastor, confess and bring it into the light that you may be healed.

Lord, I confess my desperate need for You to set me free. In You and You alone I put my faith and trust. I want to be a vessel of honor for You, to stand for Your righteousness, so that others might receive hope through me to finish the race. I am in Your mercy, Lord. Thank You for Your total restoration, making my life full of light, to the glory of Your Kingdom.

Wayne Kaufman is the pastor of Gates of Praise Ministries, Gates of Praise House Church Network, board member of: Harvest Net, The Regional Church of Lancaster County, Lancaster House of Prayer.

May

Joining together to pray for our government and community

May 1

Welcome, O King Of Glory!

"Lift up your heads, O you gates; be lifted up, you ancient doors, that the King of glory may come in. Who is this King of glory? The LORD strong and mighty, the LORD mighty in battle. Lift up your heads, O you gates; lift them up, you ancient doors, that the King of glory may come in. Who is he, this King of glory? The LORD Almighty—he is the King of glory. Selah" *Psalm 24:7–10*

As the National Day of Prayer approaches, let us pray that the Lord would be honored and lifted on high as we meet to worship and cry out to Him on behalf of our county and our nation. We welcome the King of Glory in our midst! Let us take the opportunity to participate locally in corporate prayer and invite a friend to join us.

Lord we thank You for the privilege of living in a nation that allows a National Day of Prayer. We thank You for the opportunity to blanket our county in prayer at this event and throughout the year. And we thank You, God, for Your faithfulness in answering our prayers.

Today's devotional was edited from the 2003–2004 *Throne Of Grace Prayer Guide*, a weekly guide of Lancaster County prayer concerns gathered from regional intercessors and area prayer groups.

Seek First The Kingdom

"But seek ye first the Kingdom of God, and His righteousness; and all these things shall be added unto you." *Matthew 6:33 (King James Version)*

This is one of the first scriptures that the Lord Jesus used in building my spiritual house. He simply defined my walk with Him. Always seek first the kingdom, in every thought (2 Corinthians 10:5), and in every word or action (Colossians 3:17). Be found having not my own righteousness, but rather hidden with Christ in God (Philippians 3:9, Colossians 3:3).

This scripture (and the verses that precede it) has a strong application in the thought realm. Take no thought for tomorrow! As a new believer, I was caught in the grip of the world, having experienced more of Egypt than I could stand. My thought life had been "unholy ground". Incoming scud missiles constantly assaulted me. What if? How about that! Is God really helping me? Is Jesus powerful enough to deliver me? Is Jesus powerful enough to deliver me out of my situation?

Thank God, the answer is simple. Seek first the Kingdom, and all these other things will be taken care of. Then the revelation hit me. Just believe what Jesus said. Stay simple in this. You don't have to know everything now! Faith becomes the victory. Just believing what Jesus said is what overcomes the world (1 John 5:4–5). This is the shield that stops the attack (Ephesians 6:13–15).

Now I can rest in God's love. His message is still the same. It will all work out, if I stay focused on the Kingdom. Keep it simple. Don't worry about tomorrow. Always seek first the Kingdom and His righteousness (Romans 8:28). Jesus is really in the power position. When we believe and act on what He says, then we are in that same position. Go on with that in your heart today.

Thank You Father for all that I have in Christ. Continue to give me revelation of Your truth so that I can glorify You in my time on the earth. Amen.

Ron Buch is a pastor at Breakout Ministries in Salunga.

Freedom Celebration

"When the righteous are in authority, the people rejoice: but when the wicked beareth rule the people mourn." *Proverbs 29:2 (King James Version)*

In the United States of America, we are blessed to live in a republic established by godly founding fathers who came to this new country in search of freedom to worship as they pleased. The freedoms that we celebrate in this country were paid for by the blood of patriots and require that we be diligent in their defense.

It is important that Christians seek to elect to public offices those who uphold their values. As someone who has been called to serve in the public sector, it grieves me to hear Christian people state the reasons they don't vote:

"We believe in separation of church and state"—Our founding fathers never included the words "separation", "church" or "state" in the first amendment. Even the twisted interpretation of the first amendment by the ACLU doesn't presume to keep religious people from voting or holding elected office.

"Our citizenship is in heaven"—As believers, our eternal citizenship will be in heaven, but even Christ acknowledged earthly government (Mark 12:13–17).

"We pray for our leaders and trust God to put the right ones in power"—We are commanded to pray for our leaders, and our godly elected officials do value your prayers for them, but that doesn't prohibit us from casting our vote also.

Dear God, thank You for this country in which we are blessed to live. Give us the wisdom to pass this treasure on to future generations. Be with our elected leaders, give them wisdom to make decisions, and may they surround themselves with godly advisers. Give me the wisdom when voting to cast my vote for leaders with character, conviction, and courage to seek You and to do Your will.

Randall Wenger serves as Prothonotary of Lancaster County. He lives in Elizabeth Township with wife, Barbara and two children.

Tribulation

" …but we also glory in tribulations, knowing that tribulation produces perseverance; and perseverance, character; and character, hope." *Romans 5:3–4 (New King James Version)*

Going through tribulations is a fact of life. The Greek word for "tribulation" means "pressure" or " hardship". In this day we call it stress. It can be physical, spiritual, or emotional. Why does Paul write to the Romans that tribulation produces perseverance? Because as we grow in our relationship to the Lord, we find out that He doesn't want us to love Him for what He can do for us. He wants us to love Him for who He is. Don't we all want that kind of love from others? We call it unconditional love, but it works both ways. Yes, God loves us unconditionally (as shown by sending Jesus to die for our sins) but He wants us to love Him unconditionally as well. When we go through tribulations, we have opportunities to grow in our relationship with God. Are we going to continue to love Him even if this tribulation doesn't go away?

So you see, tribulation produces perseverance. When we persevere (which means "to endure"), it creates the character qualities that God wants. By letting the Lord use our circumstance for His glory, the fruit of the Spirit develops in our lives. Finally, character produces hope. Not hope that the stressful situation (tribulation) will end, but the hope in God is strengthened. Hope in His character and His faithfulness, hope in His promises, hope in His grace and forgiveness. So next time you're going through tribulation, "glory" (rejoice) in it; because He is at work in you, conforming you to Himself (Romans 8:29).

Dear Father, I submit my will to You; and although I don't feel like it, I choose to rejoice in this circumstance, knowing that it will produce those things that You want in me, such as perseverance, character and hope. Give me wisdom Father, and grant me the grace to continue in faith."

Steve Douglass, along with his wife and children, attend New Covenant Christian Church.

May 5

Pray On All Occasions

"...pray in the Spirit on all occasions with all kinds of prayers and requests..." *Ephesians. 6:18*

S ome years ago I had the opportunity to participate in a short-term missions trip to Romania. The overseer of the visiting team was a man by the name of Ilie Corama. Ilie was a humble and very godly man.

During our time together, some team members got involved in a discussion about the morality of movies and Christians viewing them. Various opinions were raised and someone turned to Ilie to ask his opinion, "Ilie, is it okay for Christians to go to movies?" Ilie, who had been silently listening to the conversation, answered quietly in broken English, "To go to movie, to not go to movie? Nah. One should pray."

This simple statement clearly and completely answered the question that was asked, and it was answered by saying neither yes nor no, but by directing each of us to the real arbiter of such questions—God's Holy Spirit.

Jesus promised that when He left, He would send the Holy Spirit and that the Holy Spirit would guide His children into all truth (John 16:5–16). Believers are to live lives "in accordance with the Spirit and have our minds set on what the Spirit desires (Romans 8:5)." How can we know what the Holy Spirit desires? By cultivating a deep under-standing of God's word and by praying "in the Spirit on all occasions with all kinds of prayers and requests (Ephesians 6:18)."

As we face life's situations and questions, we are to pray. God will answer the prayer of a person seeking to know and do His will.

So, is it okay to do this? How about that? One should pray.

Lord, teach me to pray at all times and in every circumstance. I pray to know Your word, Your heart and the direction of Your Holy Spirit in order that I might live in a manner that is pleasing to You.

Brett R. Miller is a guidance counselor at Warwick Middle School. He and his wife, Jennifer, serve on the worship team of New Covenant Christian Church.

The Hand Of God

"For I am the Lord your God, who takes hold of your right hand and says to you, do not fear; I will help you." *Isaiah 41:13*

My wife and I were attending our daughter's graduation and were progressing through the crowd, single file, to find our seats. I was leading the way though the maze when I suddenly felt my wife's hand touch mine, obviously a signal for me to grasp her hand to keep us from being separated, as we worked our way through the crowd. My leadership was short-lived as the woman attached to the hand I was holding said, "I think you have the wrong one." That's right! I had taken another hand just because it touched mine. Fortunately, my explanations were graciously received by both of the women I was attempting to lead.

Who is leading your life right now?

Is it the hand of a stranger, who does not even know you, or is it the hand of the Lord God, the love of your life, who gently places His hand in yours and says, "Do not fear; I will help you, walk with me." The "stranger" knows only the maze of fear, anxiety, restraint, worry, discontentment and other dark paths. The Lord God knows the paths of rest, hope, freedom, joy and contentment. Today, the Lord extends His hand to you and graciously offers to lead you through the crowded activities of your day. Imagine His hand gently touching yours—now firmly gripping it. Feel the tug as He draws you to His side and hear Him whisper, "Do not fear, I will help you."

Dear God, take my hand today and lead me in paths of righteousness, for Your name's sake. Even if the path leads through dark valleys of weakness or temptation, may I feel Your gentle grip that will strengthen me and keep me from stumbling. I release my grip on the "stranger" and I accept Your offer to lead. Amen.

Lawrence Metzler is pastor of New Providence Church in Quarryville.

One

Staying Fresh Spiritually

"You have persevered and have endured hardships for my name, and have not grown weary. Yet I hold this against you: You have forsaken your first love. Remember the height from which you have fallen! Repent and do the things you did at first." *Revelation 2:3–5*

Recently, I was standing at a self-serve salad bar staring at brown-edged, limp lettuce. Although presented in a lovely crystal bowl on ice, last week's leftover lettuce could not be camouflaged. Similarly, it is just as hard to fake a leftover relationship with the Lord!

In order to stay spiritually healthy, we must stay at the feet of Jesus and be filled with the Holy Spirit. D. L. Moody, a well-known evangelist, once said that he needed to be constantly filled with the Holy Spirit because he leaked. We all leak!

The believers mentioned in Revelation 2:3–5 were doing many things right. They worked hard and had not grown weary. On the surface, they appeared to be model Christians. Yet the Lord held one thing against them. They no longer loved Him as they had when they first came to know Him. They had lost their freshness.

The Lord gives us instructions for returning to our first love:

1. Remember the height from which we have fallen
2. Repent
3. Do the things we did at first. Unless we know how far we have fallen in our love relationship with Jesus, we will not see our need to change. The Lord requires honesty and vulnerability.

How about you? Is your relationship with the Lord fresh, or do you focus on leftover spiritual experiences that are now limp? Rekindle your intimacy with God today. Don't forsake your first love!

Dear Lord, forgive me for not loving You as I did at first. Help me to realize I can do nothing without You. Amen.

Larry Kreider serves on the executive team of the Regional Church of Lancaster County and as international director of D.O.V.E. Christian Fellowship International.

May 8

Honor Thy Mother And Thy Father

"'Honor your father and mother'—which is the first commandment with a promise—'that it may go well with you and that you may enjoy long life on the earth.'" *Ephesians 6:2–3*

Pray! for Lancaster County

When we are children, and even when we become adults, this commandment remains. Let us honor (esteem and value as precious) our mothers and our fathers. And let us rejoice in the promise of an enjoyable, long life. Let us honor them with our actions and our words. Let us be aware of any of our words or actions that bring dishonor to our parents and repent.

Heavenly Father, I ask You to show me where I have not honored my parents and I repent from that. Show me specific ways to honor and bless my father and my mother this week.

Today's devotional was edited from the 2003–2004 *Throne Of Grace Prayer Guide*, a weekly guide of Lancaster County prayer concerns gathered from regional intercessors and area prayer groups.

The Power Of A Mother's Prayer

"For this is what the Lord says: I will extend peace to her like a river, and the wealth of the nations like a flooding stream; you will nurse and be carried on her arm and dandled on her knees. As a mother comforts her child, so I will comfort you; and you will be comforted over Jerusalem."
Isaiah 66:12–13

It was in the mind and heart of God to design and grace the woman He created with the capacity to nurture, teach, comfort, and give care to His little ones.

I shall always be grateful to my own mother who lovingly guided and trained me through my formative years and on to maturity in Christ. I also had other spiritual mothers as I sought to nurture and train my own children. These women stood by me and gave godly counsel and wisdom as I moved through that season of life.

One particular time I was so hungry for more of the Lord that when one of these "mothers" prayed for me, I felt the power of God coming through her in a way I had never experienced before! Of course I wanted more of what she had! She became a real mentor to me for many years, and drew me closer to God. Since that time, I have had the joy and privilege of being there for other women that needed encouragement in their lives.

We can all extend this God-given gift to nurture those young in the faith in the body of Christ, by lovingly coming alongside them and bringing them to maturity in Him.

Heavenly Father, bless each of us as we consider our role to partner with You in bringing others to wholeness, fulfillment, and fruitfulness in Your kingdom today. In doing this we will be contributing to the "wealth of the nations like a flooding stream". In Jesus' name, Amen.

Naomi Sensenig and her husband, LaMarr, serve with D.O.V.E. Christian Fellowship Westgate Celebration in Intercession and Spiritual Parenting.

May 10

God's Heartbeat

"Pray continually, give thanks in all circumstances, for this is God's will for you in Christ Jesus." *1 Thessalonians 5:17–18*

Morning hall duty. That was one of the first things I noticed when I received my teaching schedule for last year. No first period class meant an assigned "post" in the hallway or the locker bank from 7:20 to 7:40 a.m. Although I understood the need for supervision throughout the building, I groaned inwardly, mentally listing the things I could be doing if I weren't standing on the second floor landing, listening to 900 lockers banging shut and occasionally telling a kid to spit out his gum. *Waste of twenty minutes*, I thought.

One morning, however, I sensed God giving me a new perspective. As I looked down on the mob of students, backpacks slung over their shoulders, some laughing, some worried, some the center of attention and others alone, I had a glimpse of His heart for these kids. Just as Jesus looked out on the crowd long ago with compassion (Mark 6:34), He feels compassion for these seventh and eighth graders—young people bombarded with choices and challenges as they navigate the stormy waters of adolescence.

When I tune into God's heartbeat, hall duty isn't a waste of time; it's a time to pray! The second floor landing becomes my lookout, my place of intercession. As I look out over the mass of students, I pray for God's presence and protection to surround them, and for His purposes to be accomplished in their lives. I begin to see my hall duty assignment as a strategic post in the Kingdom, and I give thanks for this opportunity to make a difference through prayer.

Lord, thank You for the places You put me, even the ones I wouldn't choose. Fill me with Your compassion for people. Help me to see the opportunities You give me to advance Your Kingdom through prayer. Amen.

Andrea Adams teaches English at Manheim Township Middle School, where she is a team leader and advisor to a student-led Bible club.

May 11

Transformed By God

"So, dear brothers and sisters, you have no obligation whatsoever to do what your sinful nature urges you to do. For if you
keep on following it, you will perish. But if through the power of
the Holy Spirit you turn from it and its evil deeds, you will live.
For all who are led by the Spirit of God are children of God."
Romans 8:12–14 (New Living Translation)

Every day I see people pursuing the next "big thing" in their life.
It might be a new car, a new exercise program, or a new dress.
We always seem to be looking for something new in our lives.
These pursuits help to anesthetize us to our need to be different people
than we are. We simulate a changing life by changing our environment.
We need *real* change!

In my own words, the gospel can simply be stated, "What I am
naturally can be transformed by the supernatural power of God." In
this pivotal chapter of Romans, Paul provides great news to God's
people. We can be different people today than we were yesterday! This
does not occur through sheer determination until our natural strength is
expended and we revert to our previous actions and thoughts. It is
through our Helper, the Holy Spirit, inside us.

Through obedience to God's Word and His guiding voice, the Holy
Spirit transforms us by His supernatural power. This power is the same
power that raised Jesus from the dead (Ephesians 1:18–23). This is
phenomenal news to tired, hopeless people. It is not about fighting
against our flesh but about being mightily empowered to live beyond
the grasp of our flesh, in the love of God. We are to bask in this Love as
children in the comfort of their Father's presence. Do that today with
me!

*Father, today I choose to focus on the incredible power of your Holy
Spirit living inside of me. Help me to see Him working hour by hour.
Amen.*

Michael Shelley pastors at Lititz Christian Church and serves on the
council of the Regional Church of Lancaster County.

May 12

Harmony In Him

"Take the silver and gold and make a crown, and set it on the head of the high priest, Joshua son of Jehozadak. Tell him this is what the Lord Almighty says: 'Here is the man whose name is the Branch, and he will branch out from his place and build the temple of the Lord... And he will be a priest on his throne. And there will be harmony between the two."
Zechariah 6:11–13

This passage, by one of the minor prophets of the Old Testament, was written about the time of the return of the exiles from Babylon. It is an encouragement to the people to move forward with the restoration of the temple and speaks of a ruler and priest who are to work in harmony. This is a specific reference to Zerubbabel and Joshua who were governor and high priest respectively. Although, ultimately we know from our New Testament perspective, that the "Branch" refers to Jesus the King, I believe we can glean from this prophetic story a word that is equally true for the times that we have been blessed to live in.

We are living in a moment of history in which it appears that the Lord is calling His people, His bride, to become that pure and spotless church, in unity with Him and each other. We are the "temple", individually and corporately, when we respond to this call of God's heart. He *will* have a bride for His Son. The bride however, is composed both of those who live and minister in the physical "church" as well as those who minister and lead in the other areas of society and the marketplace.

Lord, raise up leaders in churches and marketplaces. Cause them to honor and affirm each other.

Bob Doe is the physician of the Lancaster County Prison System. An elder at In The Light Ministries, Bob serves on the Council of the Regional Church and is director of Light of Hope Community Services.

Like Job

"He will yet fill your mouth with laughter and your lips with shouts of joy." *Job 8:21*

The following is an excerpt from Paul and Sylvia Hollinger's book, *Journey of Joy*.

Although many equate Job with patience, at times, Job was more like a chronic complainer. But he endured to the end. He did not curse God and die. Job was faithful. That is why he was chosen for a time of pain, agony and suffering, followed by death, sorrow and remorse. It is our prayer that, like Job, the Lord will find us faithful to the end.

In the song *Find Us Faithful*, Jon Mohr wrote, "Oh may all who come behind us find us faithful, May the fire of our devotion light their way, May the footprints that we leave lead them to believe...inspire them to obey." This is our prayer.

Gentleness, kindness, affection and joy are the fruit of the God's Holy Spirit living inside of us. This kind of comfort cannot be experienced when everything is going just right in the warmth of a midday sun. This comfort warms us in the blackest emotions or during the wee hours of the night.

Jesus Christ suffered the loneliness and agony of sweat drops of blood in the Garden of Gethsemane. Jesus is the Eternal Comforter who knows, experientially, our every pain and suffering. That is why He alone can embrace us in His long reaching arms, tenderly wiping our tear-stained cheeks with His nail pierced hands. Jesus is the bright morning star in our universe of darkness; He is our ever-present Comforter until the dawning of the sunshine that follows every night.

Lord, help us to find joy in our trying times. You are the Eternal and Ever Present Comforter. Please let us never leave Your love, comfort and joy.

Paul Hollinger served Christ for 43 years as a manager and owner of WDAC-FM, the "Voice of Christian Radio", Lancaster.

Listen For God's Still, Small Voice

"...[sound of] a still, small voice." *1 Kings 19:12 (Amplified Bible)*

Elijah discovered that when God was not heard in the mighty wind, earthquake and fire, he heard Him speak with the sound of a gentle whisper known to his heart. The quiet whisper captured his attention because it was a tender communication from a loving Father who came to encourage Elijah in a personal way.

God often speaks quietly to our spirits, nudging us to obedience to His voice. Many times, we are looking for the Lord to speak to us in an earth-shattering way. But the Lord usually speaks to us by His Spirit, deep within our spirits by Holy Spirit-inspired impressions, thoughts and feelings. We really should pay attention to those impressions that clearly come to us.

For example, have you ever been driving down the road and had a spur-of-the-moment thought that you should pray for someone? Perhaps God is speaking in His still, small voice that you should pray for that person. My friend Keith tells of the experience he and his wife had while they were looking for a new house. As soon as they walked in the door of one particular house, they sensed it was the right one. They had an abiding peace about it and both heard the quiet voice indicating that this was the house to buy.

Rest assured that you will learn to recognize that inner voice, that impression from the Lord within that you come to know as God's voice. Let God capture your attention through a whisper. Listen for Him to speak in a still, small voice amidst the noise of human life.

Dear Lord, I know your voice is One of love and concern for my well-being. Help me to listen for Your still, small voice each day. Amen.

Larry Kreider serves on the executive team of the Regional Church of Lancaster County and as international director of D.O.V.E. Christian Fellowship International

May 15

Our County Blanketed In Prayer

"...and give him no rest till he establishes Jerusalem and makes her the praise of th earth." *Isaiah 62:7*

Pray!
for Lancaster County

"Pray continually." *1 Thessalonians 5:17*

What would happen in Lancaster County if Christians were mobilized to pray 24-hours-a-day for our region? Let us commit ourselves to joining in praying regularly for our region. And let us pray that united corporate worship, in spirit and in truth, will come forth continuously from God's people.

Lord, we ask You to continue to establish constant pray in our region. We pray that You would raise up leaders to inspire and encourage this effort and for intercessors to be released to minister before the Lord day and night.

Today's devotional was edited from the 2003–2004 *Throne Of Grace Prayer Guide*, a weekly guide of Lancaster County prayer concerns gathered from regional intercessors and area prayer groups.

May 16

Learning To Fly

"As an eagle stirs up its nest, Hovers over its young, Spreading out its wings, taking them up, Carrying them on its wings."
Deuteronomy 32:11 (New King James Version)

I recently sat across from a pastor with a picture of a large Bald Eagle on the wall behind him. Under its fierce and regal countenance a caption read "I am smiling."

Have you ever seen a large bird in flight? It seems the bigger they are, the less effort they exert, soaring sometimes out of sight with little more than a flap here and there to keep inside the updraft. One of the reasons eagles build nests so high up in trees and mountains, is to teach their young to fly. It is also a guard against predators. The way that the eagle is taught to fly is by stirring the nest and taking the young ones on rides.

These include the tumble down where mom kicks you out of the nest and you are in a free fall, flapping just as fast as you can. Then mother swoops underneath you and catches you on her back. As she mounts up to the nest, you notice something different about the place but you can't put your finger on it. The next day the same routine, breakfast a la snake or sushi and a dive over the side. Every day is a day closer to your calling on your life—to fly on wings of eagles.

Lord, Thank You that in Your mercy you get me prepared, strengthened and alert for a new direction.

Dave & Renee Queen reside in Mt Joy. They served on staff with Campus Crusade for Christ for five years and with the Josh McDowell Ministry and Global Hope Network. They currently serve with the Joseph Project.

May 17

Miracles In The Marketplace

"Take the silver and gold and make a crown, and set it on the head of the high priest, Joshua son of Jehozadak. Tell him this is what the Lord Almighty says: 'Here is the man whose name is the Branch, and he will branch out from his place and build the temple of the Lord. It is he who will build the temple of the Lord, and he will be clothed with majesty and will sit and rule on his throne. And he will be a priest on his throne. And there will be harmony between the two." *Zechariah 6:11-13*

If we are to see the Kingdom of God established in our communities, we must begin to comprehend the harmony that is described in these verses. The exiles were commanded to take from the gold and silver so as to make a crown for the "priest". This indicates an honoring of the role of the pastoral covering that God has established in our region. However, it mentions that he rules on the throne. I believe that this demonstrates the role of Zerubbabel as marketplace minister. As we come to give place and honor to both marketplace ministry leaders and to pastoral leadership, a branching out can occur into our community. No longer will ministry, supernatural power, healing and teaching be confined to a church building but manifested in schools, businesses, hospitals, prisons and other locations. This will require fivefold ministry leaders (apostles, prophets, evangelists, pastors and teachers; Ephesians 4:11) within the churches to equip the saints to go out into these arenas of our community in the power of the Word and the Spirit.

Lord, Let the saints come to maturity through equipping that results from partnering among fivefold leaders leaders. Let Your Glory fill this region.

Bob Doe is the physician of the Lancaster County Prison System. An elder at In The Light Ministries, Bob serves on the Council of the Regional Church and is director of Light of Hope Community Services.

May 18

Believing

"Whoever believes in me, as the Scripture has said, streams of living water will flow from within him." *John 7:38*

Ask yourself, as a believer, what are you believing God for today? In the world we will have trouble. We don't need to worry about tomorrow, for today will have enough trouble on its own.

No convincing is necessary on that point. Just list a few of the troubles you face right now. Are you actively believing God for His part in these dilemmas? Maybe you're like me. Often times I just try to figure out what I need to do. Other times I procrastinate and let the chips fall where they may. If there aren't issues making me feel desperate, it doesn't even enter my mind that God would want me to believe Him to give a direction.

As I consider streams of living water flowing, I am reminded that streams have a source and a destination. We also have a source and a destination. Our source is God and He would like it if we were actively believing in Him. A matter of fact, as we do the work of believing, there is a stimulating of the Holy Spirit's activity of moving and flowing in a definite direction or purpose.

The living waters, that flow from within us, are activated by our own work of believing. There are times we all feel like a dry desert, but the truth is, if we are about believing, then streams are flowing! When people come upon streams, needs are met. They are refreshed, thirst is quenched, they are cooled off and they can even be entertained. If you experience a time of dryness, ask yourself, "Am I about the work I was called to do—believing?" If not, come with me to a wonderful place of repentance.

Lord, forgive me for neglecting to believe in You again. Heal this neglect, this unbelief; help me to live a life of believing in You. Thank You for Your forgiving heart.

Anne Mellott serves on the women's leadership team at New Covenant Christian Church.

May 19

Without Faith It Is Impossible

"'Lord, if it's you,' Peter replied, 'tell me to come to you on the water.' 'Come,' he said. Then Peter got down out of the boat, walked on the water and came toward Jesus. But when he saw the wind, he was afraid and, beginning to sink, cried out, 'Lord, save me!'" *Matthew 14:28–30*

In our genuine desire to follow God, we easily pray, "Lord, let me do this to serve You." But when God begins to use us often unforeseen difficulties and obstacles come up and we begin to question if God is really leading us.

I remember asking God to give me a new job because, not only would my salary be slightly higher, but I would have more opportunity to share my faith. After working at this new job for a while I became discouraged because no one was responding to my attempts to share my faith. I began to doubt that God could or would use me in sharing my faith with others. Hebrews 11: 6 reminds us that without faith it is impossible to please God. As I read that verse I was reminded that first and foremost I was to please God whether I saw the results I wanted to see or not. Jesus told Peter, "You of little faith, why did you doubt?" Over the course of time I had many quality conversations about God with people at my job. The other Christians there also became more active in sharing their faith, and some people did respond to God's offer of eternal life through faith in Christ.

Lord Jesus, as I seek to obey and please You, please help me to keep my eyes on You and not only on the circumstances around me. Help me to learn to trust You more in the midst of the winds and storms of life. And like Peter, thank You that You hear and answer me when I cry out to You. Amen.

Tom Barnett is the pastor of D.O.V.E. Christian Fellowship in Elizabethtown.

One

"For God so loved the world that he gave his only Son that whoever believes in him should not perish but have eternal life." *John 3:16 (Revised Standard Version)*

As you wake up each day, what do you think? Perhaps it is about your job and what all you have to do this day, or is it your family and you thank God for allowing you to be able to just wake up to a new day. Whatever you are thinking, I hope and pray you look at John 3:16 above. Have you ever asked yourself, "I wonder what God is thinking?" How could He allow all the hunger and war to continue?

God loves each of us: red, yellow, black or white, Lutheran, Catholic, Methodist, Jew or Muslim. We need to ask ourselves if we believe in God. If your answer is yes, when was the last time you thanked God for what He has given you? If your answer is no, you do not believe in God, may the understanding of why you are reading this message be enough to turn your life over to God.

God gave up his Son to take all our sins away, so that we can have eternal life. Therefore, we must work as ONE so those hungry people can be fed, and so that believers of all countries work together as ONE to stop wars and live as ONE.

Dear God, thank you for giving us Your Son to take away our sins. We ask that You now give us this day to do Your will, not our own, and lead us to know each other as ONE. For we pray these things in Jesus' name. Amen.

Russell Pettyjohn, mayor of Lititz Borough, lives with his wife Irene and is a father of four children and nine grandchildren.

Breaks In The Wall

"Your prophets, O Israel, are like jackals among ruins. You have not gone up to the breaks in the wall to repair it... so that it will stand firm in the battle...." *Ezekiel 13:4–5*

These prophets were condemned for being like jackals—scavengers that feed on the remains of dead animals. Instead of building up the wall at its point of weakness, they contributed to its disrepair by *living* and *feeding* among its ruins and finding other "jackals" to join their "pack". How do you respond when you see *"breaks in the wall"*—shortcomings or offenses in another person, church, leader, or situation?

One of the enemy's subtle, but dangerous traps is to get us to *dwell* and *feed on* the ruins (breaks in the wall) that we identify in others' lives. Feeding on the dead remains of their offense or weakness, we become critical and judgmental of them. As we replay their shortcomings over in our minds, the broken wall becomes like a museum exhibit that we critique and preserve in its state of brokenness. Often, we find others to "join our pack"—sometimes under the guise of "sharing a prayer concern." Even our prayers become tainted with criticism. Instead of repairing the wall, we add to its ruin.

God says, "I looked for a man among them who would build up the wall and stand before me in the gap...(Ezekiel 2:30)." God seeks those who, when they see a *break in the wall*, step into that gap and intercede on behalf of the other's weakness or offense. Criticism is melted by compassion as we enter that place of brokenness to intercede for the wall to be rebuilt—crying out to God as though it were our own shortcoming.

God, forgive me for the times I have responded with criticism and judgment. Give me a heart that stands in the gap with life-giving intercession to repair the breaks in the wall in Jesus' name. Amen.

Dwane Reitz, prayer coordinator at Global Disciples in Lancaster, serves as an elder at Petra Christian Fellowship, New Holland.

May 22

A Church Awake

"Arise, shine, for your light has come,
and the glory of the LORD rises upon you.
See, darkness covers the earth and thick
darkness is over the peoples, but the LORD
rises upon you and his glory appears over you.
Nations will come to your light, and kings to the
brightness of your dawn."
Isaiah 60:1–3

Pray!
for Lancaster
County

"And do this, understanding the present time. The hour has
come for you to wake up from your slumber, because our
salvation is nearer now than when we first believed."
Romans 13:11

"Yet I hold this against you: You have forsaken your first love.
Remember the height from which you have fallen! Repent and
do the things you did at first. If you do not repent, I will come to
you and remove your lampstand from its place."
Revelation 2:4–5

We have a strong spiritual heritage in Lancaster County. Yet we face the same dangers as the New Testament church. We must ask the Lord to reveal apathy, complacency, and "lukewarmness" in the Church of Jesus Christ in our region. Let us ask God to wake us up and give us a zeal for His will and a passion for eternal things.

Lord this day I commit myself to returning to my first love. I will con-sider 'from where I have fallen' in my zeal for Your will and presence. By your grace, God, and in Your mercy, I will 'repent and do the first works'.

Today's devotional was edited from the 2003–2004 *Throne Of Grace Prayer Guide*, a weekly guide of Lancaster County prayer concerns gathered from regional intercessors and area prayer groups.

Extending And Expanding The Kingdom Of God

"Enlarge the place of your tent; stretch out the curtains of your dwellings, spare not; lengthen your cords and strengthen your pegs. For you will spread abroad to the right and to the left..."
Isaiah 54:2–3 (New American Standard Bible)

There are those who are called to minister among believers and those who are called to minister in the market place. Those of us who minister in the market place serve as ambassadors sent from a divine and holy kingdom. Therefore, it behooves us to adopt the mindset of the Kingdom we are sent from in our daily business transactions.

How do we develop such a mindset in business? I ask myself one simple yet profound question: In the situation I'm facing, what would Jesus do? How would He respond to this situation? Usually, I start with the golden rule: Do unto others, as you would have them do unto you. Then I ask myself how I would want to be treated if I were on the receiving end of the transaction. Finally, I ask the Holy Spirit to align this situation so that the will of my Father and the purposes of the Kingdom are advanced. By adhering to this form of diplomacy, we advance our Father's Kingdom in the market place. We also find ourselves on the receiving end of great favor and increased anointing to deal with increasingly complex and difficult situations.

Father, help me to do the right thing in every situation. Give me the courage to walk my talk in front of my business colleagues. Keep me aware of my responsibilities as Your ambassador in both word and action by showing others the respect and love that must manifest in my decision making and communications. And, as I prove my trustworthiness to You, I ask for more anointing and to be sent into situations that need of Your presence.

Elaine Warner is a nurse and attorney and works in the pharmaceutical industry. She lives with her husband Bruce in Lancaster.

Don't Stress, Just Rest

"And Jesus said to him, 'If you can? All things are possible to him who believes.'" *Mark 9:23 (New American Standard Bible)*

Today we are told: "Success comes to those who work hard enough and believe in themselves enough." I lived the first 29 years of my life with a dreaded fear of public speaking. Attempts at overcoming that fear were unsuccessful. In other areas of my life positive affirmations and determination resulted in success, but some things do not just disappear because you "wish" them away. A high school class and college speech class succeeded in creating tremendous academic stress in my schedule. Two toastmaster clubs succeeded in making my days miserable. No matter how hard I worked and believed in myself, nothing helped to eliminate the real fear I had when standing in front of people (even two people!) and speaking—no matter how prepared I was.

Over 20 years ago I counseled with my pastor, about my fear. He took me into a study in scripture about the need to grow closer to Jesus in our faith walk. He took me through verses expressing our continual need to be fed, guided and pruned. In order to be fruitful we need to remain in the presence of our Father in Heaven (the "Gardener") and attached to Jesus (the "Vine".) The branches of a vine don't have to work hard to produce fruit; they simply need to be connected to the vine, the source of their life. They don't get stressed—they rest! In faith I need to do the same.

Father God, I believe; help my unbelief. I know that my worldly attempts at success are often driven by the world's idea of success, yet are fruitful only in a worldly measure. Fill my life with fruit measured and produced on my vine by You alone. In Jesus' loving and precious Name.

Harold Godshall is a chiropractor, and a former elder of Zion Church of Millersville.

May 25

Give Generously

"Give generously, for your gifts will return later. Divide your gifts among many, for you do not know what risks might lie ahead. When the clouds are heavy, the rains come down. When a tree falls, whether south or north, there it lies. If you wait for perfect conditions, you will never get any thing done. Be sure to stay busy and plant a variety of crops, for you never know which will grow—perhaps they all will." *Ecclesiastes 1–4 (Life Application Study Bible)*

We should apply giving to all areas of ministering to others. As we are willing to step out and use what we have already been given, God increases and develops our giftings in ministry. Many times this requires us to step out of our comfort zone, but how will we know what is out there if we do not take the plunge? After all, it is not all about us, but about moving along with God to bless others. This scripture says to give generously, stay busy and plant a variety of crops. This is basically saying we are to look for opportunities to sow in many ways, in many places, living a life-style of giving. Let's keep looking for opportunities to give of what God has blessed us with. As we keep sowing, we will keep reaping. God blesses us and continues to give the increase in our ability and capacity to lead.

Father, I thank You for the opportunity to serve others in the giftings and the abilities You have already given. I desire and commit to continue to sow into other's lives to be a blessing.

Sam Smucker is the senior pastor of The Worship Center and serves on the Executive Team of the Regional Church of Lancaster County.

May 26

Good News

"He will have no fear of bad news; his heart is steadfast, trusting in the Lord." *Psalm 112:7*

Our times are filled with bad news. The daily barrage of terroristic acts, murders, fires, riots, and accidents flows from the newswires. Same-sex marriage, divorce, abortion, and illegal drug use bombard our senses. Man's inhumanity to man is a daily occurrence.

The Word of God also contains bad news. It tells of many wars, conflicts and evil actions in the Old and New Testament. It reports our sinfulness (Romans 3:23), our unrighteousness (Romans 3:10), and the death sentence we all face (Romans 6:23).

Yet, the Bible beautifully presents the "Good News", or the Gospel. It speaks of eternal life (Romans 6:23; John 3:16), justification (Romans 8:1), and redemption (Galatians 3:13). Jesus Christ (God the Son) came from God the Father to pay the price for the sins of the world. He who, for the joy set before Him, endured the cross (Hebrews 12:2), was buried (John 19:41,42), and rose again (Luke 24:6). He is now preparing a place for those who have accepted His perfect work (John 14:3) and He will come again (Revelation 22:12). The next time you hear of all the bad news, remember our Savior. He endured such bad news and hostility by sinners against Himself, so that we may not grow weary and lose heart (Hebrews 12:3).

Every newscast you hear is a prayer request. It is about people, made in the image of God, in need of salvation from Christ Jesus. So rather than complain or become discouraged, be quick to pray to Jesus, who deals with both the bad news and the good news in the right way.

Dear God, help us to remember that whether we face bad or good news, You are always there for us because of Your great love. Thank you for providing the Good News of Christ which gives us hope, peace, and stamina in a world gone bad. In Jesus' name, Amen.

Greg Barton is news director of WDAC-FM, "The Voice of Christian Radio" in Lancaster.

May 27

Walking In Trust

"Oh, taste and see that the Lord is good. Blessed is the man who trusts in Him!" *Psalm 34:8 (New King James Version)*

Whenever there is mention of the word "beatitudes" we think immediately of Matthew 5 and the teaching given there by our Lord Jesus Christ. However, in the Old Testament there are also a number of wonderful beatitudes written by various authors and inspired by the Holy Spirit. These also convey encouraging truths to those who will embrace them.

In Psalm 34 David gives expression to one of these beatitudes when he writes "blessed is the man who trusts in the Lord." In the scripture the word "trust" has several distinctive overtones. For example it can mean "to take refuge" or "to depend upon" or "to have confidence in" or "to wait expectantly." Those various dimensions of trust are expressed first of all in salvation. Paul writes "that we first trusted in Christ…(Ephesians 1:12)." Again we read, "For it is by grace you have been saved through faith…(Ephesians 2:8)."

But that trust is also demonstrated in the living of the Christian life. The scriptures declare that "the just shall live by faith." That means that we are not only saved by faith but that we are also to walk by faith. We are to live a life of trust in the Lord. That life of trust will bring blessing. Hebrews 11 gives a wonderful account of a number of the patriarchs who were saved by faith and also lived by faith. They lived a life of complete trust in the Lord and were greatly blessed of God because of it. What a testimony they have left for us to follow!

Grant, O Lord, that we may know the blessedness not only of trusting You for salvation but also the blessedness of a life of "trust" in walking with You and fulfilling Your will. In Your precious Name. Amen.

Rev. Dr. Eric G. Crichton is a pastor emeritus at Calvary Church, Lancaster.

May 28

Use Every Opportunity

"O sing to the Lord a new song; sing to the Lord, all the earth! Sing to the Lord, bless (affectionately praise) His name; show forth His salvation from day to day." *Psalm 96:1–2 (Amplified Bible)*

Paul exhorted the Ephesians to redeem the time, understanding what the will of he Lord is (Ephesians 5: 16–17). The will of the Lord is to use every opportunity to show forth His salvation from day to day. How many times, after a conversation, have I thought of ways I could have shown forth His salvation? Too many to count! Unfortunately, once the conversation is over, the opportunity has passed.

The Lord desires our words to minister grace to the hearers (Ephesians 4:29). When our mouths are full of song and praise to His name, others will benefit. They will hear about the great thing the Lord has done for us and be glad (Psalm 126:3).

Sometimes just one word or just one phrase brings life to a conversation. My prayer is that people will not intimidate me to converse only in everyday language, but that I will redeem the time looking for opportunities to speak life—not speaking condescendingly, but truly desiring to minister grace by blessing His name and showing forth His salvation from day to day.

Heavenly Father, I desire to minister grace at all times, in every situation. Direct my conversation, set a watch before my mouth and a guard before my lips. Teach me to praise You and show forth Your salvation from day to day. In Jesus' name, Amen.

Lester Eberly is small group administrator and serves on the pastoral team at D.O.V.E. Christian Fellowship Westgate Celebration.

Comfort For Those
Who Mourn

Pray!

for Lancaster County

"Praise be to the God and Father of our Lord Jesus Christ, the Father of compassion and the God of all comfort, who comforts us in all our troubles, so that we can comfort those in any trouble with the comfort we ourselves have received from God. For just as the sufferings of Christ flow over into our lives, so also through Christ our comfort overflows."
2 Corinthians 1:3–5

Suffering and sacrifice are part of the Christian life. But we have this promise from God that He will comfort us and enable us to comfort others. Many lives have been sacrificed in wars through out history and this reality continues today. Let us reach out to compassionately encourage those in our region who have lost loved ones in battle.

Lord we pray for all those who have lost loved ones in battle (recently or in wars past). We ask You, the Father of compassion and God of all comfort, to minister healing to these families. We pray also for the lives and souls of all our soldiers in harm's way.

Today's devotional was edited from the 2003–2004 *Throne Of Grace Prayer Guide*, a weekly guide of Lancaster County prayer concerns gathered from regional intercessors and area prayer groups.

May 30

A Greater Sacrifice

"But God demonstrates his own love for us in this: While we were still sinners, Christ died for us." *Romans 5:8*

On this Memorial Day we should pause and reflect on the sacrifice of those soldiers who have fought for our freedom. The blessings of liberty that our country enjoys were won by the self-giving service of those who sacrificed their freedom for ours.

The Apostle Paul says that such personal sacrifice for one's fellow country members is an amazing thing that doesn't happen very often. Nevertheless (and we can be thankful!) such sacrifice does occur (Romans 5:7). This kind of sacrifice reminds me of the movie *Saving Private Ryan* in which eight soldiers have as their noble mission the rescue of a fellow brother-in-arms. Most of them die trying to save Private Ryan.

But even more amazing, almost unbelievably, God demonstrates a personal sacrifice that goes well beyond dying for fellow comrades. God dies for his enemies! "While we were yet sinners, Christ died for us." Perhaps this could be conveyed by another movie entitled Saving Private Bin Laden!

If you think it is amazing that someone would actually sacrifice themselves for a fellow countryman, consider God's love that moves Him to die even for His enemies.

Dear Father, thank You for those who have given of themselves for my personal freedom. But I thank You even more for Jesus who gave Himself for my spiritual freedom even when I was His enemy.

Gary Griffith is the assistant pastor of Faith Reformed Presbyterian Church in Quarryville. He served as an army chaplain during Desert Storm.

Reflections On Stewardship

"His master replied, 'Well done, good and faithful servant! You have been faithful with a few things; I will put you in charge of many things. Come and share your master's happiness!'"
Matthew 25:21

The parable of the talents is a powerful reminder of the responsibility we have to wisely steward the resources that God has entrusted to us. Many times we falsely assume that the gifts of time, talent, treasure, and relationship that come from His grace are possessions that we earned, rather than a gracious and precious gift from our Heavenly Father.

To illustrate this, imagine that you worked hard and used your personal finances to purchase a gold necklace. If you lost this necklace, you might be frustrated or even disappointed, but you could eventually replace it by purchasing another. However, if a close family member or friend entrusted you with a gold necklace, with special engraving, asking you to keep it safe until they returned from a long trip, you would think about that necklace differently. If you lost that necklace, you would feel a sense of urgency that this precious possession you were asked to tend needed to be found right away! Stewardship is an act of worship by which we care for and invest wisely in the purposes of God's kingdom.

Heavenly Father, I ask that this day You will reveal Your will and way to me concerning the stewardship You have given me. Give me ears to hear and eyes to see the many good and gracious gifts that You have given me to steward for Your glory. Give me a thankful and wise heart toward the precious time, talents, treasures, and relationships You have blessed me with. In Jesus' name, Amen.

Ray Casey is the headmaster of Living Word Academy.

Supporting healthy marriages in Lancaster County

June

June 1

Abba, Father

"One thing I ask of the LORD,
this is what I seek: that I may dwell in the
house of the LORD all the days of my life, to
gaze upon the beauty of the LORD
and to seek him in his temple."
Psalm 27:4

for Lancaster
County

"As the deer pants for streams of water, so my soul pants for
you, O God. My soul thirsts for God, for the living God. When
can I go and meet with God?" *Psalm 42:1–2*

"Come near to God and he will come near to you. Wash your
hands, you sinners, and purify your hearts, you double-
minded." *James 4:8*

D avid is a wonderful example of a man seeking passionately
and desperately after God. And James includes a wonderful
promise, when we come near to God, he will come near to us!
Let us pray that the entire "Bride of Christ", the Church, will develop a
yearning for deep intimacy with her Lord and Savior. Let us pray that
this yearning would begin with us, as our souls long for God as the
thirsty deer pants for water.

*Lord, I will seek to love You with all my heart and listen for Your voice
throughout my day. I will make time to come into Your presence each
day.*

Today's devotional was edited from the 2003–2004 *Throne Of Grace
Prayer Guide*, a weekly guide of Lancaster County prayer concerns
gathered from regional intercessors and area prayer groups.

June 2

Marriage: God's Bright Idea

"...so that we may present everyone perfect in Christ."
Colossians 1:28

Marriage was God's idea. Marriage predates Christianity. Marriage is, in fact, an act of creation. But what makes marriage so different for the Christian? When two persons come together as one, what is the purpose? We would like to share not just one purpose, but what we've discovered to be *the* purpose of marriage. We have never heard it taught in a marriage seminar, and we have yet to hear it preached from the pulpit or academic broadside. Mary and I have come to believe, without a shadow of a doubt, that the purpose of marriage is to build the life of Christ in my mate.

In the book of Colossians, chapter 1, verse 28, Paul the apostle reveals his love and sacrifice for the church: to present everyone perfect in Christ. Again, he shares a similar goal with the Galatian Christians in chapter 4, verse 19: "...until Christ is formed in you."

Here you have a scriptural mandate for what we believe to be foundational to the purpose of a Christ-centered marriage—*building Christ*. To you and to me, it means that everything I do, everything I think, every look on my face is filtered through this thought: "Is what I'm thinking, is what I'm about to say, is what I'm about to do going to build Christ in my spouse?"

"To build the life of Christ" is a phrase to commit to memory until it becomes a Holy Spirit sieve in my mind and my spirit. If my goal is to build the life of Christ in my mate, then I will not hurt my mate in thought, word or deed—it's that simple.

Lord Jesus, You called us as one, just as You are one with the Father. Enable us to put our selfishness aside and begin building the life of Christ in our mate.

Steve and Mary Prokopchak serve on the Apostolic Council of D.O.V.E. Christian Fellowship International and head D.C.F.I.'s Counseling Resources.

June 3

Known But Loved

"Come, see a man who told me everything I ever did. Could
this be the Christ ?" *John 4:29*

My greatest fear before I got married was that my wife would
get to know who I really was and that would be the end of
our relationship. There were too many faults, too many disappointments, too many secrets, too many embarrassments to sustain a
relationship. In order to avoid rejection, I needed to keep pretending.

When Jesus asked the woman at the well to bring her husband, He
was cutting through her pretenses. He was telling her that He knew.

But here comes the surprise. He does not reject her like all the
others did. She had been rejected by the Jews because she was a Samaritan, by the men because she was a woman, and by her own people
because she was not living up to their moral standards. Jesus, who was
a Jew, a man and a morally upright person, had (by society's standards)
every reason to reject her—but He didn't. This is what finally convinced the woman that this Jesus was an unusual person: "Could this
be the Christ?" He knew, but He still accepted and loved. That is the
good news, which transformed the woman from someone rejected to
someone who was the bearer of life to the very people who rejected
her. She, who once was unfruitful, now became a source of life.
It is with this confidence that God wants us to live this day:
"I am known...and still loved." If you have this encounter with Christ
today, go and tell someone about it!

*Father, You search me and know me. You know everything about me,
and yet You do not reject me. Give me the confidence today that I can
be who I am with all the beauty in which You created me with and all
the flaws which You intend to mold into Your image. Amen.*

Josef Berthold is the pastor of West End Mennonite Fellowship in
Lancaster City.

June 4

A Lesson In Faith

"Brothers, I do not consider myself yet to have taken hold of it. But one thing I do: Forgetting what is behind and straining toward what is ahead, I press on toward the goal to win the prize for which God has called me heavenward in Christ Jesus." *Philippians 3:13–14*

I learned a lesson in faith from my daughter and her dog. For years, my youngest daughter Kristen's closest animal friend was her Pomeranian dog, Tiny. Wherever Kristen wandered, Tiny went.

At times I was concerned about what would happen to Kristen if something ever happened to Tiny. Then one day when Kristen was in school, it happened. Tiny ran out onto the road and was killed. When Kristen came home from school, Shirley and I both sat down and told her what had happened. There were many tears of sorrow.

Later that night, I went into her room to comfort and pray with her. Upon entering her room, I saw a large cage beside the head of her bed, with a fresh bowl of food and water in it. I said, "Kristen, what are the cage, water and food for?" She said, "It is for my next dog."

That statement spoke volumes into my life, not only that night, but also five years later when the Sight & Sound Entertainment center burned down. I recalled her words with childlike faith: "It is for my next dog." That statement increased my faith to press on. The message was that an accident or a fire may destroy a dog or a theater, but it can't destroy a dream or a vision. God is bigger. God is greater.

As God honored Kristen's faith in giving her another dog (named Taffy), so God honored my faith in giving me another theatre named the Millennium Theatre.

My prayer is forgetting what is behind and reaching forward to what lies ahead. I press on toward the goal for the prize of the upward call of God which is in Christ Jesus.

Glenn Eshelman is the executive producer and founder of Sight and Sound Ministries.

June 5

I Believe

"Immediately the father of the child cried out and said, 'I believe; help my unbelief!'" *Mark 9:24 (Revised Standard Version)*

Many years ago (over 20, now), I counseled with my pastor about my fear of public speaking. He ended our time together by handing me poem on a card: "Footprints in the Sand." He left me to ponder the verses and encouraged me to believe that Jesus would be carrying me whenever I felt alone or unable to cope with a challenge in my life. Weeks later I spoke to a group of close to 500 people, and—with the sense of the presence of the Holy Spirit— I finished without the use of the many notes I had always required in the past.

I praise God for the many times I've sensed His presence throughout my life. Having a personal relationship with such a loving Father is so important as we go through our lives. We can feel safe and secure living our lives, though we may actually be in the eye of a hurricane, knowing that the turmoil around us won't sweep us up. We must keep in mind that we are nothing but branches, a part of the "True Vine", and fruit will be added to our branch when, and only when, the Father decides to add it.

Father God, I pray for Your Hand to be guiding me so that I may always be sensitive to Your leading. Thank You for all that You bring to me and guard me from the belief that I can multiply without Your blueprint being followed. In Jesus' loving and precious Name.

Harold Godshall is a child of God, a chiropractor, and a former elder of Zion Church of Millersville.

June 6

A Single Success Strategy

"Love is patient, love is kind. It does not envy, it does not boast, it is not proud. It is not rude, it is not self-seeking, it is not easily angered, it keeps no record of wrongs. Love does not delight in evil but rejoices with the truth. It always protects, always trusts, always hopes, always perseveres. Love never fails." *1 Corinthians 13:4–8*

If you could adopt a single strategy for success, if you could choose only one course of action to overcome problems in your life, if you had to select one and only one approach to resolving a difficult situation, the answer is clear. Choose love. Why? Because love *NEVER* fails! Love will always produce success.

This truth became revelation to me as a young manager sitting in a business seminar and hearing about a hierarchy of behavior starting with "understanding" that leads to "trust" that culminates with "caring". In discussing this model, I asked the instructor if what was being presented as newfangled business strategy wasn't already covered in the Bible's discussion of love. He answered, "Yes. However, the idea of "love" is not one that is easily discussed in the workplace." The "yes" was all I needed! Over 20 years later, I can tell you I have taught the success strategy of LOVE as being the surest and most infallible approach to business as well as personal success. You see, it is true. Love NEVER fails!

Lord, I thank You for the truth of Your Word which provides clear and simple strategy for our success. Grant us a deeper understanding of the overcoming power of love. By the power of Your Holy Spirit, enable us to proclaim this truth in every situation, to everyone we meet, wherever we go. In Jesus' name, Amen!

George Mobarak serves as vice president of development for Signature Custom Cabinetry in Ephrata.

June 7

She Knew Him

"...she came and worshiped Him, saying, "Lord, help me!" But He answered and said, "It is not good to take the children's bread and throw it to the little dogs." And she said, "Yes, Lord, yet even the little dogs eat the crumbs which fall from their masters' table." *Matthew 15:25–27 (New King James Version)*

I have marveled at Jesus' seemingly brazen treatment of this Gentile woman. He ignored her, "answering not a word", because he was called only to the Jews. Then, as she worships at His feet, He essentially equates her with a dog.

But if we understand the Scripture's play on words, we will realize Jesus' true response. *Strong's Concordance* defines her worship as "to kiss, like a dog licking his master's hand." Have you ever watched a hopeful dog at his loving master's feet? When it wants something, it wags its tail, prances, barks, licks, jumps...with full expectation of receiving from his hand. A dog knows its master's character.

In the same way, this woman knew Jesus' character. She had probably seen His tears as He touched lepers, or heard His joyful laughter as lame men leaped about. She fully expected that He rewarded those who sought Him (Hebrews 11:6), just as a dog happily licks its master's hand.

Jesus saw her expectation and His heart melted. He softly responds, "the children's bread should not be given to the puppies" (a literal translation of dog). She sees His adoring eyes and says eagerly, "Yes, Master, but even the puppies eat the children's crumbs." Though she wasn't a Jew, she knew He deeply loved all people.

Full of joy, Jesus replies, "O woman! You have great trust! You have what you desired!" And her daughter was healed immediately.

Lord, give me this woman's faith! Pour into my heart a revelation of You as my Kind Rewarder. Enable me to live expecting Your goodness. Thank You, Jesus. Amen.

Janet Richards, author, actor, intercessor, is currently called to regional intercession and to reconciliation of the Anabaptists with the Swiss Reformed church.

June 8

Whatever You Do, Do It As Unto The Lord

Pray!
for Lancaster County

"Also, seek the peace and prosperity of the city to which I have carried you into exile. Pray to the LORD for it, because if it prospers, you too will prosper." *Jeremiah 29:7*

"And whatever you do, whether in word or deed, do it all in the name of the Lord Jesus, giving thanks to God the Father through him. … Whatever you do, work at it with all your heart, as working for the Lord, not for men, since you know that you will receive an inheritance from the Lord as a reward. It is the Lord Christ you are serving." *Colossians 3:17–24*

"Do everything without complaining or arguing, so that you may become blameless and pure, children of God without fault in a crooked and depraved generation, in which you shine like stars in the universe as you hold out the word of life—in order that I may boast on the day of Christ that I did not run or labor for nothing." *Philippians 2:14–16*

So often, when we have an assignment or obligation, we focus on the demand of the one who made the assignment. The quality of our work may depend on our esteem of that person. In the above verses we are reminded that we must "do it all for the glory of God." Wow—what would happen if all the Christians in our region lived by this principle? Let us pray that we all will be faithful stewards and servants in every situation and in every relationship the Lord has given us (families, friends, neighborhoods, workplaces, and congregations).

Lord, I will 'press on' to obey You and to see Your purposes accomplished in my life, my home, my neighborhood, and in Lancaster County.

Today's devotional was edited from the 2003–2004 *Throne Of Grace Prayer Guide*, a weekly guide of Lancaster County prayer concerns gathered from regional intercessors and area prayer.

June 9

Abiding In Him

"I am the vine; you are the branches. If a man remains in me and I in him, he will bear much fruit; apart from me you can do nothing." *John 15:5*

I went into a personal retreat day full of questions—seeking vision for the new school year, clarity about church ministry, and guidance for personal relationships. I longed for clear direction. *Just tell me what to do, God, and I'll do it,* I kept praying. Nothing came. No word, no plan, no goals for the year ahead. Nothing.

As I sat quietly, I felt God's Spirit whisper, *Just come and be with Me. You are seeking information. Seek My face. I do not shout words of wisdom or marching orders at you from a distance. I call you by My Spirit to come close, to hear My heartbeat. I will show you things you don't see. My embrace is the place of instruction and wisdom.*

I'd become so goal-oriented, so intent on accomplishing God's purposes and moving forward, that I'd neglected the most precious treasure—intimacy with God. I'd been wanting Him to tell me what to do so I could run off and get busy doing it—and He just wanted me to be with Him. I was seeking answers rather than seeking God.

My own intensity and demanding schedule still sometimes drive me toward "answer seeking" rather than intimacy with the Father. Yet, I know that my work will be unfruitful if I'm not closely connected to the Vine, the source of life. I want to make my home in Him, living out my days in a relationship of deep, loving communion.

Lord, draw me close to You. I want my life to bear the fruit of abiding in You. When I come seeking answers, turn my heart to seek Your face.

Andrea Adams teaches English at Manheim Township Middle School, where she is a team leader and advisor to a student-led Bible club.

Hard Press

"Not that I have already attained, or am already perfected, but I press on, that I may lay hold of that for which Christ Jesus has also laid hold of me." *Philippians 3:12–13 (New King James Version)*

Wow, I thought Paul had it together: "NOT THAT I HAVE ALREADY ATTAINED?"

How can the most "successful" Christian that has ever existed proclaim that he is reaching forward to those things that are ahead? Do we realize the significance of that statement? There is always greater purpose for us. We cannot reach the end of everything we can know. There is no top of the mountain! The most dedicated servants of God can pour out their lives and never get to a place where they can go no more. There is always more.

This is refreshing to me. I get bored easily.

Once, my brother and I went to an amusement park in Ohio. We went on all the big rides first and were bored by noon.

So, I begin to think. For what things has Jesus laid hold of me? He chose me for a purpose. Jesus did not choose someone else and have to take me as well. He chose *me*. I know He did not choose me that I would die in obscurity never knowing God or making an impact for His kingdom. He did not lay hold of me so I would live in hopeless misery and never be able to walk in freedom from what has bound me. He did not lay hold of me so that I would be "lucky" to really accomplish anything, but He laid hold of me to walk in the powerful provisions made available to me through His life, death and resurrection.

Jesus, thank You for laying hold of me. Help me to press on toward Your purposes and not to give up. May I use my life to the fullness through all You have provided for me.

Shawn Weaver served over two years as the director of Oasis Youth Services in Manheim and has been recently called into Lancaster City.

June 11

Real Love

"I waited patiently for the LORD; he turned to me and heard my cry. He lifted me out of the slimy pit, out of the mud and mire; he set my feet on a rock and gave me a firm place to stand. He put a new song in my mouth, a hymn of praise to our God. Many will see and fear and put their trust in the LORD."
Psalm 40:1–3

A neighbor girl and I were speaking one day and I was startled when she asked me if I had "beaten my wife lately"! I responded by telling her that I had *never* beaten my wife. She was amazed and asked me "Why not?" I replied that I *loved* my wife and I wouldn't beat her. She then asked, "What does it mean to love someone?"

We live in a world full of hurt and suffering. Every moment of every day contains heartache. Sexual abuse. Divorce. Addiction. Homelessness. Poverty. Fractured families. Materialism. And there is a little girl in my neighborhood who describes parental love as harsh words and the jagged end of a broom handle.

We live in a society where love is defined as a feeling, an urge, an impulse without commitment, and a vague but admittedly nice idea. Our culture gropes for significance in everything but God. Even so, as we follow God in our daily lives, we can offer God's love to hurting people around us—whether they are in the boardroom or the prison cell! This love is not the unrealistic hope of Hollywood, but the real hope that Jesus offers us in the midst of the nitty-gritty of life! If each of us would love others as Jesus does, maybe a little girl in your neighborhood might come to understand that she's loved by God, too!

Dear God, show me how to see those who are hurting around me with Your eyes and love with Your heart.

Steve Brubaker is the director of residential programs for the Water Street Rescue Mission in Lancaster.

June 12

Looking Glass

"Search me, O God and know my heart...lead me in the way everlasting." *Psalm 139:23–24*

In life, we find ourselves going through the motions of being Christian. We are smiling at all the right times. We know how to respond to any question asked us on Sunday morning.

When we look in the mirror of His Word, we hear Him calling us to meet Him in that secret place of intimacy. He calls us patiently, compassionately, to drink of His water and sit at His table. He calls us to a place of peace and rest in Him. We know it's Him, yet we do not come. Oh, we tell Him, "We will be right there." We justify our reasons for being late; reminding Him it's because of our service for Him and the responsibilities we carry in this world. Yet, even when we think these thoughts, they come out hollow and empty without the truth of real justification. The accuser of the brethren stands close at hand to whisper accusations in our ears, stirring the storms of defeat that spiral us down into the valley of despair. Our heart begins to condemn us for our slothfulness and neglect. The coldness of our heart amazes us. We are left in the loneliest of all places—with ourselves.

In this abyss of emptiness and defeat, the voice of His Holy Spirit reminds us of His Word, "If our heart condemns us, He is greater than our heart (1 John 3:20)."

Dear God, Search my heart and know me in all my ways. My desire is to know You and please You. Root out of my heart any hidden slothfulness that keeps me from You. I repent of my faithlessness and slothfulness in seeking You first. Help me to have courage to follow You in the way everlasting. Amen.

He is forever faithful!

Wayne Kaufman is the founder of Gates of Praise Ministries/House Church Network, serves on the boards of Harvest Net Ministries, the Regional Church of Lancaster County and advisory board of the Lancaster House of Prayer.

June 13

Hiding Place

"He who dwells in the secret place of the Most High shall abide under the shadow of the Almighty" *Psalm 91:1 (New King James Version)*

Jesus exhorts us to carefully steward the resources the Father has given us. Time is one of the most precious resources that we have been given. We each get the same amount of time every day—24 hours—no more, no less. I have often thought to myself or heard others say, "If only I could have more time…" Since we cannot create more time it is wise for us to consider how we steward the time that we do have.

As I have considered this challenge I have examined Jesus' life here on the earth. Meetings consumed his days with needy people, difficult co-workers and encounters with those who opposed him—yet Jesus did not bow to frustration or complain that he needed more time. In fact He thrived—filled with joy—in spite of the intense demands on his time. How did he do it?

In Matthew 6, Jesus gives us a clue: he references a time in the secret place with the Father. Could it be that the key to Jesus' fruitfulness on the earth was exactly that—his secret life of prayer with the Father? Could it be that my own willingness to draw away into that secret place with the Father is the key to my own ability to fulfill all that God has for me each day?

As I seek to grow in my times alone with the Father, the Psalmist's words invite me to consider the secret place—a place of security, peace and revelation: "He who dwells in the secret place of the Most High shall abide under the shadow of the Almighty."

Father, continue to reveal to me the importance of the secret place. Help me to understand how encountering You in that place changes my perspective of my life, my needs and those I come into contact with. Amen.

Matt Buckwalter is the director of Lancaster House of Prayer.

June 14

Personal Power Encounter

"Your problem is that you don't know the Scriptures, and you don't know the power of God." *Matthew 22:29 (New Living Translation)*

Ouch! What an insulting indictment Jesus handed to the religious leaders of His day. They may have been proud of their knowledge of the scriptures and yet He was saying that these leaders really didn't understand them. They did not have experiential knowledge of the power of God. When we are not really connecting to the living God, what we end up with is "religion!"

Religion is pretty easy for any of us to fall into isn't it? Addressing the Pharisees another time, Jesus said, "You search the Scriptures because you think that in them you have eternal life; it is these that testify about Me; and you are unwilling to come to Me so that you may have life (John 5:39–40 NAS)."

While the Pharisees were experts in the scriptures, Jesus saw that they were studying for the wrong reasons. The scriptures have been given to lead us to God. Yes, they are His words to us and carry His full authority. But He wants us to have a personal relationship with Him, not just a book or a religious system. While the Bible certainly is a road map, God has given us the Holy Spirit as a Guide to interpret the map.

Have you ever been told not to seek experiences? Sure. And there is good reason for that advice. However, God does want us to experience Him. What is wrong with a life-changing experience with God?

Dear God, I want to connect with You when I read the scriptures. And I desperately need life-changing experiences with You. Forgive me for slipping into religious mode at times. I really want an authentic relationship. Today, I will practice Your presence while I go about my work. Let's talk during the day! Amen.

Barry Wissler is the senior pastor of Ephrata Community Church and heads HarvestNet, a resource ministry linking churches and ministries as partners in the harvest.

June 15

Men Of God

"He will turn the hearts of the fathers to
their children, and the hearts of the
children to their fathers; or else I will come
and strike the land with a curse." *Malachi 4:6*

for Lancaster
County

"You then, my son, be strong in the grace that is in
Christ Jesus. And the things you have heard me say
in the presence of many witnesses entrust to reliable men who
will also be qualified to teach others." *2 Timothy 2:1–2*

A child's view of the Father God is greatly influenced by his or her earthly father. Yet in our country the role of fathers is often discouraged and undervalued. The joy of fatherhood is also neglected in the pursuit of worldly goals. Let us pray that men across our region will recognize their crucial role in their families and be godly leaders in their homes. Let us pray that the Lord will turn the hearts of the fathers to their children, and the hearts of the children to their fathers.

Lord, as a man, I recommit myself to living as a godly man in my roles as husband, father, and especially follower of You!

Lord, as a woman, I ask You to show me how to value and encourage men as they seek to fulfill their godly roles.

Today's devotional was edited from the 2003–2004 *Throne Of Grace Prayer Guide*, a weekly guide of Lancaster County prayer concerns gathered from regional intercessors and area prayer groups.

June 16

Blossoms And Fruit

Read John 15:1–6

As a Lancastrian, I feel a need each Spring to be a "gardener". Since I live in the city my growing arena is extremely limited, so I grow about three tomato plants every year. Observing the growth of this wonderful fruit has helped me to understand both the spiritual life and evangelism a little better.

God creates blossoms as well as fruit. The blossoms are beautiful, but they are not the fruit. Picking and sharing the blossoms would be premature and destroy the fruit. We cannot be premature about sharing what God is creating in our lives.

Fruit contains seeds. Blossoms do not. Inside each seed are many more tomatoes. The blossom looks attractive, but does not contain the life of the seeds. Fruit can reproduce because it has seeds. Blossoms cannot reproduce. When we let God finish building the character of Jesus in us the product contains reproducible life.

Tomato plants do not eat their own fruit. If the fruit stays on the vine too long it will rot. Fruit must be picked on time and given away. The seeds inside each fruit contain many more tomatoes. When the fruit is given away it has potential to produce by the hundreds similar fruit. We are "given-away" people who must share the character of Christ when it has matured in us.

The Gospel must mature in our lives first. There must be a divine imprint of the character of Jesus on our lives. But when this character is present, we must not keep it to ourselves. The Christian Life is meant to be shared—lived in front of our neighbors and spoken in a way that invites them to taste and see that the Lord is good.

Jesus, help me to disregard the vanity of blossoms, and desire the fruit that You are producing in me. May You produce Your Holy Seed in me and in the Christians in Lancaster County that Your glorious Gospel would take root. Amen.

Dan Snyder is the executive director of Lancaster Youth Network of Churches.

June 17

A Model For Forgiveness

"Be ye kind one to another, tenderhearted, forgiving one another, even as God for Christ's sake hath forgiven you."
Ephesians 4:32 (King James Version)

I s forgiveness an "event" or a "process"? As a counselor, I have spent much time believing that forgiveness is a "process", a principle strongly supported by my profession. Many counselors justify a client's anger toward their offenders, and support the idea that forgiveness takes a long time. Some coach people not to forgive until their offender repents, or he/she makes changes in their behavior.

My clients also believe that forgiveness is a "process", and they justify that it may take months, or even years, for them to forgive. They forgive by degrees. Some *never* come to the place of forgiveness as they walk in bitterness toward their offenders.

God gives us a correct model for forgiveness in the way he relates to us. Ephesians 4:32 makes us ask, "How did God forgive us?" Is it by degrees, or is it a once and done deal? Does God forgive us only after we have changed?

I am convinced that in God's kingdom forgiveness is an event, an act of the will. If we are to be like God, we cannot afford to forgive in "degrees" or live in bitterness as we work toward forgiveness. We must forgive—*then* we are free to reconcile, bring restitution, work through emotions and resolve relationships. Believers rejoice in the fact that forgiveness from God is instantaneous and complete. As we forgive as God has forgiven us, we will see forgiveness more as an "event" and less as a "process".

Dear Lord, please help us to forgive others as You have forgiven us. Help us to see forgiveness as an act of a will, and act accordingly. May we walk in love and forgiveness and reconciliation with those who have offended us.

Dr James Johnson, director of Shepherd's Touch Counseling Ministry, Dr. Johnson hosts the Counselors Notebook, a radio broadcast on WJTL, Sundays at 1:20 pm.

June 18

Embrace His Fullness

"Not that I have already obtained all this or have already been made perfect, but I press on to take hold of that for which Christ Jesus took hold of me." *Philippians 3:12*

Are we daily pressing into the boundless, fathomless, and incalculable riches of Christ (Ephesians 3:8), strengthened with his power in the inner man and daily living empowered by His Holy Spirit (Ephesians 3:16), and deeply rooted in His love (Philippians 3:17)?

Paul, the revered saint, asked himself that question (Philippians 3) and answered it with a resounding, "No". If anyone could conceivably think he or she had "arrived" it was he. He had the pedigree, the passion and the zeal. Outwardly all seemed in order but there was (and is) so much more. Acknowledging there was much more that God had available for him, he chose to "press on" to take hold of every bit of it.

Today each of us is the recipient of the glorious inheritance of a great adventure with the God of the universe. What a great privilege! Do we embrace His fullness with unqualified words such as *all*, *every*, and *always*? Is His praise *always* on our lips (Psalm 34:1)? Do we give thanks in *all* circumstances (1 Thessalonians 5:18)? Do we cast *all* our cares and burdens on him (1 Peter 5:7)? Do we trust in Him with *all* our heart and acknowledge him in *all* our ways (Proverbs 3:5–6)? Do we comprehend His promise that *everyone* who asks and seeks in His name receives and finds (Matthew 7:8)?

Thank you Lord for Your gracious, persistent heart that daily calls us into Your presence. Today we choose to yield more fully, wait in Your presence more expectantly, rejoice more fervently and take hold of You as You take hold of us. Thank you, Jesus.

John R. Gibbel serves in marketplace ministry as a partner in Gibbel, Kraybill & Hess.

June 19

Calm The Storm

"The disciples went and woke him, saying, 'Lord, save us!
We're going to drown!' He replied, 'You of little faith, why are
you so afraid?' Then he got up and rebuked the winds and the
waves, and it was completely calm." *Matthew 8:25–26*

When I was about six years old, my family took a trip to Disney World. On our flight home, the plane encountered a typical summer thunderstorm. Normally, airplanes try to avoid such problems, but our pilot attempted to beat the storm into Baltimore. He didn't make it. Instead of a nice peaceful landing, the plane was bounced around a lot. My parents told me later that they were afraid the plane was going to crash. I say they told me this because I was not awake during the ordeal. As a small child who had just had an exhausting/fun week of vacation, I peacefully slept through the entire commotion. While others were fearful for their lives, I was oblivious. Only as I sleepily walked off the plane and saw the looks on adults' faces did I know there was a problem.

The disciples faced a great storm through which they couldn't sleep. Instead, they worried that they would drown. Only Jesus had the peace and presence to remain calm. Jesus was unafraid because He knew the storm didn't have complete control. He saw the storm's power, but He knew God was greater.

As the storms of our lives rage about us, how do we respond? Do we have that childlike faith to put ourselves completely in God's hands? Or, do we try to get ourselves through it? The Lord wants to bring peace into our lives, as we trust Him.

*Lord, help me in my unbelief. I may not understand what is happening,
but I know You are absolutely trustworthy. Help me to rest in You in
spite of the storms I face. Amen.*

Jonathan Mikesell is the pastor of Lititz Wesleyan Church. He and his
wife Jennifer have a one-year-old son named Matthew.

June 20

Faith Calisthenics

"Now the just shall live by faith..." *Hebrews 10:38 (New King James Version)*

It seems physical exercise is a high priority to many people these days. It is a priority for me as well, but a far greater personal priority is to exercise my faith as a life-style. The scriptures declare that without faith it is impossible to please God (Hebrews 11:6). God is so good! Everything He mandates us to do is purposed to (1) bring blessing to us; (2) advance His wonderful kingdom on the earth; and (3) bring glory to His name. He personally desires to enable us to fulfill every assignment and opportunity He gives us. When we first came to Christ, He gave us a measure of His very own faith (Romans 12:3; Mark 11:22). He is instructing us to use that faith to access His kingdom provision as a way of daily life. This brings pleasure to our Father's heart and is a testimony to those who know only the world's system.

When I have trouble in my relationships, distress in my family, unhealthy symptoms in my body, pressure in my finances, or desire to impact the needy in the world around me, I seek to remember only one question. "Nevertheless, what does God's Word say concerning this (Matthew 4:4)?" Then, by an act of my will, I apply my faith to that Word. Finally, I persist with a heart of gratitude. I keep on hearing and keep on speaking what God has said (Romans 10:17). By His grace, I do not fling away my fearless confidence for it carries a great and glorious reward (Hebrews 10:35)!

Father God, thank You for being so good. I praise You for giving Your very own faith to me to use. Father, let Your kingdom come and Your will be done on earth—right here in my life—just as it is in heaven. I love You, Father, and I receive Your awesome love for me.

Ann S. Gibbel serves in the areas of prayer and healing.

June 21

Even If He Does Not

"If we are thrown into the blazing furnace, the God we serve is able to save us... But even if he does not, we want you to know, O king, that we will not serve your gods..."
Daniel 3:17–18

There is a type of "faith" that declares, "God will do this!" Staunchly closing out all other options and declaring the will of God is an attitude that I once admired from afar. Yet what happens to this faith when God does not heal, save or provide? When I trusted God for two years for something that did *not* come to pass, I began in my brokenness to realize presumption and misplaced trust. I cannot trust God *to do something*; I need to trust *God*. My faith cannot be in one outcome; it must be in God, "even if He does not...."

Three young Israelites boldly, humbly told the Babylonian king, "Our God is able to save us... but even if He does not... we will trust Him." Jesus also agonized when facing death, yet victoriously brought His will into His Father's. "Father, if you are willing to take this cup from me; yet not my will, but yours be done...glorify your name (Luke 22:42, John 12:28)!" God chose to save Shadrach, Meshach, and Abednego from death. He did not choose to save Jesus. Yet in both situations, He used evil for good and glorified Himself.

When I don't know how to pray, I am learning to say:
• God, You are able to do this.
• Even if You do not, I trust You.
• Father, glorify Your Name.

"God, You are able to _____. Nothing is impossible with You. I ask You to do this to show Yourself glorious. Yet, Lord, Your ways are higher than mine. Even if You do not answer as I desire, I trust You. Glorify Yourself through this situation."

Melanie Nofziger, wife of Wendell Nofziger, works at Global Disciples Network and serves as leadership team member and youth leader at West End Mennonite Fellowship.

June 22

Father, May They Be One...

Pray!

for Lancaster County

"...First go and be reconciled to your brother; then come and offer your gift."
Matthew 5:24

"You have heard that it was said, 'Love your neighbor and hate your enemy.' But I tell you: Love your enemies and pray for those who persecute you, that you may be sons of your Father in heaven. He causes his sun to rise on the evil and the good, and sends rain on the righteous and the unrighteous. If you love those who love you, what reward will you get? Are not even the tax collectors doing that? And if you greet only your brothers, what are you doing more than others? Do not even pagans do that? Be perfect, therefore, as your heavenly Father is perfect." *Matthew 5:43–48*

"May the God who gives endurance and encouragement give you a spirit of unity among yourselves as you follow Christ Jesus, so that with one heart and mouth you may glorify the God and Father of our Lord Jesus Christ. Accept one another, then, just as Christ accepted you, in order to bring praise to God." *Romans 15:5–7*

The world judges the church by the quality of our relationships. Are we different? Let us take these scriptures to heart, to glorify God with *one heart and mouth.* This will require our commitment to reconciliation in the body of Christ. It will require that we give up our rights to be offended, and that we seek open communication with one another. Let us pray for each other and for our region that broken relationships would be mended.

Lord, search the motives of my heart toward my brothers and sisters in Christ. Prepare and change my heart to love in greater ways.

Today's devotional was edited from the 2003–2004 *Throne Of Grace Prayer Guide*, a weekly guide of Lancaster County prayer concerns gathered from regional intercessors and area prayer groups.

June 23

Extravagant Devotion

"Leave her alone," said Jesus. "Why are you bothering her? She has done a beautiful thing to me." *Mark 14:6*

Imagine the King of Kings and Lord of Lords coming to your defense in this manner. How would you feel, knowing His love for you, His affection, His pleasure with your life? This woman stepped out and anointed Jesus' head. She poured out a year's worth of wages, *before* she knew what His response would be! She thought it was going to be a beautiful act of obedience, and she knew it was on *her* heart to do it, but what would *He* think? How would *He* respond? She didn't know, yet she chose to walk in extravagant obedience. She made the choice to step out, and Jesus called it "beautiful".

Am I willing to be misunderstood by a few, to know the pleasure of my Lord? The fruit that obedience produces in our lives is always sweet, yet it remains a challenge. Which side of this story will I be on? Will I be one of the ones who deem Him worthy? Or will I join those who criticize out of misunderstanding, fear and jealousy? Let's choose faith and obedience today, and be amazed at what the Lord does through our simple acts of faithfulness.

Father, we ask in the name of Jesus for boldness, strength and passion to walk in devotion toward You today. We ask for opportunities to model obedience and devotion to You, so that others might recognize the reality of Your Lordship in our lives. We love You, and we thank You for Your devotion to us in spite of our shortcomings. In Jesus' Name, Amen.

Mark Buckwalter lives in Lancaster city with his wife Heather and their son Moses. They are members of the leadership team at Lancaster House of Prayer and are working to see young leaders equipped in the Body of Christ in Lancaster.

June 24

Living By The Book

"All authority in heaven and on earth has been given to me."
Matthew 28:18

The time in which we live requires that the church have a revelation of what living under Jesus' authority looks like. First let's look at the definition of authority. It is the power or right to act or command; Jesus has both the power and the right.

When we, the church, are submitted to Jesus' authority we are free to live obediently, boldly, confidently, and fearlessly. The disciples knew this and turned the world upside down. The people said of Jesus that he spoke with such authority (Luke 4: 32,36). The church will be able to love others unconditionally and speak authoritatively to the degree that we allow Jesus to be our final authority. There is no theory, idea, teaching or movement among humanity that the authority of Jesus cannot expose or refute when it is false or deceptive.

God the Father gave Jesus his authority. Therefore Jesus sends us by his authority. His power and authority go together. We have neither of these by our own exertion. When the authority of Jesus is present everyone knows it. Legitimate authority commands respect simply by its presence. The church under Jesus' authority will, by our living, promote respect for God whereever we are.

When I remember whom my authority is it alters how I think and act, how I approach a situation. I used to have what doctors call, "white coat syndrome": my blood pressure went up in a doctor's office. After hearing a speaker explain God's complete authority, my blood pressure is under control. I now remind myself who my authority is and my blood pressure stays down. If we hear and obey Jesus' instructions, we will minister life to people.

Father, by Your Spirit, You keep us remembering that Jesus said, "All authority in heaven and on earth has been given to me. Go therefore and make disciples of all nations."

Kathleen Hollinger has served in several leadership roles with ACTS Covenant Christian Fellowship.

June 25

The Posture Of Faith

"I have been crucified with Christ; it is no longer I who live, but Christ lives in me; and the life which I now live in the flesh I live by faith..." *Galatians 2:20 (New King James Version)*

While this Scripture is not traditionally used to address unbelief, several months ago, the Lord began to speak to me to use it concerning the presence of unbelief in my own heart. It is actually a form of "faith" that entails putting trust in one's own abilities rather than God and His abilities. It is an issue concerning not the absence of faith, but the posture of faith. A man who is riddled with unbelief ought not to pray for more faith, for his issue is not an inability to believe, but rather the interference of *self*—the one in whom he has placed his confidence (or lack there of). He would do better to ask for death of selfish desires. Only after he dies to his desire to control his own destiny will he be able to place his faith in the One who is able to help him achieve it. Paul discovered that death to self is the key to living by faith.

At the root of unbelief is pride, the conviction that self knows better and is in fact more reliable. Pride places human limitations on God, making God a man and man his own god.

Father, help us to place our faith in Your strength and give us the grace to die to our own strength. Replace self-sufficiency with God-dependency. Make us a people utterly reliant on You in everything.

Jonathan Jacobs serves on the leadership teams of The Lancaster House of Prayer, Consuming Fire Ministries, Morning Star Satellite School, and The Gemeinschaft.

June 26

The Heart Of Worship

"... Then he fell to the ground in worship and said: '...The LORD gave and the LORD has taken away; may the name of the LORD be praised.'" *Job 1:20–21*

W hen thinking about notable passages of worship or praise from scriptures, I guess I have a pre-conceived notion of what worship should look like. Recently, I was impressed with a very powerful expression of worship that took place in the most unusual circumstances.

God allowed Satan to test Job, for Satan was convinced Job was righteous only because he was rich. In a moment, all of Job's possessions were stripped away. I can just imagine Satan watching with cynical glee as each of the "messengers of doom" informed Job of his losses (Job 1:13-19). I can almost hear Job's accuser joyfully predict, "Now Job will stand, shake his fist in the air, and curse God!" Satan was not prepared for what actually happened next.

Instead of fist-shaking, Satan saw Job on the ground *worshiping!* Job was devastated and battered but not destroyed or broken.

This seems to be a crystal-clear insight into the heart of worship. It is a simple acknowledgment that God is God and remains in control, regardless of what we're feeling or experiencing. Was Job smiling, singing or dancing? No. But was he still worshiping? Absolutely! Was Job filled with pain, questions, and all sorts of anguish? Certainly. Was he still worshiping? Amazingly, the answer is still yes!

Does your current situation find you contemplating shaking your fist at God? Why not come to your creator in worship? You say you can't smile, sing or even begin to pray? Allow your tears to communicate the following:

God, You are God, and in the midst of my confusion You are still God. God, You are good, and in the midst of my pain, You are still good. Even in my devastation, I worship You.

Ron Ressler, with his wife Molly, serves as an overseer/coach for cell group leaders at Living Hope Community Church, west of Lancaster City.

A.L.I.V.E.

"Not that I have already attained, or am already perfected: but I press on, that I may lay hold of that for which Christ Jesus has also laid hold of me...forgetting those things which are behind and reaching forward to those things which are ahead, I press toward the goal for the prize of the upward call of God in Christ Jesus." *Philippians 3:12–14 (New King James Version)*

Think about it: **A**lways **L**iving **I**n **V**iew of **E**ternity. Reaching toward that which is ahead. What would you be like if you kept the eternal perspective on life? How would your character change? What about non-believers, how would you view them? Are you pressing on towards all that God has for you in eternity?

As Jesus walked the Earth, he kept an eternal perspective. He knew where He came from and where He was going (John 8:14). He kept His sight on the goal. He did not worry about what others thought of Him because He knew that in eternity it would not matter (John 5:41). He knew it only mattered what His Heavenly Father thought of him.

My challenge to you today is to consider what you can change in your life to keep the eternal perspective. It is natural for us to worry about what others think. Are you willing to worry about what your Heavenly Father thinks? I urge you to press on towards the goal the Lord has for you. Press on towards the call of God and forget about those things which are behind. Receive the prize your Heavenly Father has for you!

Oh God, I pray that we would never lose sight of the goal that You have placed before us. Father, continue to remind us to live in view of eternity. I pray our mindset would be on eternity when we are placed in difficult situations throughout the day. Help us to remember that You are all that matters, Father!

Lesley Johnson is the publications assistant for House to House Publications and the D.C.F.I. youth team communication coordinator.

June 28

Refreshing Words

"Throw your net on the right side of the boat and you will find some. When they did, they were unable to haul the net in because of the large number of fish." *John 21:6*

The scene is the Sea of Galilee with five weary disciples returning from a bad night of fishing. Feelings of frustration were likely manifesting themselves. Their hopes were dashed without even a single fish to show for their fishing abilities. Weary and defeated they show up on the shore with an empty boat.

That morning five discouraged fisherman discovered what a difference a fresh word from God could make for their day. Christ gave them the word, they responded without much hesitation, and it changed their day.

Oh, how easy it is to become discouraged from all our efforts to be faithful followers of Christ and tireless servants in His Kingdom! When I am exhausted from trying, or despaired from failing, I know it will make a difference if I steer my boat toward the shore where Jesus is waiting and watching. It is in those times that I desperately need a fresh word from God. And that can make all the difference if I take Him at His word.

Dear Father, forgive me when I allow my perspective of a situation to lead me to discouragement instead of to You for Your refreshing word. I thank you that You are the source of my strength, the bread for my soul, and the water for my spirit—available for me beyond fathomable measure. As I bend my ear to hear Your voice, and crack the cover of Your written pages, give me a fresh word that renews me to fulfill your purposes in me this day. In Jesus' name, Amen.

Lloyd Hoover is a Mennonite bishop/overseer of the Groffdale district and secretary of Lancaster Mennonite Conference.

June 29
Locked Up
"...I was in prison and you came to visit Me." Matthew 25:36

Many of us struggle with engaging ourselves with the message of this verse. In fact, it appears that the church as a whole, because of being silent, has actually taken a "lock 'em up, throw away the key" mentality. In doing so, we have lost our message of hope and restoration.

We have been silent. In our lack of mercy, forgiveness, compassion and wisdom, our eyes are blinded to the needs of a prison system sanctioned to punish wrong doers—and we are now witnessing the destruction of many families. This, I'm sure, saddens the heart of God, especially in light of the fact that over fifty percent of those incarcerated are non-violent. Many of these individuals are looking for hope and an opportunity to redeem their name and to build a new reputation. Children of the incarcerated are six times more likely to follow in their parents' steps unless someone steps in to help them.

Are we bold enough to allow ourselves to see the truth of what is happening and to ask God for forgiveness for turning our hearts away? Can we dare to open our hearts to love the unlovable and possibly to be let down from time to time? I believe God is calling us to truly become a church of compassion and restoration, to reach out to those who have fallen and tenderly bring healing into their lives. It is such a glorious experience to witness one who was lost and is now found.

Dear Father, forgive me for turning a blind eye to those who are incarcerated. Restore in me a heart of compassion, of healing, of hope and of restoration. May I be a vessel in your hands today to reach out in love to someone who is hurting.

Tom Armstrong is the Chairman of Public Policy, Justice & Mercy; executive director of New Person, Inc.; worship leader at First Assembly of God, Columbia; former State Representative.

June 30

Only In The Cross

"May I never boast except in the cross of our Lord Jesus Christ, through which the world has been crucified to me, and I to the world." *Galatians 6:14*

One morning in a small country church in England, the Prime Minister came to worship with the congregation. The pastor was so honored that instead of preaching the sermon he had scheduled for that Sunday, he spent the entire time praising the gentleman in the congregation. After church a lady approached the minister and asked, "Where was the cross of Christ in your sermon? All you talked about was the Prime Minister and nothing was said about Christ!" The minister got the point and placed a cross in the back of the church so that every time he got in the pulpit he could see the cross and remember that he must always preach on it.

Although this incident happened several years ago it still speaks to us. We need to concentrate on the cross of Jesus Christ. It is in the cross of Christ we glory because we regard it as the matchless exhibition of the love of God. We see God providing a way of salvation for the entire world. We must always keep our attention on what Christ did on that old rugged cross for us! We need to remember that Jesus Christ took our sins upon Himself and that the world has been crucified to us and us to the world. We need to boast in the cross of our Lord Jesus Christ!

Dear God, may we ever look to You and not to others or to ourselves! May the eyes of our hearts and our minds be sharp enough to catch the ever-present glimpse of the CROSS OF JESUS CHRIST! In Jesus' name, Amen.

Rev. Alan J. Yudt is the pastor of the Jerusalem United Church of Christ in Penryn.

July

Enjoying life and friendship
in Lancaster County

July 1

Let Freedom Ring

"...He has sent me to bind up the broken-hearted, to proclaim freedom for the captives and release from darkness for the prisoners, to proclaim the year of the Lord's favor and the day of vengeance of our God..." *Isaiah 61:1–2*

for Lancaster County

"Now the Lord is the Spirit, and where the Spirit of the Lord is, there is freedom." *2 Corinthians 3:17–18*

We praise God for the many freedoms we enjoy in this country. Yet, there are many who are being held captive by lies of the enemy. They remain bound in darkness in need of someone to release them from their prisons. May we pray this passage from Isaiah 61 for Lancaster County. Let us proclaim that this would be the year of the Lord's favor in our region. May the Spirit of the Lord come and bring true freedom.

Father, we are so grateful for our country, and for the freedoms with which You have blessed us. Help us not to take our freedom for granted. May we be beacons of light to those who are bound by darkness. Today, enable us to bring hope and deliverance to all those who are yearning to be free.

Today's devotional was edited from the 2003–2004 *Throne Of Grace Prayer Guide*, a weekly guide of Lancaster County prayer concerns gathered from regional intercessors and area prayer groups.

July 2

Who Do You Trust?

"And we know that all things work together for good to those who love God, to those who are called according to His purpose." Romans 8:28

2nd Chronicles 14 through 16 talks about King Asa of Judah. The story is complete, but the lesson contained in chapter 16 is too obvious to miss. When an opportunity happened upon the king to trust God for deliverance, instead, and despite God having just shown His awesome power to deliver, Asa chose to trust a worldly kingdom for protection. Because of this, God forsook him in this situation.

Quite literally, every day we are faced with uncertainty and opportunities to be dishonest, embarrassed, or disappointed. We are threatened with the prospect of failure or things just not going our way. The easy way is not always the right way out. Did you receive that? *The easy way is not always the right way out.* This is a "rubber-meets-the-road" time. This is where you have a real life chance to "walk the talk."

Do you trust in yourself to conjure an excuse and then have the gullibility to believe your own excuse is justified? Maybe you chose a white lie to bend the situation in your favor and give you that fleeting illusion of a personal wall of safety. If you have, God will not honor and bless you in any sinful approach to a problem. However, if you trust God for deliverance and His power to work things out, He will never forsake you.

Father, I am in a situation that scares me, threatens me and makes me feel uncomfortable. I don't know the best way to handle it. Help me not to make excuses, rely on my own devises, or sin to get through it. Please give me the faith to trust in Your promise of Romans 8:28. I trust You, God. You are my Deliverer, my Fortress, my Shield, and the outcome is in Your eternal and loving hands. Amen!

Diana Oliphant is a small group minister, missionary and servant/leader from The Worship Center.

July 3

Dependence On God

"Then Moses said to him, 'If Your presence does not go with us, do not lead us up from here'" *Exodus 33:15 (New American Standard Bible)*

Moses is making a passionate and desperate plea before his God. He recognizes the enormity of the task before him and his total inadequacy to accomplish what God has called him to do. However, in wisdom, he also sees and knows Whom it is he serves, and in trembling humility, he bows, confessing utter dependence.

How do we respond when faced with similar, albeit much smaller, situations? Is our response to fall on our faces and cry out to God to be merciful and not abandon us? How about our pursuit of deeper intimacy with Him? Do we work for it or do we surrender, recognizing that all we desire is being freely offered.

So many times I have retreated to the shallow reservoir of my own talents and strength, only to be frustrated and humiliated by circumstances that God never intended me to handle on my own. But pride is strong. God knows that to learn trust, a man must be broken. What I sometimes forget is that even Moses failed. It was only after a prolonged desert experience, that he came to know his Lord and learned that he could not go on without Him.

I have found that when I have exhausted every avenue of self-effort, I discover one reassuring truth. He is there, waiting for my surrender so that He can lead me in the way I should go.

Father, I am so grateful for Your promise to never leave or forsake us. Continue to lead us into desert places where we can learn utter dependence upon You.

Rick Reed formerly served New Covenant Christian Church in the deaconate, men's ministry and eldership. He currently co-leads a care group of high school and young adults.

One

July 4

Set Me Free

"In my anguish I cried to the Lord, and he answered by setting me free." *Psalm 118:5*

L egend has it that King George of England ended his royal duties on July 4, 1776, with the journal entry, "Nothing of note happened today." Without the benefit of email or satellite news coverage, the king drifted to sleep unaware that history had changed. Across the Atlantic, a new nation was being born.

Like the eighteenth century monarch, we probably miss moments of life-changing transformation. It is possible that somewhere in a small congregation on the other side of the county, a husband will be set free from alcohol today. In a support group a mother will break the bondage of anger. A pregnant teenager will be set free from the stronghold of fear. Might God be breaking the chains of a college student's depression even as you read this?

The Psalmist writes simply, "the Lord set me free." He knew that something of note happened in response to his anguished cry for help. Sometimes, like King George, we expect business as usual in people's lives or in the spiritual condition of our county. We don't expect much change.

Then suddenly freedom surprises us. Quietly, the Lord sets someone free. The news arrives of dramatic growth in a once-struggling congregation. An old neighborhood bar goes bankrupt. A divorce procedure is abandoned. Is there ever a day when God's great grace is *not* liberating someone? It seems a king ought always to bid the day farewell with, "Somewhere, something of note happened today, I'm sure of it."

Dear God, don't let me sleep through Your acts of mercy. Awaken my expectation that today You are freeing captives, and that today You could free me if I, too, would call on Your name. Amen.

Dave Witmer, church planter, writer, musician, husband and father, serves with Living Hope Community Church west of Lancaster City.

July 5

Gone Fishing...Again

"Simon answered, 'Master, we've worked hard all night and haven't caught anything. But because you say so, I will let down the nets.'" Luke 5:5

During the night no fish had ventured into Simon's fishing nets. When Jesus suggested that he put his nets into the water again, I imagine that Simon thought the idea crazy. Yet, out of respect for Jesus, he did what he was told. He trusted Jesus enough to do what He said, even when it didn't make sense.

When the nets had been let down, Simon and his friends caught so many fish their nets began to break. Simon was amazed at this miracle. His first response was to feel his own insignificance compared to Jesus' greatness. "When Simon Peter saw this, he fell at Jesus' knees and said, 'Go away from me, Lord; I am a sinful man (Luke 5:8)!'"

A few months ago God spoke to me through these verses. It was as if He was saying to me, "Daughter, you are tired from fishing all night only to find your nets empty. Trust Me and My plans for you. Do not run away from what I have for you, your family, and neighborhood." I found rest as I obeyed the Lord's instructions. In a fresh way I was able to trust that Jesus is the one that works the miracle of redemption in my life and in others that I love in this city.

Dear God, without You I am nothing and have nothing to offer to the broken in this city. With You, I am somebody and have something to offer to those that have no hope. Help me not to run away from what You have for me, but to trust You, Jesus, for the miracle of redemption in my life and in others. Amen.

Jennie Groff serves with her family to give leadership to a developing house church network under Hope Net in the western part of Lancaster.

July 6

Don't Look Back

"As soon as they had brought them out, one of them said, 'Flee for your lives! Don't look back and don't stop anywhere in the plain!'" *Genesis 19:17*

In chapter 19 of Genesis we find Lot living in Sodom, which is depicted in scripture as a very wicked and sinful city. In fact God was about to destroy the city, and He sent two angels to get Lot and his family out so they too would not be destroyed.

As the family left the city, they were given strict instruction by the angels, "Do not look back." We know that Lot's wife did look back and became a pillar of salt. But why did she look back? What was so appealing about Sodom? Was it that she left family behind? Was it that she had left friends behind and feared what they might think of her? Was it because her home and her established routines represented security that was now lost? Was it because there were pleasures there she would no longer enjoy as a stranger in a strange place?

It is easy for me to question her motives. But why am I tempted to look back? What is it about Sodom (sin) that so readily tempts any of us to look back?

Jesus said, "No man, having put his hand to the plough, and looking back, is fit for the kingdom of God (Luke 9:62)." Where I look is an indication of where my heart is. The Apostle Paul said that he was forgetting what was behind and looking ahead, he was pressing on towards the goal of the high calling of God in Christ Jesus. His eyes were fixed on Jesus, the author and finisher of our faith. May this be true for each of us.

Father, forgive us for our desire to look back. Remove from us the appeal of sin and fill us with the singular purpose of keeping our eyes on You.

Elvin J. Ressler is bishop of the Millwood District of the Lancaster Mennonite Conference.

Choosing Rest

"But He was in the stern, asleep on a pillow. And they awoke Him and said to Him, 'Teacher, do You not care that we are perishing?' Then He arose and rebuked the wind and said to the sea, 'Peace, be still!' And the wind ceased and there was great calm. But He said to them, 'Why are you so fearful? How is it that you have no faith?'" *Mark 4:38–40 (New King James Version)*

A life-threatening family crisis was set in motion. Crying out to the Lord, reading His word, and seeking an answer, my friend turned to Mark's account of the wind and waves obeying Jesus. Pondering His word, the question came, "Lord, what else could the disciples have done?" The still, small voice came forth, "They could have lain down to sleep with Me."

The hard places of work and family, the broken relationships and crisis seasons are what define and expose our absolute inability to do anything on our own. Jesus truly made the way for us. He has unlimited love to cushion, fill and replace our hard places inside. Wisdom, insight and understanding beyond our comprehension are available. Strength and grace will rise up and sustain us hour after hour. Sometimes, just the ability to put one foot in front of the other is the miraculous evidence of God's keeping hand upon us.

Why is it so difficult to lie down in our testing times? What, within us, bids ourselves to stand burdened, instead of resting in and with the Lord? Jesus modeled resting close to our Father God in the good times as well as the tough times.

Dear Jesus, even You said, "I can of Myself do nothing." You are my Lord, Savior, Supply and Source. I ask You to guide me into a greater rest and dependence upon You. Teach me, Lord, to live as You lived, dependent upon Father God. Direct and enable me—in thought, word and deed, reflect Your character and purpose moment by moment in my life. Amen.

Diana Oliphant is a small group minister, missionary and servant/ leader from The Worship Center.

July 8

Power In The House

"I pray also that the eyes of your heart may be enlightened in order that you may know the hope to which he has called you, the riches of his glorious inheritance in the saints, and his incomparably great power for us who believe. That power is like the working of his mighty strength, which he exerted in Christ when he raised him from the dead and seated him at his right hand in the heavenly realms." *Ephesians 1:18–20*

Pray!
for Lancaster County

"With this in mind, we constantly pray for you, that our God may count you worthy of his calling and that by his power he may fulfill every good purpose of yours and every act prompted by your faith." *2 Thessalonians 1:11*

There is *incomparably great power* available for us who believe. It is by this power that God will fulfill every purpose He has for us. And not only will He fulfill His plan for us individually, but that same power will be utilized to complete His purpose for the whole region. May our eyes be opened to this hope, and to this rich inheritance. May we be empowered through faith to live worthy of the calling.

Lord Jesus, show me Your purposes for my life, and give me the power to fulfill them. Help me not to be a slacker, but to receive your incomparable great power so that I will be able to do all You have called me to do.

Today's devotional was edited from the 2003–2004 *Throne Of Grace Prayer Guide*, a weekly guide of Lancaster County prayer concerns gathered from regional intercessors and area prayer groups.

July 9

Safe In The Storm

"Because you have made the LORD, who is my refuge, even the Most High, your dwelling place, no evil shall befall you, nor shall any plague come near your dwelling." *Psalm 91:9–10 (New King James Version)*

My dog, Max, is getting old and is becoming quite fearful of many things. Some years ago he became very frightened by thunder—not because anything bad happened to him, but just because it scared him. Now, when he hears strong winds or even just when he smells rain in the air, he becomes very afraid and wanders around the house cowering, trying to find some place to hide. What he doesn't seem to realize is that he has never been (and, in all likelihood, never will be) harmed by a storm. He's well protected inside the house. The storm is outside.

When we place our faith in God, in His Word and in His Christ, we are well protected regardless of what our five senses seem to indicate. We may smell the rain and we may hear the storm beginning to howl. We may even hear the deafening crack of the thunder, but we must speak to ourselves and remind ourselves of what this Psalm—indeed, what *all* of scripture—tells us.

If we will trust God—which includes following through on His instructions to us—we can count on Him to protect and care for us. When trusting and obeying God it seems like it will put something in our lives in jeopardy, we must rely *not* on what we see or feel, but on what God has told us: "…If God is for us, who can be against us (Romans 8:31)?"

Dear Lord, You are the Great Shepherd. You are my dwelling place, and I trust in You to protect me from all evil no matter what I may see or feel. I praise You for Your great love for me and Your power at work in and around me.

Jim Gambini pastors the Mount Pleasant Brethren in Christ Church in Mount Joy.

One

July 10

Maturity

"No prolonged infancies among us, please...God wants us to grow up, to know the whole truth and tell it in love—like Christ in everything. We take our lead from Christ, who is the source of everything we do. He keeps us in step with one another. His very breath and blood flow through us, nourishing us so that we grow up healthy in God, robust in love." *Ephesians 4:14–16 (The Message)*

I just could not wait until that summer morning when the tomatoes were ready to be picked in my grandfather's back yard in a North Philadelphia row house. We had planted in early spring, and watched as the buds sprouted little green tomatoes and matured into a meal fit for a king. Anyone who loves lettuce and tomatoes on fresh bread with mayo knows what I'm talking about!

As I grow into my new role at Water Street Rescue Mission, I have been impressed over and over that Christ desires maturity in me. Paul's admonishment "no longer to be children, tossed here and there..." suggests maturity in thought. Not for the purpose of pride, no, it's "for the building up of the body in love." Yet, I must not get impatient waiting for it to happen in others; I am called to walk with Christ, *in step with others*, allowing Him to nourish me that I might grow up healthy *along with the rest of the body*.

Paul begins this chapter with a discussion on maturity and ends with a reminder that it is not about us, but all about Jesus. As I live focused on Christ and the glorification of His Church, allowing Him to bring me to maturity, will not the world hunger for more?

Lord, I look to You for wisdom, guidance, and direction. Place me alongside people in the furnace of life's situations, that I might become mature—all that You want me to be—that I might serve You completely. In Jesus' precious name, Amen.

Reverend Rick Rutter is the outreach ministries coordinator at Water Street Rescue Mission in Lancaster.

July 11

All Things New

"A Message from the high and towering God, who lives in Eternity, whose name is Holy: "I live in the high and holy places, but also with the low-spirited, the spirit—crushed, And what I do is put new spirit in them, get them up and on their feet again." *Isaiah 57:15 (The Message)*

There are depths in our heart that can only be accessed through brokenness. Brokenness is not being sad about how bad things are (or could be), but it is an awareness of an awesome God's presence in the midst of life's deepest valleys. Isaiah 66:2 says that God esteems "the humble and contrite in spirit." In 2 Corinthians 12:10 Paul says, "for when I am weak, then I am strong." God's strength is perfected in human weakness and brokenness before him. Even when we do everything right according to "the Book" things may not always go our way or even the "right" way. God is still sovereign. A broken heart is a heart that knows this truth experientially.

The events of the past cannot be changed, but our perspective on the events can change. John and Paula Sandford write, "Christian healing comes then not by making a broken thing good enough to work, but by delivering us from the power of that broken thing so that it can no longer rule us, and by teaching us to trust his righteousness to shine in and through that very thing."

It is difficult to allow God to reveal things about our past in order for root issues to be addressed. I have resisted admitting the pain caused by others hurting me. But the times I allow God to break through my stony heart, I feel His deep cleansing love and acceptance that makes my spirit soar to the heights of an eagle.

Lord, help me see You as the awesome and caring God You are. Grant me a heart to respond to You in new ways and depths of cleansing and healing for Your Kingdom's sake.

Ed Hersh provides counseling and healing prayer ministry to individuals and families, trains lay counselors here and abroad, and helps wounded leaders receive spiritual renewal.

One

July 12
Cash Your Check

"As God's fellow workers we urge you not to receive God's grace in vain." *2 Corinthians 6:1*

In a very practical sense, "grace" is "God's ability for the situation at hand." Daily we face issues which are beyond our ability to handle. But God comes to us in Jesus Christ and offers us His ability to deal with our impossibilities. In light of God's generosity it is critical that we not receive His grace in vain. To receive His grace in vain is to fail to "cash the check" entitling us to His grace. Naaman received healing instructions (God's grace) from Elisha but the healing was not given as he had expected. His servants urged him to follow the instructions and dip seven times in the Jordan River. In effect they urged Naaman not to receive the grace of God in vain.

Some time ago while jogging I had the sudden thought that God wanted me to knock on the door of a stranger and tell whoever came to the door that God wanted to come into the house if they would open the door. I convinced myself that this was a ludicrous thought. My son later said, "Dad, that was God!"

I finally took courage, drove back to the house and delivered the word I had received from God. The wife said, "I cannot believe you came, for just three days ago I was preparing to leave my husband because he is a heroin addict. I sensed that I should wait and that I would soon receive direction." In response to this experience both the wife and her addicted husband became Christians.

I ponder. How many times has God given me His grace and I have not used His ability for the situation at hand. I have received His grace in vain.

Dear Father, You have been so generous in giving Yourself to me. Forgive me for not allowing Your ability to transform my everyday situations.

Enos Martin, M.D. is the professor of psychiatry at Penn State University and a bishop in Lancaster Mennonite Conference.

July 13

The Amazing Word

"For the word of God is quick, and powerful, and sharper than any two-edged sword, piercing even to the dividing asunder of soul and spirit, and of the joints and marrow, and is a discerner of the thoughts and intents of the heart." *Hebrews 4:12 (King James Version)*

During my childhood I was baptized at an early age. My family did not attend church, so it wasn't until my adult life that I was baptized again and I developed a relationship with the Lord. The lessons that I have learned since developing a relationship with the Lord have helped me tremendously. Reading God's Word, praying, attending church, and the fellowship I experience with my family, friends, and co-workers helps me grow spiritually. I think about my early childhood and wonder what my life would have been like if I had had a relationship with the Lord then.

God speaks to me through His Word. When I read my Bible out loud I receive inspiration. I don't know what it is, but hearing God's Word has an effect on my heart. I receive encouragement, hope, and understanding when I read the Bible. Reading God's Word helps me discern. In the course of my daily job, I have to make difficult decisions and before I make my decisions I try to follow the lead of the Lord through prayer or reading my Bible. When I read God's Word I am amazed at the wisdom and lessons in life that I discover.

Dear Heavenly Father, I thank You for Your Word and Your guidance that helps us live our lives glorifying You. As You speak to us through the Bible, help us to receive Your Words into our hearts and put them into action through our thoughts, words, and deeds. In Jesus Christ we pray, Amen.

Jeff Pierce serves as fire chief for the city of Lancaster. His desire is to serve his community as Jesus Christ would want him to.

One

Good Marriage...On Purpose

"...each one of you also must love his wife as he loves himself, and the wife must respect her husband." Ephesians 5:33

Our communities will only be as strong as our families. Putting families *first* so that they *last* is a real task, but not so difficult that it can't be done. I feel passionate about the health and well being of marriages in our community and believe that we should work together to bring out the best in our spouses. I am a better person than I could ever be by myself, thanks to my wife's contributions.

"Christian married love is a persistent effort on the part of two people to create for each other the circumstances that enable the very best to come forth. This enables two people to create for each other the circumstances in which each can become the person God intended him or her to be," says Richard Dobbins. *Persistent effort means you have a deliberate definite plan. I discovered in life I get more good things done* **on purpose** *than any other way.*

In marriage, couples can help each other recognize where their best gifts lie. The marriage benefits from the best each has to offer. We must encourage each other in the expression of these gifts so that we can become the people God intended us to be.

Make a deliberate plan that will bring out the best in your spouse:

- Release your mate to be the person God intended.
- Recognize his/her best gifts.
- Enable the very best to come forth.
- Contribute something weekly to facilitate love in your marriage.
- Be deliberate about your family being more important than anything you do.

Lord, help me to pray for my mate daily, to release him/her to fully become the person You intended. Bring forth our best gifts and give us creative ideas to facilitate Christian married love. Amen.

Jonas Beiler is the founder of the Family Resource and Counseling Center.

July 15

Hope For Believers

"May the God of hope fill you with all joy and peace as you trust in him, so that you may overflow with hope by the power of the Holy Spirit." *Romans 15:13*

for Lancaster County

Much of the world today seems to be characterized by despair, depression and conflict. Yet this scripture indicates that as we trust in God, the door is opened to hope, joy and peace. In fact, the power of the Holy Spirit is able to make us *overflow* with hope. So believers can walk in sharp contrast to the prevailing spirit of the day. We don't have to rely on ourselves or live in the hopelessness that a self-sufficient mindset ultimately brings. As we open ourselves up to that overflowing hope, we can ask God to flood our whole county with a force that will literally drown oppression, discouragement and fear and replace it with hope!

Father, thank You for giving us the Holy Spirit, and for the promise of joy, peace, and hope that He brings. Please fill us as we choose to put our trust in You. Let every believer in Lancaster County resonate a hope-filled life, and let that hope infiltrate every circumstance we encounter...for Your glory and praise.

Today's devotional was edited from the 2003–2004 *Throne Of Grace Prayer Guide*, a weekly guide of Lancaster County prayer concerns gathered from regional intercessors and area prayer groups.

July 16

Relationships

"...I have come that they may have life, and have it to the full."
John 10:10

My favorite thing to do is teach the "homeless" folks who flock to Holy Trinity Lutheran Church every Sunday at 8:00 am. Trinity is an urban church, and so is within easy walking distance for those who don't have cars.

These friends don't have a whole lot else either, except for fears of eviction, bench warrants, tooth abscesses, and getting mugged. So when I talk about Jesus as being someone you can *count on*, they're all ears. Most of these folks know some scripture. They know about Jesus dying for their sin and removing it as far as east is from west. As comforting as that is to them, when I speak of how much we can trust Jesus for the present times and trials, they want to know more.

"Suppose someone asked you why you got married, and you said that you wanted to have someone to care for you when you're old and decrepit," I posed one bright Sunday morning. "Well, sure, I guess," I continued, "but what about a *relationship* with someone who loves you, someone you can talk to and work things out with. See, that's what we have in Jesus. In fact, He goes so far as to call us His bride!"

Think of it: we're on intimate terms with the Lord of the universe. I don't even begin to understand it. But I'm beginning to enjoy it.

Lord, You've opened our eyes to the truth of Your salvation which we've claimed and have forever. Don't stop there, dear Lord, but let us see You touching our lives everyday. And, please, let us know it was You.

Tim Wentworth is founder and director of the Christian Library of Lancaster County.

July 17

The Blessing Of Being Weak

"And He said to me... 'My strength is made perfect in weakness.' Therefore most gladly I will boast in my infirmities, that the power of Christ may rest upon me.... For when I am weak, then I am strong." *2 Corinthians 12:9–10 (New King James Version)*

I grew up in a family of achievers where good grades, lots of extracurricular activities, and obtaining a college education were the norm. I presented myself as confident and competent and did my best to hide any insecurity or inadequacy.

But a new leadership position threatened to erode my confidence. Overwhelmed by the weighty responsibility, thoughts of quitting bombarded my mind. In God's providence, I attended a conference for leaders of similar ministries. On the first night, a speaker did a role play with a young woman who was brand new to her ministry and felt so inadequate she was ready to quit. To my amazement, the speaker said, "It's good you feel weak and inadequate. Now you can learn to depend on God for more than just your salvation."

Gulp. Is that what I'd been doing? Paul's words flashed through my mind, "When I am weak, then I am strong." I realized I'd never understood that verse and that I actually hated being weak, which is why I hid it from myself, others, and even the Lord.

I went back to my room and began admitting to God all my weaknesses, inadequacies, and insecurities. At the end of a long, tearful time, I felt like an absolute worm. I told God that was all I truly was, but if He could still use me to lead the ministry, I was willing. At that moment, a flood of love and power poured from God's heart to mine, and I knew that I would stay at the ministry. But instead of covering weaknesses, I would admit them, seek God's strength, and let His power flow through me.

Father, I still feel weak sometimes. Help me to release my weakness to You and walk in Your perfect strength.

Lisa Hosler is president of Susquehanna Valley Pregnancy Services.

July 18

A Different Currency

"It takes more than bread to stay alive. It takes a steady stream of words from God's mouth." *Matthew 4:4 (The Message)*

After fasting 40 days, Jesus is hungry, almost starving. Satan tempts Jesus saying, "If you are so powerful, why don't you end your suffering right here? Change bricks to bread!"

This question tempts us all. Since Job became the first poster child of undeserved suffering, people want to know why a good God does not put an end to the many forms of human pain. In this confrontation with Satan, Jesus can lay to rest our temptation to believe that God is not really in control. Instead, He chooses to suffer. Jesus can create nourishment, but He will do it only on His own terms. Not while suffering, but while enjoying a party, He changes water to wine. He has the necessary power to end the suffering of the whole world if He wants to.

So what is the message in Jesus' temptation and suffering?

"Evil's fundamental temptation of man," says Dallas Willard, "is to believe that the physical and public side of the human universe can sustain man's existence." Jesus' temptation teaches us that no matter how much we are willing to give in order to receive relief from suffering, man cannot live and thrive as God intends by seeking relief from every point of pain. We cannot live the God-life depending on the currency of this universe alone. The physical universe cannot deliver the Son of Man from His suffering and it cannot deliver us from ours. It does not matter how much "bread" we get, we must have some kind of spiritual connection. This is why most of the world believes in God—they cannot live without Him, or at least without the idea of Him.

Father, soften my heart that it might absorb Your love, sharpen my mind that it might understand Your complexity, open my eyes that they might see Your beauty.

Robert Woodcock has served as a missionary, pastor, and professor and is a centurion in The Wilberforce Forum.

July 19

He's Already Here

"In a desert land he found him, in a barren and howling waste. He shielded him and cared for him; he guarded him as the apple of his eye." *Deuteronomy 32:10*

Recently, I complained, "God, where are You? It feels like You are hiding from me!"

I sensed God responding, "Stop trying to find me. Start living as though I have already been found. Stop praying as though you are trying to persuade Me to come and listen to you. Start telling Me your needs as though I have already come to you and am hearing and understanding you."

It's amazing all the humanly devised methods and strategies we create to try to find God, when God claims to have already found us! Today, you may feel like you are living in a desert land. Listen to the voice of God, "I have found you!" It may feel like your land is barren and like a howling waste. But listen to God saying, "I am shielding you, caring for you, and guarding you as the apple of my eye!"

God says, "I want you even more than you want Me. I want to make you whole, to teach you truth, to comfort your hurts, to help you bear fruit." God says, "I am real, not just someone you imagined or created in your mind. I am real, more real than the muscles on your fingers, more real than the blinking of your eyelids. Treasure Me! Put your hope in Me. I can be seen. I am pouring My spirit and My life into you. Be attentive to how I am with you!"

Dear Lord, thank You for finding me, for caring for me, and for guarding me as the apple of Your eye. In the midst of my desert land, give me faith to respond to Your faithful presence. Amen.

Ron Zook serves as the pastor of New Holland Mennonite Church.

July 20

Weed Whacker

"...tear down your father's altar to Baal and cut down the Asherah pole beside it. Then build a proper kind of altar to the Lord your God on the top of this height..." *Judges 6:25–26*

When I was a dairy farmer, I remember hot summer days "going around" electric fences with my weed whacker. I cut down the grass and small trees and poison ivy that grew up into the wire so the electricity would not "short out." When I was doing that work I was "Gideon," which means "cutter down".

Gideon was mulling over the idolatrous conditions around him, and was crying out to God for help. And God heard, and visited him. Joash, Gideon's father, was an idolater. His name means "Yahweh has bestowed". Think about it. Yahweh has bestowed *to an idolater* a son who is a "cutter downer". And that's the first thing Gideon did. He cut down the idols in his father's house!

I need "Gideons" for my life. There are false gods (Baals) all around me; some of them seem to creep into my own house, into my own life. It is so sneaky how that happens. I need "Gideons" to come as cutter downers,"Gideons" to confront me about the things that get in the way of worship of the Only True God of Heaven and Earth: Father, Son, and Holy Spirit. I don't want to be "shorted out!"

Good news! God has bestowed "Gideons." He has given us:

*   the Scriptures, the revealed and written-down Word of God, that cuts down strongholds.
*   Jesus, the Word of God made flesh: "Thy Word is Truth"; "I am the way, the truth, and the life."
*   the Holy Spirit to guide us into the truth.
*   the centuries of prayer, worship, and witness of the Church.

What "Baal" is in your life? God *will* send a "Gideon."

Lord Jesus, reveal those things in my life that "short out" my love and passion for You, and in Your mercy, cut them down. Amen.

Ray Reitz pastors Mountville Mennonite Church.

July 21

Two Kinds Of Believers

"At that time many will turn away from the faith and will betray and hate each other . . . And this gospel of the kingdom will be preached in the whole world as a testimony to all nations, and then the end will come." *Matthew 24:10,14*

There are two types of believers. One type sees problems, the other is part of God's solution. The stark contrast Jesus describes is between believers who turn away from the faith and others who carry the gospel of the kingdom to the nations. The former are busy fighting against the people of God. Problems in relationships or jealousy in position have drawn their attention. Their fervor is poured into hating other believers, possibly with the "righteous intent" of exposing problems or straightening out doctrine.

The latter have a focus on the nations yet to be reached with the news of Jesus. For them, the all-encompassing drive is to bring Jesus to those who have not yet heard the life-giving message. The second group Jesus mentioned actually ushers in the end of the world as we know it today. Is this the passion that grips your soul?

Where were your efforts directed over the last year? The choice is yours today. It will be your choice tomorrow. Choose to reject the temptation to argue about non-essential doctrinal details and focus instead on the people who still need to hear the message of life and forgiveness. Ask yourself, "Have I wrongly picked up a petty grievance and taken my eyes off of the calling of God to love my brother and reach the lost?"

Lord Jesus, I ask that Your burden for the nations become my burden. Lead me to involvement with people still sitting in darkness, unaware of Your light. I pray for Your strength as my life is reordered with Your purpose. I deliver myself afresh into Your hands to be shaped and made useful.

Bruce Heckman serves on the leadership team of Immerge, preparing people for cross-cultural ministries.

July 22

Righteousness Restored

Pray!
for Lancaster County

"And this is my prayer: that your love may abound more and more in knowledge and depth of insight, so that you may be able to discern what is best and may be pure and blameless until the day of Christ, filled with the fruit of righteousness that comes through Jesus Christ—to the glory and praise of God."
Philippians 1:9–11

As God's love abounds in our hearts, a numbers of practical results will follow. We will have deeper insights into situations that will enable us to discern what is best, and consequently make wise decisions. We will develop in Christian purity as His love teaches us to say no to ungodliness. We will also be filled with biblical righteousness that declares us blameless on the Day of Judgment. Finally all this will bring glory to God and honor to Jesus Christ.

Lord, grant me insight into unrighteous areas in my life and walk. I repent of these areas, and I receive Your mercy and power to walk uprightly in thought, word, and deed. May the righteousness that You are restoring in me result in great glory, honor and praise to Your name.

Today's devotional was edited from the 2003–2004 *Throne Of Grace Prayer Guide*, a weekly guide of Lancaster County prayer concerns gathered from regional intercessors and area prayer groups.

July 23

Fear

"Though the fig tree does not bud and there are no grapes on the vines, though the olive crop fails and the fields produce no food, though there are no sheep in the pen and no cattle in the stalls, yet I will rejoice in the LORD, I will be joyful in God my Savior. The Sovereign LORD is my strength; he makes my feet like the feet of a deer, he enables me to go on the heights."
Habakkuk 3:17–19

Have you ever fearfully considered the future and what it might hold for you or your family? Have you worried about losing your job or business? We hear of wars and earthquakes, hurricanes and floods, terrorists and tidal waves—and the list goes on. Is it any wonder that men's hearts fail them for fear? That fear sometimes grips *my* heart.

Most of my fears are not even based in reality but they still dramatically affect my peace of mind. In light of these fears, I am drawn to today's verse. What is the rock that I can stand on, what is the hope in the midst of all pain and fear? If I have not faced these situations in my life, what right do I have to speak about these things? A runner does not wait till the day before the race to begin training, and so we have the opportunity to prepare for whatever may come our way. The Lord is my strength! We can learn to rejoice in Him and be joyful in small inconveniences now, so that having been faithful in little, we will—by His grace—be faithful in much.

Father, I am so thankful that I do not have to worry about what the future holds, that I can instead put my confidence in You. Help me to never forget that You are my strength and my joy. Thank You for the peace that You give me as I face the future.

Fred Esbenshade serves with information systems and sales at Esbenshade's Greenhouse, Brickerville.

July 24

All Men Will Know

"A new command I give you: Love one another. As I have loved you, so you must love one another. By this all men will know that you are my disciples, if you love one another."
John 13:34–35

P rovocative bumper stickers...thoughtfully worded T-shirt messages...the "Christian fish" symbol. There is nothing wrong with incorporating some modern-day methods in our quest to let those around us know that we belong to Jesus. However, are we guilty of hoping this "lick and stick" approach to evangelism will somehow fulfill our obligation to the Great Commission? In contrast, the Gospels are full of accounts showing Jesus catching people's attention by what He said and did.

Jesus did not love people passively. Consider the adulterous woman, Zacchaeus the tax collector, and how about Peter after he denied his Lord? Jesus got right in there, up close and personal. These examples of how Jesus loves people make this verse all the more potent. To love each other as Jesus loves us would break the age-old stereotypes that the world holds of the church. It would also mean obedience to God, since Jesus "commands" us to love one another.

God loves us. His kingdom is built on love. His desire is that all people would come to know Him and enter His kingdom of love (John 3:16). *The way we relate to each other as Christians can be the demonstration of God's love that the world needs to see.* Loving each other, as Jesus modeled for us, will be the what we are looking for in a world of throwaway relationships...and, we get to keep our bumpers clear.

Father God, help us as a regional church to be known for a love that could only have its source in You. May we be a generation that allows You to work a unity in Your body that draws people to You, so that the world may know. Amen.

Bob Snyder is the senior elder of Elanco D.O.V.E. Christian Fellowship, Terre Hill.

The Truth

"...They perish because they refused to love the truth and so be saved. For this reason God sends them a powerful delusion so that they will believe the lie." 2 Thessalonians 2:10–11

The truth is" ...haven't we all at one time or another said: "I wish they had just been honest and told me the truth from the start?" In reality, most of our closest friends know pretty accurately how much truth we will receive, and at what point truth pushes our wound or reaction button. But how much more precisely does Jesus know our tolerance levels? And, while He is the truth, revealing new life each day with His presence, He remains patient while bringing truth to our weaknesses.

How many reoccurring encounters with truth will we have where, in hindsight, we wish that we would have welcomed the blessed "wounds of our friends"? (Proverbs 27:6) We read in 2 Thessalonians 2:11 that an ongoing pattern of rejecting the truth invokes a delusion from God until we believe the lie. That explains why repeated sins soon lose the precious work of the conscience for daily life.

Truth on the other hand, brings life, over the smell of death for those who are being saved as described by Paul in 2 Corinthians 2:15. That living fragrance emanates from those who love the truth as an ointment of healing, restoration, and daily freedom. Today the truth is that the Lord is still in His mercy redeeming us from our delusions just as when we were first saved.

This day Lord I renew my trust in You and Your unfailing love. I offer myself to receive Your truth as life for today and protection from the delusion of my own thoughts.

Chip Toews is first a servant of the Lord Jesus Christ and then assigned to pastor the greatest folks around: the members of New Covenant Christian Church.

July 26

Let's Celebrate!

"Rejoice in the Lord always. I will say it again: Rejoice!"
Philippians 4:4

My son Anthony and I traveled to our capital city to take in a baseball game. I don't remember who played the home team that night but I do recall the level of enthusiasm as I watched the fans arrive. Before the game even started there was an excitement, an anticipation that could almost be felt in the park. But as our National Anthem ended and the umpire yelled, "Play Ball!" the atmosphere became even more charged. The enthusiasm for what was about to take place multiplied a hundred fold over the pre-game activity.

As I took all this in I remember wondering, with all that Jesus has done for us, what is it that we should be centering on as we gather in our churches, in our small groups, or even as we fellowship around the dinner table? What is it that Jesus has done for each of us that has literally changed the course of our lives?

Is it simply that He lived an exemplary life or was an outstanding teacher or even that He healed the sick? After all many folks have lived model lives, taught good lessons and even, in some cases, performed miracles. What is it about Jesus Christ that is so noteworthy? "For God so loved the world that He gave…" God has given His son to die in our place so that we might have eternal life. And Jesus was pleased to comply so that "…whoever believes can have eternal life". The price has been paid and we are saved!

If baseball fans have so much to shout about, how much more do we, as believers, have a reason to be excited? Should we not make our gatherings times of celebration of unexplainable proportions? I, for one, must enthusiastically shout YES!

Lord Jesus, may we overflow with rejoicing as we consider all You have done.

Frank Ferrari, director of Transformation Ministries, Lancaster County.

July 27
Well Done
"Well done, good and faithful servant!" *Matthew 25:21*

My goal for all that I am and all that I do is to please God, forget about myself and focus on Him, using the good gifts He has entrusted to me.

This passage is the "punch line" of the parable of the talents (Matthew 25:16–22). God entrusts us with gifts that we might discover how to risk using them every day. God expects the fruit of His gifts (and His glory in them) to compound over time, like money left on deposit at interest. Since God has given you the gifts, He expects that you're risking, growing, failing, and succeeding by exercising these gifts. Your gifts may include faith, or prayer, or encouragement, or being a channel for His healing, or sharing His love and drawing people into a personal relationship with Him (Ephesians 4:11).

Gifts are entrusted to further God's mission. Each person has their unique part to play. There are things God has designed me to do. They aren't always easy for me to do. But God knows how my serving— alongside my laborers in Christ—can achieve His results.

His plan is NOT for everyone to do the same thing. Instead He wants each servant to be faithful to the particular task entrusted. God asks us to listen in His Word, the Bible, and listen in prayer for how to serve others in His name and bring someone into personal relationship with Him.

Most giving and forgiving God, grant that I many honor You by bringing someone to know You personally. Develop us together as devoted, effective, focused servants of Jesus. By the power of Your Holy Spirit, equip and encourage us to step outside our comfort zones in sharing our faith and serving others in Jesus' name. Center us in prayer and Your Word. Make us active caring listeners, in the name of the Father, Son and Holy Spirit. Amen.

Bill Eberle is servant pastor of St. Thomas Episcopal Church, a community focused in prayer and healing, mentoring and partnering with other congregations.

July 28
Riding With The Master
"When we put bits into the mouths of horses to make them obey us, we can turn the whole animal." *James 3:3*

Horses are dignified and graceful, each having a unique personality. A well-trained, loved horse will freely gallop through the meadow or routinely follow the animal ahead of him on a trail. However, frightened wild horses pose a challenge. I watched a horse, scared and tense, respond to the persistent, soft voice and tender, gentle touch of a horse whisperer. The cocky, feisty spirit of the horse lessened as he began to relax. Realizing the human was there to love him, not beat him, the horse began to obey the commands of the trainer.

Monty Roberts, author of *Horse Sense for People*, encourages people to rethink the way they use power over others. He challenges us to use a gentle manner instead of a controlling, demanding attitude when dealing with them. According to James 3:3, a horse can be tamed, controlled and made to obey with just a simple bit in its mouth. Like horses, sometimes people blaze their own trail, but if we submit to God, He will change our lives.

As a horse responds to his master and after his day of activity returns to his home, the barn, so we look forward to going to our heavenly home after our lives of surrender. "At that time, I will gather you, I will bring you home..." says Zephaniah 3:20.

Heavenly Father, as my Master Trainer, give direction to my life. As I submit to You, I become as obedient as a bridled horse waiting to greet You in Your heavenly home. As Revelations 19:11 says, "I saw heaven standing open and there before me was a white horse, whose rider is called Faithful and True." Oh God, what a glorious day that will be when I saddle up and ride with you, My Master! Amen.

Dona L. Fisher is chairperson for the Lancaster County National Day of Prayer Task Force. She is vice-president of Friendship Foundation, Inc.

July 29

Even The Gates Of Hell Will Not Prevail

Pray!

for Lancaster County

"The Lord will open the heavens, the storehouse of his bounty, to send rain on your land in season and to bless all the work of your hands. You will lend to many nations but will borrow from none. The Lord will make you the head, not the tail. If you pay attention to the commands of the Lord your God that I give you this day and carefully follow them, you will always be at the top, never at the bottom." *Deuteronomy 28:12–13*

"...and upon this rock I will build my church; and the gates of hell shall not prevail against it." *Matthew 16:18 (King James Version)*

If the Church rises in obedience to the commands of the Lord, we are assured of victory over the forces of darkness in our area. His Word promises that blessing and bounty will flow, so much so that we will always be on top of things, never at the bottom. God's design for His people is that we would be the leaders...*the head and not the tail.* As the Church goes about the business of advancing the Kingdom of God, the influence of darkness will wane and the gates of hell—no matter how ominous and perilous they seem to be— will not stand.

Lord Jesus, Thank You for the call to obedience and the fruit of following Your commands. Help me, today, to obey You in a greater measure. Grant fellow believers the assurance that even the gates of hell will not prevail against us when we choose radical obedience and bold commitment to Your Word.

Today's devotional was edited from the 2003–2004 *Throne Of Grace Prayer Guide*, a weekly guide of Lancaster County prayer concerns gathered from regional intercessors and area prayer groups.

July 30

God Delights In You

"The Lord your God is with you, He is mighty to save. He will take great delight in you, He will quiet you with His love, He will rejoice over you with singing." *Zephaniah 3:17*

These words portray a picture of God as a loving parent that is with us, will save us, delights in us, quiets us with love and sings a song about us because He is so glad that we are His children. This is not the picture of God that I had for many years. I knew God was able to save me, but I also knew that he was a God of judgment. I lived in fear that God would strike my name out of His "Book of Life" and prayed that He would re-enter it after I confessed all my sins. I just hoped that I remembered all of the sins and that I would not die before I had the chance to confess.

Zephaniah pictures instead a God who is cheering for us much like I do for my children from the bleachers as I watch them play volleyball or basketball. I tell them what a great job they did. Even when they make mistakes, they are still my children. I comfort them after a difficult game where they made some bad choices so that they can get back in the game and play better the next time.

God is your cheerleader, encouraging you in the game of life. Do you feel discouraged? Spend some minutes listening to God's words of delight that He lovingly sings about you. God will save you and will be with you "no matter what" as you turn toward Him.

Dear God, Thank You for Your love and encouragement, for Your presence, for Your song of rejoicing. Open my ears to hear Your words and my mouth to share You with those around me. Amen.

Judy Zook is the associate pastor of New Holland Mennonite Church.

July 31

Divine Connections

"Simon Peter climbed aboard and dragged the net ashore. It was full of large fish, 153, but even with so many the net was not torn." *John 21:11*

Simon Peter and the other four disciples had just returned from a frustrating night of fishing. It would have been extremely disappointing and fruitless had they not followed the word of Jesus. Then they experienced the miracle, 153 fish. The second miracle in the scene is that even under the stress of this amazing load the net did not tear.

The definition of a net is a network of multiple cords intertwined and connected together for purpose. Could it be that this fishing scheme is a picture of the way Christ is building the church today? Might He be divinely connecting multiple cords in network arrangements in our communities? Under the stress of reaching our communities for Christ, can these relational ties keep the network from tearing?

Jesus is still dong miracles today and as we partner and encourage each other in God's work, we will be overjoyed at the miracles we will get to see. After this experience with Jesus, Simon Peter and his friends would never be the same. They caught 153 large fish and the net was not torn.

Father, I am blessed to realize that I am never alone as I follow You, for You will never leave me nor forsake me. I also thank You for the privilege to be a part of Your vast family, and I pray that You will surround me with individuals in meaningful relationships that increase my spiritual vitality. I pray that I, too, will have the grace and the opportunities to connect with other believers so we can impact in our world as we spread the message of good news. Amen.

Lloyd Hoover is a bishop overseer of the Groffdale District of Churches of Lancaster Mennonite Conference.

One

August

Leaving our borders to serve in world missions

August 1

Laborers For The Harvest

"The harvest is plentiful but the workers are few. Ask the Lord of the harvest, therefore, to send out workers into his harvest field."
Matthew 9:37–38

Possibly one of the most effective deceptions of the enemy has been to convince the Church that the harvest is not ripe. Even though it is in direct contradiction to the Word of God, we have difficulty believing that souls are ready to hear the good news. The truth, however, stands: *the harvest is ripe*. It was ripe when Jesus spoke those words, and it remains ripe today. Multitudes are waiting for the laborers to come. Our task is to pray that those laborers would be equipped and sent to the fields. We can pray also that each of us, our leaders especially, will have the heart of God concerning the lost in our region and around the world. And perhaps we might even join the prophet Isaiah who said, "Send me."

Dear Lord, forgive my lack of compassion for the lost. Open my eyes and birth in me an urgency to wade out into the fields and bring in the harvest. Don't let me be deceived any longer, but help me labor wherever I am and whenever I can.

Today's devotional was edited from the 2003–2004 *Throne Of Grace Prayer Guide*, a weekly guide of Lancaster County prayer concerns gathered from regional intercessors and area prayer groups.

One

I Gladly Bow

"Great and marvelous are Yours works, O Lord God, the Almighty; Righteous and true are your ways, King of the nations. Who will not fear, O Lord and glorify Your name? For you alone are holy; For all the nations will come and worship before you, for your righteous acts have been revealed."
Revelation 15:3–4 (New American Standard Bible)

Did you ever think about why all peoples and nations of the earth will bow their knees in worship to the living God? We will bow because we will see that God has done right concerning each of us in every situation of our lives. God is doing the right thing at this moment for each of us, for our families, cities, nation and the world. One day, all who are angry with God and shake their fists at Him, will see that He had their best at heart. This will so humble us that we will stop accusing and say "Only you are righteous and only You have the right to rule."

One night as I was getting ready for bed, complaining to God because we didn't have the money to pay off our YWAM property, God whispered in my ear, "You are going to be embarrassed someday when I reveal why I didn't give you the money yet." Because I couldn't understand God's timing, I accused God of not handling my situation correctly. Someday God is going to show us His righteous acts and we are going to understand that He is omnipotent. Our Father God is handling all of our affairs. I quickly got down on my knees and said,

"Heavenly Father forgive me for accusing you of not handling things rightly. You know what is best even when I can't understand it. I entrust my life to You—help me to trust You more. I gladly bow my knee to You, the only righteous and living God." In Jesus' Name, Amen.

Bill Landis from Lancaster County, serving with Youth With A Mission as the Jamaica/Caribbean Director.

August 3

Measuring Stick

"Yes, a person is a fool to store up earthly wealth but not have a rich relationship with God." *Luke 12:21 (New Living Translation)*

Jesus was telling a parable about a certain farmer who had a harvest beyond his wildest dreams. The first response and consuming reaction of this farmer was to build *himself* bigger barns, sit *himself* down, and allow *himself* the extravagant luxury of eating, drinking, and merry-making. The farmer never considered that this blessing could be about anyone other than himself. In the end, his life is demanded of him and his abundant harvest is lost to him.

I am at one of those decade markers in my life journey. More than at any other time I have felt compulsion to assess issues of success and value. Invariably I have been tempted to rely on empirical measures and consequently have found myself comparing myself to others. Jesus' directive to prioritize a rich relationship with God in the parable of the farmer has been a great challenge in reassessing my approach to this decade marker.

In God's eyes, I am rich toward God as I recognize that all I am and all I have are gifts from God. Secondly, I am rich toward God as I understand that every gift of God is given to equip me for God's purposes and not for my hoarding. Unlike the farmer, I can live in complete gratitude for the wonderful gifts He has given to me, asking Him to open my eyes to every opportunity, great and small, to utilize these gifts for His purposes. This is the true measure of a person!

Gracious Father, thank You for every blessing I have received from Your hand. Help me always to have an attitude of gratitude. Open my eyes to see how You would have me utilize these gifts, and grant me a willing spirit to step into what I see. Through Jesus Christ, my Lord. Amen!

Joe Hyatt is pastor of the Speedwell Heights Brethren in Christ Church in Lititz and Secretary/Treasurer of the Warwick Ministerium.

One

August 4

I Make Myself A Slave

"Though I am free and belong to no man, I make myself a slave to everyone, to win as many as possible."
1 Corinthians 9:19

How will they know, if no one tells them? "How beautiful are the feet of those who bring good news" (Romans 10:15). Christians need to take the gospel to those who haven't heard. These people are everywhere we go. Usually, the lost don't come to us—we need to go to them. They don't know what it is that they're missing, so how will they know where to look for it (Romans 10:13–15)?

In my own humanity, I have already asked God why He called me to leave my home and everything I knew to take the gospel to Brazil, or why He couldn't use Brazilians to reach Brazilians. I can't say that I heard a clear answer, or that I will know the answers on this side of heaven. But I do know that when one of the baby Christians I am discipling says "Thank you so much for coming here... I don't know where I'd be if God hadn't sent you..." those other questions become obsolete. Impacting lives for eternity is much more important than our personal comfort! If you step out of your comfort zone to go where God is calling you, He will cause you to grow incredibly and to become more dependent on Him. I have seen this principle at work so much in my life.

Paul shows us in 1 Corinthians 9:19–23 how he conformed to the cultures of different people groups (without compromising Christ) in order to share the gospel with them. He gives us a great model to follow.

Lord Jesus, take me where You have called me to go. Help me to be a witness for You today and everyday, everywhere. Show me how to become a slave to those around me so that they will come to know You. Amen.

Christine Miller is a missionary/church planter serving in Fortaleza, Brazil alongside her husband, Chad.

August 5
Tune In To God

"Then you will call upon me and go and pray to me, and I will listen to you. You will seek me and find me, when you seek me with all your heart." *Jeremiah 29:12–13*

I could hear the muffled voices of a group of girls having a party upstairs. Among the muted sounds of the girls laughing and talking, I kept hearing a reoccurring, distinct voice that captured my attention. "Do you know whose voice that is?" I inquired of a friend. He knew the girl's voice because it was a friend of his—LaVerne. It was the first time I had heard her voice, and I was intrigued. In fact, I was so intrigued that I married her seven years later, and now I know her loving voice anywhere.

Jesus told His disciples one day, "My sheep know my voice (John 10:4)." How did they know His voice? They built a relationship with Him. They learned from experience to trust the voice of their shepherd.

God's distinct voice stands out. To hear God's voice clearly, we must have a growing love relationship with God. Learning to discern God's voice takes effort on our part. We can get so involved in the affairs of this natural world that we forget to listen. In our scripture verse for today, the Bible instructs us to make a concerted effort to meet with the Lord, thereby placing ourselves in a position to hear from Him. God will reveal Himself to those who humbly seek Him. The more often we meet with God and talk to Him about the concerns on our heart, the clearer His voice becomes.

God desires to communicate with His children. Take the time to hear from Him. He yearns for you to hear His loving, distinct voice.

Dear Jesus, Help me to take the time to hear from You daily. Amen.

Larry Kreider serves on the executive team of the Regional Church of Lancaster County and as international director of D.O.V.E. Christian Fellowship International.

August 6

Living Sacrifices

"Therefore I urge you, brothers [and sisters], in view of God's mercy, to offer your bodies as living sacrifices, holy and pleasing to God—this is your spiritual act of worship. But be transformed by the renewing of your mind..." *Romans 12:1–2*

I love this season of late summer and early fall. This transformation of nature happens season after season. Each time, it is a *God wonder* that reminds us, renews our trust, and revives our hope and worship of our Creator. Currently I am in a season of pastoral "Sabbath rest," created to revive and transform me. This verse serves as a centering focus for my personal devotion, renewal, and worship.

The apostle Paul uses an interesting phrase—"living sacrifice"— to describe our lives as disciples of Jesus Christ. We are to offer our total selves as daily sacrifices that are holy and pleasing to God.

As we "offer ourselves up" at the altar of God, we are changed. Old Testament sacrifices were changed and transformed into an acceptable gift to God by the refining fire. We too are to be transformed daily. Paul suggests that this change comes about by the daily "renewing of our mind in Christ Jesus." Peterson's *The Message* says, "we are to take our everyday, ordinary lives—our sleeping, eating, going to work, and walking around life—and place it before God as an offering." In doing so we are changed from the "inside out."

It is my prayer to be changed into the likeness of Christ by the renewing of my mind through meditation, prayer, rest, and reading, understanding and obeying the scriptures.

Dear God, may my life be a living sacrifice that serves and honors You as a sweet smelling aroma, and may it attract and invite others to come to know You. In the name of the Living Christ I pray. Amen.

John H. Denlinger serves as pastor at Ridgeview Mennonite Church . John is married to Deborah Ann Young Denlinger and they have three adult children, Jeremiah, Jonalyn and Julie.

August 7

Ask, Seek, Knock

"Ask and it will be given to you; seek and you will find, knock and the door will be opened to you." *Matthew 7:7*

Ihave a cool poster on my bedroom wall picturing a large, ancient looking door surrounded by billowing fog. Written over the picture are the words: "Ask and it will be given to you, seek and you will find; knock and the door will be opened to you (Matthew 7:7)."

How many times have I not taken the truth of these words to heart and fell asleep under them while harboring frustration about an 'unsolvable' issue in my life? More than I'd like to admit.

What is the difference between those experiencing God move in their lives and those experiencing hum-drum Christian lives? Those who are asking, seeking and knocking with a persistent heart are the ones receiving from God.

What would our lives look like if we would ask until we received? What would our churches look like if we would seek until we found? What would our county look like if we would knock until the door is opened?

Effective prayer is prayer that attains what it seeks.
It is prayer that moves God, effecting its end.
—Charles G. Finney

He who fails to pray does not cheat God, he cheats himself.
—George Failing

Father, I ask You to fill my heart with the desire to pray. Show me the urgency of the times that we are living in and how You want to use my prayers to cause Your kingdom to come and Your will to be done. Give me a persistent heart that doesn't give up until I receive Your promises. Thank You, Lord.

Kevin Hurst is part owner of Simply Sweet candy stand located in Central Market, Lancaster city. He also assists in leading a Geimenshaft small group.

August 8

Jesus In The Marketplace

"We are therefore Christ's ambassadors, as though God were making His appeal through us. We implore you on Christ's behalf: Be reconciled to God." *2 Corinthians 5:20*

Pray! for Lancaster County

"...enable your servants to speak Your word with great boldness. Stretch our Your hand to heal and perform miraculous signs and wonders through the name of Your holy servant Jesus." *Acts 4:29–30*

Christian leadership is to be demonstrated far beyond the walls of the "church." We are designated as His ambassadors, sent to inform those in a distant land of another country, and implore them to be reconciled with its King. Those in the workforce have a unique opportunity to share the hope of Christ at their places of work. Business leaders have the privilege of demonstrating righteousness and compassion in their many interactions with unbelievers. May they receive the support and accountability they need from their pastors and congregations. Let's pray for boldness for these workers. Let's even ask God to work miraculous signs and wonders right there in the marketplace. May many be drawn to Christ through their witness.

Lord God, thank You for calling me to be Your ambassador. I ask that You would make Your appeal through me at my place of work. Give me the boldness I need to declare Your goodness. Bless those business leaders that I know. Help them to be examples of integrity and godliness as they, too, proclaim the message of reconciliation.

Today's devotional was edited from the 2003–2004 *Throne Of Grace Prayer Guide*, a weekly guide of Lancaster County prayer concerns gathered from regional intercessors and area prayer groups.

August 9

Practicing God's Presence

"The LORD replied, 'My Presence will go with you, and I will give you rest.'" *Exodus 33:14*

In a book entitled *The Practice of the Presence of God*, Brother Lawrence, who served as a cook in a monastery over 300 years ago, talks about the concept of practicing God's presence as a life-changing experience. He used the word "practice" because it is not something that we naturally do. We need to sharpen our spiritual senses by practicing our awareness of God's presence with us every minute of our day. God is not only present in our church services but present with us at home, at work, at school, while we drive, while we play and sleep.

We practice God's presence by talking to Him while we go about our daily activities.

Brother Lawrence writes, "during any daily duty lift your heart up to him, because even the least little remembrance will please him. You don't have to pray out loud; He's nearer then you can imagine."

We practice God's presence by thanking Him for everything all day long. If you practice gratitude, it will not only put you more in tune with God's presence, it will also change your attitude toward life.

We practice God's presence by asking God to help us with little things all day long.

"Help me drive safely." "Help me as I prepare this meal." "Help me do a good job." "Help me be friendly to this customer" Practicing God's presence is a continual flow of conversation with God who is with you. The promise that comes with His Presence is rest in a stressed-out world. "My Presence will go with you, and I will give you rest."

Heavenly Father, I thank You that You have promised never to leave me or forsake me. Help me to be aware of Your presence all day long and to know Your still small voice throughout the day. Amen.

Lester Zimmerman is senior pastor of Petra Christian Fellowship in New Holland.

234   *One*

August 10

What Really Matters

"Whom have I in heaven but you? And earth has nothing I desire besides you. My flesh and my heart may fail, but God is the strength of my heart and my portion forever."
Psalm 73:25–26

I've heard it said many times that we should live each day as if it were our last. If you think of that, how much would your daily activities change to compensate that idea? You wouldn't do a lot of the everyday things that take so much of your time. We need to pay the bills, drop the kids off at soccer, go to school, etc. We are not physically able to stop everything that needs to happen; however, we are able to change our mindsets.

It's all about Him. That is why we live, whether we recognize that or not. We were created for His purposes. Our lives are not our own. Our possessions are not our own. We sometimes get the mindset that we accomplish things on our own strength. God's hand is continually in our lives, leading, guiding, and providing. If we begin to grasp the big picture, it can definitely change our way of living. Live in view of eternity. Focus your thoughts on the things that really matter—the Lord's will for your day and life, your family, friends, neighbors, and co-workers.

My mother has seven children and when asked why she had so many kids, she responds by saying, "It's the only thing I have on this earth that I will be able to take with me to heaven." It's the truth. Our saved families and friends will also be the only thing we have in heaven that we have here. Challenge yourself to start focusing on eternal things.

Lord, help me to focus on You and seek Your will for today. Help me to take time for the things that are important in this life and not get caught up with the things of this world.

Jamie Groff is a worship leader at D.O.V.E. Christian Fellowship Westgate Celebration.

August 11

Interdependent People

"And, behold men brought in a bed a man which was taken with palsy [paralyzed] and they sought means to bring him in, and lay him before [Jesus]." *Luke 5:18 (King James Version)*

I have lived under the false impression that for one to be a Christian of distinction, one must be strong in faith and resolute in purpose. While these are admirable characteristics they are not the foundation of a growing relationship with Christ. Real fruitfulness in Christ happens when I and those around me live out the example of this verse. The Bible clearly calls all of us of the household of faith to bear one another's burdens and to submit one to another. In other words, God calls us to carry others and asks us to allow ourselves to be carried. There is no such thing as a strong Christian who operates outside of the give and take of a fellowship that embraces each believer's strengths, while ministering to each believer's weaknesses. To strengthen my relationship with Jesus I must give my strength unselfishly to those who are "paralyzed" while allowing others to carry me in my moments of paralysis or powerlessness.

There are times when I need to be carried and times when I need to help carry others. In these days of the so-called self-made and independent Christian, what we need is a Christianity that moves beyond the flexing of doctrinal muscles, to the full disclosure that I need you and you need me as we work out the salvation of our souls.

Dear Lord, in the name of Your precious Son, let us as Christians be unashamed of those places where we are weak, and unselfish with our strengths as we work out Your purpose for the church in this life. Amen.

Edward Bailey is the pastor of Bethel African Methodist Episcopal Church in the heart of "Churchtowne" in Lancaster City.

August 12

Beautiful Dreamer

"Forget what happened long ago! Don't think about the past. I am creating something new. There it is! Do you see it? I have put roads in deserts, streams in thirsty lands." *Isaiah 43:18–19 (Contemporary English Version)*

In December of 2000 my family and I traveled from our home in Calgary, Alberta, towards Pennsylvania. We had accepted the call of a church in the New Holland area to be their pastor. As we drove, there was a sadness—we were leaving all of our family behind, moving to a new country where we didn't really know anyone—but there was an excitement that propelled us. I am convinced that the same thing that propelled us to make a big move should be the same thing that propels us as believers and churches…a dream! Marcel Proust wrote in his book *The Eyes of a Dreamer,* "Christians today desperately need the eyes of dreamers. Solutions lie not in focusing upon the rocks in the path, but on the possibilities ahead."

In this passage God describes His dream for His people. He describes the way He wants to impact His people and their future. He shows us there is hope for a new dream in the darkest of circumstances. God promises through the prophet Isaiah to bring something wonderful, gracious, spectacular and new into their lives. It's not going to be more of the same—exile, despondency, hopelessness—but release from captivity and hope for tomorrow. God said to the Israelites and God says to us, "I will show you the way in the desert, I will give you streams in the wasteland. When life, when ministry, when relationships, when work, when money all seem hopeless, I will provide a dream…I will provide a way…I will bring you into streams of living water."

Dear God, in the midst of my struggle and my pain help me to see the dream You have for my life.

Douglas P. Sider is the senior pastor of Summit View Church in the New Holland and Octorara communities.

Passion Under Control

"Everyone should be quick to listen, slow to speak and slow to become angry, for man's anger does not bring about the righteous life that God desires." *James 1:19–20*

W e all have things we are passionate about—desires we wish to see realized. These may be expressed as goals or "Action Steps." Although the "desires" mentioned in James 1:14 include evil desires, it broadly refers to any strong passion (note Jesus' desire in Luke 22:15). So, none of our desires should be excluded. James warns that any strong desire can tempt us to sin in order to see it accomplished.

Sandwiched between the verses on temptation and anger are verses 16 and 17. We can be deceived to think that the achievement of these "good and perfect" things depends on us—rather on a sovereign God.

So how does this relate to anger? Anger happens when passion meets resistance. The emotion may be triggered by people, by inanimate objects or events. Our anger, frustration, irritation (or whatever we wish to call it) drives us to take things into our own hands—and solve the problem now—because it appears that God needs our help! But James categorically states that the *expression* of our anger will never accomplish God's purposes. For Moses (in Numbers 20), his anger resulted in his disqualification as a leader.

What are the sources of irritation and anger in our own lives? What desires are we tempted to meet because God seems to need our help? Once we can deal with our emotion, what steps does God hold us responsible for to see this desire met for His glory?

Dear God, please show me where anger is tempting me to achieve Your purposes through actions and words motivated by anger. Please keep me from justifying my anger just because the cause may be understandable. I commit myself to fulfilling Your purposes—Your way—for Your glory. Amen.

David Muchmore is international director for Asia for CrossWorld and Adjunct Professor of Missions at Lancaster Bible College.

August 14

It's Okay To Be Different

"They are like children sitting in the marketplace and calling out to each other: 'We played the flute for you and you did not dance; we sang a dirge, and you did not cry.'" *Luke 7:32*

Jesus spoke these words to people who had rejected John the Baptist and who were now rejecting him. Both were seen as radical in their opinions and both were rejected by many (Luke 7:33–34). John lived and ministered in the wilderness. Jesus was seen eating and drinking with people who were considered "bad company".

Similar attitudes surround us today. If we stop to listen for God's voice, and we step forward in obedience, we are often drawn away from what many would see as the most likely path. This can bring about misunderstanding and even rejection by some people because we may not "fit the mold". It is foolish, however, to think that everyone's service to God will look the same. Not everyone who ministers will have an "official title" that is recognized by the world.

So, how can we know that God is speaking and we're not just crazy? Trusted friends in Christ can be an encouragement. More time listening in prayer can't hurt; but faith in Jesus who has spoken to us must be our foundation.

Relax! Even John the Baptist had doubts about his calling (Luke 7:18–20). Be encouraged that your service in obedience to the Master will bring reward and vindication. That is why Jesus closed his conversation on this matter with these words: "wisdom is proved right by all her children (Luke 7:35)."

Lord Jesus, grant me the faith and clarity of mind to hear Your vision for my life no matter how different it may seem from "the norm." Encourage me and grant me friends who I can trust to keep me going in the direction that You have called me. In Jesus' name, Amen.

August 15

A Region Of Refuge

"'The glory of this present house will be greater than the glory of the former house,' says the Lord Almighty. 'And in this place I will grant peace,' declares the Lord Almighty." *Haggai 2:9*

for Lancaster County

"Then the church throughout Judea, Galilee and Samaria enjoyed a time of peace. It was strengthened; and encouraged by the Holy Spirit, it grew in numbers, living in the fear of the Lord." *Acts 9:31*

It is the Lord who grants peace and gives encouragement. We can ask Him to establish Lancaster County as a region of racial and relational reconciliation, restoration and refuge. We can envision our region as a haven of spiritual rest and a place of peace among believers, neighbors and communities. In such an environment, the church is free to multiply, and as it does, we can anticipate glory in His house.

Heavenly Father, we want Your glory to be revealed in our lives, our churches and our communities. Help us actively seek, by our words and actions toward others, to create places of peace. Make us peacemakers *who are able to bring reconciliation and healing to those who are estranged.*

Today's devotional was edited from the 2003–2004 *Throne Of Grace Prayer Guide*, a weekly guide of Lancaster County prayer concerns gathered from regional intercessors and area prayer groups.

240   *One*

August 16
One Day At A Time

"Awake, O Lord! Why do you sleep? Rouse yourself! Do not reject us forever…". *Psalm 44:23–24*

In the 80's, author Phillip Yancey boldly brought the body of Christ to attention with his now classic work, *Disappointment with God.* Yancey affirmed our need to be honest and open with God with our deepest needs and complaints; however, most of us feel that it's sacrilegious to openly express disappointment with God because He is sovereign and all-powerful.

In Psalm 44, David expresses profound disappointment with God, even claiming that all the troubles befalling Israel were not the nation's fault. "All this happened to us, though we had not forgotten you or been false to your covenant (v. 17)." One wonders about this statement considering the wayward history of Israel—surely David was pouring out an honest complaint from his heart. From his perspective he felt that God had not stood up to defend them, though he could have.

Have you experienced the bitterness of disappointment this year? I have. I have been misunderstood, falsely condemned, and mistreated. I have seen my labors treated with contempt. I have had those I love turn their back on me. I have been grieved at our nation's slide into depravity. I have been disappointed with the compromises of the church of Jesus. How about you? Have you brought your disappointments before the Lord? Be honest with Him! He knows your heart and will understand your complaint. And don't forget to listen to His answers. They may surprise you. Lean hard on Jesus; He experienced disappointments deeper than anything we will ever know!

Dear Father, help me to be honest with You about all that is in my heart. I don't want to sugarcoat how I'm thinking. You already know what's in my heart…help me to tell You all about it. I love You, Jesus. Amen.

Scott Lanser is the pastor of New Hope Church in East Hempfield. He has served in youth ministry leadership in Lancaster County for over 20 years.

Servants All

"The Spirit of the Lord is upon me…to give unto them beauty for ashes…that they might be called the trees of righteousness, the planting of the Lord, that he might be glorified."
Isaiah 61:1,3 (King James Version)

So many people come into the church with "disqualified" branded on their souls. Their weaknesses, inadequacies and fears shout louder than the preacher, and so they find an obscure pew and settle in for their weekly dose of "religion". We've got to look them in the eye and say, "We're in this together!" Jesus didn't care whether Peter smelled like dead fish or not! He said, "Come on! Let's go fish for men!"

When people work beside their leaders in the harvest, they learn that God can compensate for their inadequacies; where they are weak, He is strong! In ministry to others, they find a new heart beating within, a new soul being born. They begin to see themselves as servants, as useful.

When people die to self and live for others, the life of Christ blooms in their midst. Trampled twigs become trees of righteousness. Love, joy, peace, patience, kindness, goodness, faithfulness, gentleness and self-control (Galatians 5:22–24) blossom in their souls. They grow; they reproduce.

And God shows up, because He loves hanging out where love is growing. When God shows up, the lights come on. When the lights come on, those people lost in darkness come in search of life. And as the world sees the love of God in action, through the people of God in unity, spiritual scales fall from their eyes and they suddenly believe that the Father sent the Son (John 17:20–23).

All this happens through a church where everyone is a minister.

Jesus—servant of all though Lord of all—give me a servant's soul that I may impart it through service to others. Amen.

Adapted from *God's Heart for Ministering to God's People* by **Phil Hernandez and Mark Ammerman**. Phil pastors In The Light Ministries in Lancaster City; Mark serves on the leadership team.

August 18
"YES"

"...Let your YES be YES..." *James 5:12*

Recently my mother received a left hip joint replacement at Ephrata Community Hospital. Before wheeling her to the operating room, the nurse wrote in bold permanent marker "YES" at the exact spot on her body where she needed surgery. Thus, the surgeon could make no mistake as to which hip needed to be replaced.

The Lord reminded me that He wants us to approach Him boldly, letting Him know what areas of our lives need healing. We need to come to the throne of grace in no uncertain terms and proclaim, "YES" to all that He has for us. The Bible tells us that "...we have not because we ask not... (James 4:2)." "Which of you, if his son asks for bread, will give him a stone? Or if he asks for a fish, will give him a snake? If you, then, though you are evil know how to give good gifts to your children, how much more will your Father in heaven give good gifts to those who ask Him (Matthew 7:9–11)." So won't you totally surrender to the Father? He is on call 24/7, desiring to minister to you.

Dear Heavenly Father, today if there is any area of my life that needs a touch from the Great Physician, or if I need to totally surrender to the Lordship of Jesus, give me the grace to "...let my YES be YES... (James 5:12)."

T. Scott Jackson, M.D. is a physician at Crossroads Family Medical Center.

Check Your gauges!

"...May your whole spirit, soul and body be kept blameless..."
1 Thessalonians 5:23

Several years ago, my daughter and I had the extraordinary experience of destroying the engines in both our cars on the same day. I had become so busy "building the kingdom," I forgot to check the oil in the vehicles. Both our cars' engines overheated and were ruined beyond repair. Since that time, I learned the importance of keeping a close watch on the critical gauges on the dashboards of our cars!

I believe that, like the gauges in our cars, God has given three specific spiritual gauges to help us live passionately for Jesus while maintaining a proper life balance so we do not burn out in the process. One gauge is for the spirit, one for the soul and one for the body.

Spirit gauge: Some time ago, a group of church leaders in an underground church in Central Asia asked me how much time I spend alone with the Lord each day. The Lord used this question to cause me to deeply search my heart and repent and press into God daily in a fresh way. How much time do you spend alone with God each day?

Soul gauge: Our soul needs to be cleansed and revitalized regularly. Is there anyone you have bitterness against? Keep short accounts. Forgive them, and keep your soul healthy.

Body gauge: Jesus knew when to withdraw from the crowds to rest and rejuvenate His body. A healthy body gives us more stamina for spiritual warfare.

Constant maintenance is needed in order to stay spiritually healthy to live out our destiny in the kingdom of God. Run the race—but check your gauges! It could save your life.

Dear Lord, help me to maintain a proper life balance—body, soul and spirit. Amen.

Larry Kreider serves on the executive team of the Regional Church of Lancaster County and as international director of D.O.V.E. Christian Fellowship International.

August 20

This Is A Call

"Very early in the morning, while it was still dark, Jesus got up, left the house and went off to a solitary place, where he prayed." *Mark 1:35*

In the early 1990's, Dr. David Yonggi Cho spoke at Lancaster Mennonite High School. Cho pioneered a church in Seoul, South Korea. At that time it had grown to about 700,000 members. He said two things made his church grow—small groups and prayer. He explained the role prayer played in his church's growth. Every day his entire congregation assembled at the church about 4 a.m. to pray before going to work. Most Americans find it challenging to make a 10 A.M. Sunday Worship Service. Imagine your entire congregation coming together for prayer every morning before going to work. I wondered what motivated these people?

Cho went on to tell about a time he overslept. The alarm went off, but instead of turning the snooze alarm on he turned it off. Suddenly, the ringing of the phone awakened him. It was his mother-in-law. "Cho, where are you? What are you doing? Everyone is waiting for you!" Cho answered, "I overslept". "What is wrong with you?" she replied. "Are you no longer Christian?" Having been chastened, he jumped out of bed and ran to the church. When he arrived on stage, everyone laughed at him. He looked down to discover he was still in his pajamas. How do you respond to the call to prayer?

There is an ancient saying: Lex orandi, lex credindi; est. It literally means, "The rule of prayer is the rule of faith." In other words, show me how you pray and I'll tell you what you really believe. Jesus' ministry was rooted in prayer. Everything He did flowed out of prayer.

Dear God, put within me a desire to pray like Jesus. Strengthen my faith through prayer, so that all I do reflects Your will and not mine.

Rev. Craig Snow, pastor of Swamp UCC, Reinholds, member of Cocalico Ministers Prayer Group.

Lavish Grace

"Blessed be the God and Father of our Lord Jesus Christ, who has blessed us with every spiritual blessing in the heavenly places in Christ...before the foundation of the world, that we should be holy and without blame before Him in love."
Ephesians 1:3–4 (New King James Version)

Have you considered that God loved you so much that He devised a way to bless you before you were created? Not only for your sake, but we read in Isaiah 43:25 that "I, even I, am He who blots out your transgressions for my own sake."

With a tremendous desire to include you in His eternal plans, God predestined you to be adopted as His son through Christ Jesus. It was His good pleasure to lavish His grace upon you, redeeming you, forgiving your sins and making you accepted in the Beloved. As if this was not enough, in Him you have an inheritance and you were sealed with the Holy Spirit of promise to the praise of His Glory!

Don't you know that your body is the temple of Almighty God, that you were created for His glory? A carrier of the Anointed One, a holy vessel set aside for the express purpose of spreading the good news of the love of God, in word and in deed? Lighting dark places, giving hope to the hopeless, allowing the presence of the Lord within you to be seen in your actions, countenance and words?

As He has loved, forgiven and accepted us—so that we could have a future—let us become a catalyst in our community, so that they too can know the love and blessing of the Lord.

Dear God, I thank You for every spiritual gift, not because I deserved it, but in Your great mercy and grace You chose to freely give it. Therefore, let me be a vessel of Your glory, so that Your love and salvation may be spread abroad among our community. In the name of Jesus Christ, Amen.

Allan Chambers gives apostolic oversight to Global Covenant Ministries.

August 22

Our Schools

"Don't let anyone look down on you
because you are young, but set an example for the believers in speech, in life, in
love, in faith, and in purity." *1 Timothy 4:12*

for Lancaster
County

"I pray that out of his glorious riches he may
strengthen you with power through his Spirit in your
inner being." *Ephesians 3:16*

The educating of our young people is one of the most daunting
tasks we face. Whether they attend public or private schools,
whether they are home-schooled, in trade schools, or university settings, their educational experiences will shape not only their
future, but that of our country. As a new year begins to unfold for
schools, let's pray that God would invade our educational institutions.
Let's lift up believing teachers and students and pray that they would
be powerful influences for Christ. Let's ask the Lord to give them inner
strength through His Spirit. May the truth of the gospel they proclaim
interrupt and impede any negative forces that would try to overtake
them or their school.

*Lord, we pray for everyone involved in the educational process—stu-
dents, teachers, administrators, coaches, youth leaders, parents, and
school boards. We ask that You bless them and help them to move Your
purposes forward.*

Today's devotional was edited from the 2003–2004 *Throne Of Grace
Prayer Guide*, a weekly guide of Lancaster County prayer concerns
gathered from regional intercessors and area prayer groups.

August 23

Mission Statement

"The Spirit of the Lord is on me, because he has anointed me to preach good news to the poor. He has sent me to proclaim freedom for the prisoners and recovery of sight for the blind, to release the oppressed, to proclaim the year of the Lord's favor." *Luke 4:18*

Here we have the mission statement of the life of Jesus Christ. Jesus read this text from the prophet Isaiah to describe himself. While adapting this mission of Jesus to be our own mission, it can also be a great source of personal encouragement. Spiritual poverty, blindness, imprisonment, and oppression are all things we battle. We may have been given bad news, lack vision, feel trapped or unjustly treated, but God, in the person of Jesus Christ, came to reveal justice and mercy to an undeserving humanity. If we are trusting Christ as our Savior, Jesus is the only One anointed to give us spiritual wealth, freedom, vision, relief and favor. When I give Him free reign to use the things I possess and to reveal my blind spots, to step into my heart's prison and to release the hurting words and actions of others in forgiveness, then I can truly experience His favor and accept His love (Psalm 23). The further I travel in life's journey, the more I realize that even the faith to accept His gracious work in my life is a free gift from His mighty hand (Ephesians 2:8–9).

Lord, help me to accept my life experiences today as divinely ordered and anointed to produce spiritual fruit. Lord, where I am poor, give me riches, where my heart is in bondage, break the chains, where my vision is lacking, grant me eyes to see, and where I am holding on to bitterness or unforgiveness, help me to release the offender to Your measure of justice.

Ed Hersh provides counseling and healing prayer ministry to individuals and families, trains lay counselors here and abroad, and helps wounded leaders receive spiritual renewal.

August 24
Plant The Word

"A farmer went out to sow his seed. The farmer sows the word." *Mark 4:3,14*

Some people are gifted with plants and are said to have a "green thumb", while other people seem to kill every plant they try to grow. Jesus often used plants and farmers as examples for His parables. In the parable of the seed and the sower, Jesus tells us that the seed that is sown is the Word of God. The farmer goes out and sows the Word. It falls on different soils with different results, but that does not keep the farmer from sowing His seeds.

Are you like the farmer? Do you go out and sow the seeds of the Word? We need to continually sow seeds into the world, no matter where in the soil they fall. Because you cannot see into the heart of another person, you do not know if the seed that you sow will take root and blossom into a life changed by the power of the Gospel. On the other hand, the person you meet may possess a hard heart that is not ready to receive the Word, but that does not mean that you should not sow it. There are many ways to sow seed. These include leaving tracts, sharing a kind word with someone having a rough day, or providing refreshment in Jesus' name, to name a few. I encourage you to use your God-given personality to sow the Word in ways that best suit you. Remember, faith comes from hearing the message and the message is the Word of Christ. Go and share it.

Dear God, may You give me opportunities each day to sow Your Word into lives around me. Prepare each heart for the Word that will be sown. Give me courage and wisdom to carry out this mission in Jesus' name. Amen.

Kevin Kirkpatrick, former evangelist with The Pocket Testament League, is the pastor of Berean Bible Fellowship Church in Terre Hill.

August 25

I Am Gentle

"Come to me, all who are weary and burdened, and I will give you rest. Take my yoke upon you and learn from me, for I am gentle and humble in heart, and you will find rest for your souls. For my yoke is easy and my burden is light."
Matthew 11:28–30

Modern day agriculture has little understanding of the meaning of the word "yoke". What does this first century illustration have to say to the 21st century church? I am a bi-vocational pastor who not only shepherds the flock at my local church, but oversees the management of a dairy farm with my brother. We farm the land to feed the cows using modern day equipment. Long ago our ancestors said good-bye to the yokes and welcomed the invention of gasoline and diesel powered tractors.

In the first century a yoke was essential to getting the job accomplished. The two or more cattle that were connected by what was known as a yoke were obligated to work together to get the job done. Anything done contrary to working together would be considered offensive and contrary to the purpose and goals of the farmer. In Matthew 11, Jesus invites you and me to take his yoke upon us. The work and the burden associated with the work belong not to us, but to the Lord. Therefore, when we take his yoke upon us we must remember that it indeed is His yoke and not my invitation to the Lord Jesus to take on my yoke.

Father, I pray that today You would rest my soul in the knowledge that the work is Yours, the weight of this work is Yours and the "yoke" is Yours. By faith, I ask You to connect me to Your unlimited resources so that Your power can be at work through me. In Jesus' name Amen.

Pastor Joe C. Garber, Byerland Mennonite Church, Western Lancaster County Pastors Prayer Group

August 26

Called By God

"The Spirit of the Lord God is upon me, because the Lord has anointed me to bring good news to the afflicted; He has sent me to bind up the brokenhearted, to proclaim liberty to captives, and freedom to prisoners; to proclaim the favorable year of the Lord, and the day of vengeance of our God; to comfort all who mourn." *Isaiah 61:1–2 (New American Standard Bible)*

I heard someone say that America is called by God to release the captives. I believe that this calling is not for America, but for the body of Jesus Christ. Brother Paul calls the body of Christ to live simply so that our excess can be given to others. We may live thinking that this is our land, but the earth is the Lord's and the fullness thereof. He reminded the Israelites the importance of justice for the aliens who were in their land—because they knew what it was like to be aliens themselves. If we want to be a righteous nation again, then we must remember that God will not bless us merely because of our history, but because of our willingness to bind up the brokenhearted, whether they live here in our borders or in a foreign land.

Lord God, give me enough that I may not steal or beg and dishonor Your name, but keep me from so much that I become proud and ignore You. My daily bread is the portion that You have promised me. Help me to live on that today.

Phil Reynolds is the pastor of the Mohler Church of the Brethren in Ephrata. His passion is evangelism and justice.

Uniquely Loved

"How great is the love the Father has lavished on us, that we should be called children of God!" *1 John 3:1*

On a warm August day, my family and I gathered around our mother's bed to say good-bye—one last time. The following Thursday we gathered to remember her precious life. Woven throughout the tapestry of stories and sentiments was one common thread—my mother's love. She had a way of loving us that made us feel incredibly special. She loved us uniquely and cherished the nuances that made us individuals. While we all shared common memories of our life with her, we each had private memories—memories that brought comfort to the deepest part of our aching hearts.

Greater far than a mother's love is the love of our heavenly Father. He did not just love "the world", He loved you—uniquely. So much so, that He sent His only Son to die for you so that you might have eternal, abundant life (John 3:16–17). His love created your inmost being (Psalms 139). His love chose you before the creation of the world (Ephesians 1:4), and nothing will ever separate you from His love (Romans 8:38,39). Allow that incredible thought to go from your head to your heart and then celebrate His love for you today. But do not stop there!

You are not the only one He loves uniquely. He loves the woman who scans your groceries. He loves the stranger on the street. He loves your neighbor. He loves all of them uniquely. So today, ask God how He can reveal His unique love through you to someone who really needs to be comforted in the deepest part of his or her aching heart.

Father, thank You for loving me uniquely. Please enable me to grasp Your love for me in a deeper way today. Show me how to convey Your unique love to someone else today.

Terri Miller is the Executive Director of Love INC (Love In the Name of Christ).

August 28

Pilgrim Or Settler

"Blessed are those whose strength is in you, who have set their hearts on pilgrimage." Psalm 84:5

God has called us to set our hearts on pilgrimage with Him. The heart attitude needed to fulfill our destiny in God is the attitude of a pilgrim. A pilgrim's heart longs for something more. Instead of settling for the status quo there is a passion to experience more of God.

"My soul yearns, even faints, for the courts of the LORD; my heart and my flesh cry out for the living God (Psalm 84:2)."

Pilgrimage is not easy. Psalm 84 refers to the valley that we need to walk through, a place of sorrow, pain and dryness. Yet in the midst of our journey God provides springs in the desert to strengthen and encourage us.

"As they pass through the Valley of Baca, they make it a place of springs; the autumn rains also cover it with pools. They go from strength to strength, till each appears before God in Zion (Psalm 84:6–7)."

The opposite of being a pilgrim is being a settler. A settler is one that stops journeying, stops dreaming, stops taking risks, and longs for the comfortable and familiar. You and I can settle where it's safe and comfortable or we can set our hearts on pilgrimage and discover what an awesome God we serve as He takes us through the dark valleys and up, up to the high majestic mountains.

Heavenly Father, I want to have the heart of a pilgrim as I journey with you. Give me the strength to overcome the obstacles and find those times of refreshment in Your presence.

Lester Zimmerman is the senior pastor of Petra Christian Fellowship in New Holland

August 29

Sabbath Rest

"Come to me, all you who are weary and burdened, and I will give you rest. Take my yoke upon you and learn from me, for I am gentle and humble in heart, and you will find rest for your souls. For my yoke is easy and my burden is light."
Matthew 11:28–30.

Rest! What picture comes to your mind? Solitude in the mountains, walking a deserted beach, or sleeping late? Recently I asked a group that I was teaching how many thought they needed rest. Over half the group raised their hands immediately!

Are you weary? Do you need rest?

Rest is an idea among 21st century Americans that is greatly pursued yet many times missed. In our family, we find we need to guard against over-busyness that wants to overtake us. Does the enemy want to keep us busy while neglecting our "rest time" with the Lord? Our family carefully plans and prioritizes between soccer and baton practice, school events, extended family events, church activities and so on. Sometimes we have to say "no" to good things.

God was thinking of us when He gave the principle of a weekly Sabbath Day of rest. Jesus had us in mind when he called the weary and busy to Him for rest. Here is not just rest for our tired bodies; here is rest for worried minds and troubled spirits.

Jesus is saying, "You search for rest in many places. Now it is time to come to Me for true rest. I alone can ease your burdens in mind and spirit, your worries, disappointments, fears, troubles and regrets. Come to Me, cast your cares and burdens on Me, and I will lighten your load."

Lord, I come to You for rest. I choose to cast my cares on You and receive Your rest, peace and provision. I ask for Your wisdom in helping me live a life-style of rest and peace. Thank You for new life, strength, vision and victory in You! Amen.

Allen Dise serves as senior elder of D.O.V.E.Christian Fellowship Manheim. He and his wife, Lucinda, have two children, David and Elana.

August 30

Stepping Out

"Forget about what's happened; don't keep going over old history. Be alert, be present. I'm about to do something brand new. It's bursting out! Don't you see it?" *Isaiah 43:18–19 (The Message)*

I mark up my Bible. Whenever I am reading in it and come across a passage that resonates with me, I underline it. I first marked this passage in Isaiah 43 on December 21, 1996. At that time, I had been a youth pastor for 19 years. Something was stirring in me. I felt it was time to do something different. As I read this passage, I felt God wanted to lead me to a new arena of ministry. But I did not know where. The picture was fuzzy. As I read Isaiah 43:19 where it says, *See, I am doing a new thing! Now it springs up; do you not perceive it?* I replied, "No, I do not see it. Help me, please."

For the next year, my wife, Rila, and I talked a lot about what we wanted for our family and future. We sought counsel and direction through praying together and meeting weekly with a small group of friends for reflection and prayer. We pursued job leads and weighed them out in terms of our values and priorities. Slowly the picture became clear. I interviewed at First Presbyterian Church in Lancaster in November of 1997. After many conversations, visits, and wrestling in prayer, we sensed Lancaster was our next ministry assignment.

Since that time I have gone back and marked that Isaiah 43 passage six more times. In many ways I see the "new thing" God is doing. God's grace can be experienced in many ways. One way I found is that God always gives me enough guidance to make the next step.

Thank you, God, that You care about me. Lead me today, so I can joyfully serve You and experience Your grace in new ways. In Jesus' Name, Amen.

Donald Hackett is an associate pastor at First Presbyterian Church on Orange Street and works with Cherry Street Worship.

August 31

Powerful Weakness

"Three times I pleaded with the Lord to take it [thorn] away from me. But he said to me, 'My grace is sufficient for you, for my power is made perfect in weakness.' Therefore I will boast all the more gladly about my weaknesses, so that Christ's power may rest on me. That is why, for Christ's sake, I delight in weaknesses, in insults, in hardships, in persecutions, in difficulties. For when I am weak, then I am strong."
2 Corinthians 12:8–10

Thorns are an inevitable part of life experience. Jesus came, not to see us free from skin, but sin.

Paul welcomed his weaknesses, so that Christ's power could manifest through him. Paul was an ordinary person who allowed extraordinary revelation and power to change his life. Paul wanted God to perform a "miracle" in taking away his thorn. If his thorn were a health problem, I'm sure he sought complete healing. If it was financial lack, he would have prayed for replaced financial security. God wanted to show his power in helping Paul overcome his weakness in supernatural ways. Sometimes a miracle is not defined as the quickest and most comprehensive relief possible, but rather God's provision of the daily strength to endure one's losses and to trust God for provision.

Our imperfections and inabilities give God the perfect platform to demonstrate His abilities. In my own life, it is often when I feel most vulnerable and powerless that God shows himself the strongest. I'm not always cooperative with this process, but when I finally "let go and let God", I see a fruitful turn in the circumstances, or even a supreme victory to God's glory.

Lord, work in us a desire to see Your strength exalted above ours. Free us from Satan's lie that we must be "strong" to be useful in God's Kingdom. Teach us how to accept Your divine provision for the purpose of bringing glory to You (not to ourselves) in our lives.

Ed Hersch provides counseling and healing prayer ministry to individuals and families, trains lay counselors here and abroad, and helps wounded leaders receive spiritual renewal.

September

September 1

Be Still And Know
That I Am God

Pray!

for Lancaster
County

"Be still and know that I am God; I will be
exalted among the nations, I will be exalted in
the earth." *Psalm 46:10*

"The fruit of righteousness will be peace; the effect
of righteousness will be quietness and confidence forever."
Isaiah 32:17

There is a promise of rest for the people of God. The righteous will walk in peace, quietness and confidence. But for that to be realized, we must first make the time and find the place to be still before the Lord. There is an increased rest in His presence, and goodness that will be missed if we fail to make the *effort* to stop, listen for His voice, and be washed in His grace. As we seek His presence for ourselves, let us pray the same blessing for the church of Jesus Christ in our region.

Father, help me today to quiet myself from all the busyness and be still before You. May I bear the fruit of righteousness because of being in Your presence. Then, as the psalmist says, You will be exalted among the nations and in the earth.

Today's devotional was edited from the 2003–2004 *Throne Of Grace Prayer Guide*, a weekly guide of Lancaster County prayer concerns gathered from regional intercessors and area prayer groups.

September 2

Sit Down

"Jesus said, 'Have the people sit down.' Now there was much grass in the place. So the men sat down, about five thousand in number. Jesus then took the loaves, and when He had given thanks, He distributed them to those who were seated. So also the fish, as much as they wanted." *John 6:10–11 (English Standard Version)*

This is a wonderful, old story. Jesus was sensitive to the needs of the people who followed Him. He provided more than enough, with many baskets left over. Jesus did miracles and the people were amazed.

Recently, I saw a new truth in this old story. Jesus said, "Have the people sit down." He asked for a step of obedience before He provided. I don't know if the people knew there was no food. I don't know if the disciples said that lunch was coming. I suspect they didn't. I think the people were just told to sit, with no explanation. It was not a hard thing that the Lord asked. There was "much grass" in the place. He did not ask them to sit on rocks, dirt, or mud. They were standing around and they sat down. And then, Jesus fed those who were seated. Those that obeyed experienced the miracle.

In the past few years I have been desperate for many things. I have needed God to feed me materially. I have needed God to feed me spiritually. I have needed God. I have worked frantically to get what I needed. How often, as I struggled, did I miss the instruction, "sit down"? Sometimes I felt too desperate, too needy. I believed I must work harder and do it on my own. I forgot that when I sit before the Lord, trusting in Him, He always feeds me.

Lord, remind me to sit down in Your presence. Give me faith to believe that You will provide more than enough. Let me rest in Your grassy place.

Karen Boyd is a member of Pennsylvania Homeschoolers Accreditation Agency Board and WITF Educational Advisory Board.

September 3
Learning To Rest In God
"...on the seventh day he rested from all his work."
Genesis 2:2

My parents were hard workers. My father was a full-time pastor, and my mother was a housewife who led the charge of "keeping house" for five boys, a girl and a husband—not to mention the responsibilities that came along with being a pastor's wife. I will never forget how tired they would get on some evenings. They were both wonderful conversationalists, and loved to talk, but there were nights when their bodies would just give in. Sometimes my parents would fall asleep right in the middle of me talking, or worse yet, in the middle of them answering. "Mom," I would cry, "you're not listening." The irony of this whole experience is that now I have three sons, and there are days that I hear them exclaim, "Dad, you're not listening; you're sleeping."

The fact is that the body needs rest. God created a day for resting to show its significance. Rest is a beautiful symbol of what must occur in our spiritual lives if we are to grow in our faith and relationship with Christ. Three basic things happen when we go to sleep: exhibition of trust, release of control, and freedom to dream. Sleep is the ultimate physical act of trust. We trust our surroundings enough to shut down our awareness of them and consequently be vulnerable. We are no longer in control. And as a result of this trust and release of control, our minds are free to dream and go places we can't go when we are awake.

God calls us to rest in all of our challenges and circumstances in life. Just like when we go to sleep, He wants us to learn to trust Him totally to work things out for the good. Only then will we be able to realize His dreams for us.

Father, this day, may we learn to rest in Your sovereign plan for our lives.

Irvin L. Scott is the principal of McCaskey East High School.

A *Reap* Is Coming

"And let us not grow weary while doing good, for in due season we shall reap if we do not lose heart." *Galatians 6:9 (New King James Version)*

My husband Jim and I have been in ministry for over 30 years. In the course of time we have had many mountain top experiences as well as times of great weariness. The mountain tops have inspired us, but working our way through the weariness has caused great growth. Do not run from weariness, but learn from it. The weariness is a time for God to get our attention. Often it is a time for rest and to be called away by God. As we obey we are renewed and changed. The promise of this scripture as a reap will come.

Our ministry over the years has been serving pregnant and single parent women. We have lived with over 200 birthmothers. Many of these women have placed their children in adoption. We have cared for and loved these mothers and have been blessed to give life and to influence future generations. In this journey there have been periods of weariness.

Recently we received a call from a young woman who had been placed in adoption 25 years ago. I was able to tell her I was in the delivery room when she was born and have prayed for her all these years. She asked if she and her adopted parents could meet us at the Olive Garden for dinner. If you were at the Olive Garden that night you would probably not have noticed us, but a "reap" was occurring. To see her face to face, meet her parents and see how well she has done was a wonderful moment for us.

Dear Lord, may we come to You in our weariness and be refreshed and changed. May we continue to do good knowing that in Your perfect timing a "reap" is on the way.

Anne Pierson is executive director of Loving and Caring, Inc.

September 5

Obedience Through Suffering

"Though He was a Son, yet He learned obedience by the things He suffered, and having been perfected, He became the author of eternal salvation to all who obey Him."
Hebrews 5:8–9 (New King James Version)

Why does God let us suffer so much? The purpose of suffering is to help us learn obedience. We often learn most by experiencing the consequences of our mistakes. Jesus, however, never made a mistake or a wrong choice, yet even He had to learn obedience by suffering. Why, and how is that?

Jesus was perfect, yet He had to be "perfected" to become the author of salvation. His greatest work and act of obedience to the Father came at the very end of His life. It was because He spent a lifetime learning how to be obedient in the midst of suffering that He had strength for the cross.

Jesus identified with us in every way. He suffered through the same learning process of life experiences we do, but He never sinned going through them. He never returned evil for evil. He didn't get mad at God. He didn't defend Himself. He trusted God in every circumstance. With each increase of suffering, Jesus learned to a greater degree how to remain under the control of the Holy Spirit. He learned the fruit of meekness. He learned how to obey His Father, not His own will or desires, in every situation. The result was that Jesus was prepared for His greatest hour.

Are you facing tremendous struggles? Remember, the greater the suffering, the greater the work God is preparing for you. Let the suffering teach you how to trust Him. Let the fruit of meekness grow, teaching you how to live each moment in obedience to God's Spirit.

Oh God, I want to fulfill the destiny You have chosen for me. Please help me to live in total obedience to Your Spirit's leading, no matter how much I am suffering. Thank You Lord, Amen.

Dean Witmer recently completed his pastorate at Living Truth Fellowship, Christiana, and helped form the Lancaster Transformation Network.

September 6
The Pygmalion Effect
"Follow my example, as I follow the example of Christ."
1 Corinthians 11:1

I know that we are to imitate Christ, but honestly, it seems a bit arrogant of Paul to write, "Follow my example." The ironic twist to this is that our example is one of the most powerful ways of influencing people. What's that got to do with Pygmalion, and what is the effect? In Greek mythology, the sculptor Pygmalion carved a statue of a beautiful woman, fell in love with the statue, and brought it to life by the strength of his perceptions. One might say that he had such high expectations of this statue, that the force of those expectations brought life. "Leaders play Pygmalion-like roles in developing people" write Kouzes & Posner in their book, *The Leadership Challenge.* "Research on the phenomenon of self-fulfilling prophecies provides ample evidence that other people act in ways that are consistent with our expectations of them. If we expect others to fail, they probably will." Bennie Goodwin in his book, *The Effective Leader,* writes, "People have a tendency to try to live up to the genuine expectations of those they admire and respect."

This Pygmalion Effect places two challenges on leaders. One, do we have high expectations of people we are training? (Not so high that they are out of reach, but high enough that they know we believe they can reach them.) Second, do we model our lives in such a way that people admire us and want to live up to the godly expectations? Fortunately, the Holy Spirit is our helper. He empowers us, making us both attractive and genuinely challenging to others. Pygmalion is a great story, a wonderful myth. But praise God for the reality of Christ, who brings into being things that are not.

Thank You Lord Jesus, for Your life model that propels us forward into ministry. I pray for perspective in our lives that we can provide godly encouragement and be a Christ-like model.

Dan Hoellwarth pastors ACTS Covenant Fellowship in Lancaster.

September 7

Check Your Heart

"Judge not, and you shall not be judged. Condemn not, and you shall not be condemned. Forgive, and you will be forgiven. Give, and it will be given to you: good measure, pressed down, shaken together, and running over will be put into your bosom. For with the same measure that you use, it will be measured back to you." *Luke 6:37–38 (New King James Version)*

Our thoughts and the words that result have great impact. By our words we are justified or condemned. They are containers of life or death. When we are tempted to judge and speak judgment, we must learn to give mercy. When we want to condemn, we must offer grace. When we have been wounded and want to retaliate, we must forgive. The measure of a life lived in the presence of Jesus is the reflection of His character in our daily lives. As we voice our thoughts in family relationships, as we witness to the sinners on the street, as we interact with the people in our churches, it is what we say that improves or destroys life. John 15 says that we must be so in Jesus that His words abide in us. A bad tree cannot produce good fruit and a good tree cannot produce bad fruit. To produce good fruit, we must abide in the vine, in His words. As we allow them to be the ready answer when we are tempted to judgment, we will have the joy He has promised in John 15. Out of the abundance of the heart the mouth speaks. What is in your heart today?

Father, we desire to obey Your word and not judge or condemn others. We ask Your forgiveness for words of death that we have spoken. Holy Spirit we invite You to remind us to speak blessing over others, to speak forgiveness over wounds, and to give of ourselves willingly to love one another. Thank You for grace to change our lives in Jesus' name!

Abigail King is pastor administrator at The Lord's House of Prayer in Lancaster.

One

September 8

Souls Saved

"He has blinded their eyes and deadened their hearts, so they can neither see
with their eyes, nor understand with their
hearts, nor turn—and I would heal them."
John 12:40

for Lancaster
County

"Jesus answered, 'I am the way and the truth and
the life. No one comes to the Father except through me.'"
John 14:6

"Finally, brothers, pray for us that the message of the Lord may
spread rapidly and be honored, just as it was with you."
2 Thessalonians 3:1

According to Scripture, a veil of unbelief covers eyes that are
blinded by sin. But as believers share Jesus as the Way, the
Truth, and the Life, that veil will be lifted. The power of the
gospel will enable those who are blinded and deadened to turn and be
healed. As we think of the potential harvest in our region, let us pray
that the message of the Lord may indeed spread rapidly and be honored.

*Lord, please use us to lift the veil from sin-blinded eyes this week. Set
up "divine appointments" for us to bring the message of salvation.
Help us listen for Your timing and* plan *our witness that Your Kingdom
may be advanced.*

Today's devotional was edited from the 2003–2004 *Throne Of Grace
Prayer Guide*, a weekly guide of Lancaster County prayer concerns
gathered from regional intercessors and area prayer groups.

September 9
Brazen Claim

"This is what the LORD says: 'Let not the wise man boast of his wisdom or the strong man boast of his strength or the rich man boast of his riches, but let him who boasts boast about this: that he understands and knows me, that I am the LORD, who exercises kindness, justice and righteousness on earth, for in these I delight,' declares the LORD." *Jeremiah 9:23-24*

I am the greatest!" reoccurs occasionally among some sporting figures! Most of us would not make such a brazen claim…or do we? We may not say we are the best, but we act as if we can handle life and its unknowns on our own! How often do we dress ourselves up in our "Sunday best" and act as if we are in control? How often do we try to convince ourselves we can handle an uncertain future?

The problem lies precisely when we try to live securely apart from God. Oh, we would never admit to that exactly. We claim to need God, but then we live without any concern or honest devotion to Him. We pray to Him, but react as if we do not know Him! We are like the fly on the earthmover, looking back and saying, "Wow, look at all the dust I can kick up!" We take credit for ourselves instead of giving credit to the Creator.

We "boast in God" when we live to honor *Him* and therefore find our security in *Him*! Have I shown the kindness, justice and righteousness that God delights in this past week? When I am under pressure, do I live to please God or to survive? Does it show in my words and actions?

Dear God, help me to see when I am trusting in myself and not in You. Forgive me for putting myself above You and help me to find my joy in who You are, rather than who I am apart from You. Amen.

John Soden is the associate professor of Bible at Lancaster Bible College.

One

September 10

Relationship: Life's #1 Priority

"Love the Lord your God with all your heart and with all your soul and with all your mind. This is the first and greatest commandment. And the second is like it: Love your neighbor as yourself." *Matthew 22:37–39*

The Son of God was asked the question, "…which is the greatest commandment…(Matthew 22:36)?" How would the Creator of the universe answer this query? How would the One who established the law as well as fulfilled it, answer such a broad question? Would Jesus hesitate; would He say they're *all* important? Without hesitation He fired back, "love God and love people"—Relationship.

Relationship was broken through the fall of man. This fall brought about curse-filled relationships. Curse-filled relationships are full of selfish desire (James 3:13–16).

Healthy relationship has some major ingredients as well. At the core of meaningful relationships are similar or shared values, unselfish love and openness. We may not enjoy all the same hobbies or music, but at our core we share similar values. Without comparison, we love unselfishly. We do not love for a return of love; we love because Jesus first loves us. We are open in communicating our lives and our shortcomings. We go beyond "small talk" to emotions, because openness draws us together and fear of rejection in relationship separates us.

Relationship is the most important thing in life. Money cannot buy it, "things" cannot keep it and distance cannot destroy it—but without it there is little purpose.

Father, I confess my need for relationship with You and those You have placed in my life. Help me to move beyond selfish desire, comparison, performance and reflection to shared values, unselfish love and openness in my relationships.

Steve and Mary Prokopchak serve on the apostolic council of D.O.V.E. Christian Fellowship International and heads D.C.F.I.'s Counseling Resources.

September 11
When Danger Comes Ashore

"Peace I leave with you; My peace I give to you; not as the world gives do I give to you. Let not your heart be troubled, nor let it be fearful." *John 14:27 (New American Standard Bible)*

The world changed on September 11, 2001. The threat of war always existed, but distance was our ally. Wars took place in foreign lands. Suddenly, the danger came ashore on American soil. And many people got scared.

What we referred to as "peace" was no longer a given. Or was it? Perhaps we did not understand or were simply failing to appropriate peace in our lives. A church proclaimed this message: "Peace is not the absence of war; true peace is the presence of God. Where does such peace come from and why so great a confidence in it? When Jesus walked the earth, He spoke of many things. Peace was one of them."

"Peace I leave with you; My peace I give to you; not as the world gives, do I give to you. Let not your heart be troubled, nor let it be fearful (John 14:27)." Notably, this verse follows Jesus' introduction of the Holy Spirit as the Helper who will come to guide the true follower of Christ. True peace then can only come from God. It is the result of obedience to Him and allowing the Holy Spirit to reign in our lives. Paul further demonstrates this in Galatians 5:22, writing that a natural by-product of walking in the Spirit is peace. Still, the world can be overwhelming, especially knowing that Christ indicated there would be tribulation here (John 16:33). We can, however, experience...turmoil, by simply applying the principles of Philippians 4:4–6: a) praise—giving When we do, peace will result, "And the peace of God, which surpasses all comprehension, shall guard your hearts and your minds in Christ Jesus (Philippians 4:7)."

Dear God, teach us Your peace that our hearts and minds may be guarded in Christ. Amen.

Brad Hoopes is the director of development at Dayspring Christian Academy and has served as a pastor here in Lancaster County.

One

September 12

Confidence

"This is the confidence we have in approaching God: that if we ask anything according to his will, he hears us. And if we know that he hears us—whatever we ask—we know that we have what we asked of him." *1 John 5:14–15*

Because of our Father's incredible love for us, He listens to us His children, and desires to make His will known to us. He longs to communicate His heart and desires to His people. He graciously waits for us to slow down, pull away, and take time in His presence. From the beginning, God so lovingly has planned and allowed us to partner with Him in accomplishing His purposes on the earth. He reveals His will and purpose to people who will in turn declare into existence what He plans to do (Amos 3:7). What an awesome privilege to come boldly before His throne of grace (Hebrews 4:16) declaring His word and will into situations. How powerful that His word never returns to Him empty, but always accomplishes His desire and achieves the purpose for which He sent it (Isaiah 55:11).

Job 22:28 says that we will decree a thing and it will be established for us. Why not declare destiny seeds over our families and salvation seeds in our workplaces? How about sowing unity seeds over our congregations and freedom seeds in our neighborhoods? As we sprinkle the seed of His word we can expect a great harvest!

Gracious Father, reveal Your heart and will to me today. May I respond to You with faith and expectancy, and pray into existence those things that You desire of me today. Grant me a childlike faith to trust You fully. In Jesus' precious name, Amen.

Bonita Keener helps lead prayer initiatives in the region and serves on the leadership team at New Life Fellowship in Ephrata.

September 13

Accepted

"... made us accepted in the Beloved." *Ephesians 1:6 (New King James Version)*

What a privileged relationship we have with God! It includes our forgiveness, justification, righteousness and acceptance before God. Acceptance means to be admitted and welcomed, like into a club as a member. God's acceptance means that we are the recipients of divine satisfaction, and even of divine delight. In Christ we are accepted by God. We are accepted "in the beloved."

Sometimes Christians feel accepted when, in our own experience, we are full of hope and expectation of a good future or a successful day. Sometimes we succumb to fear, anxiety, or temptation and conclude that we are no longer accepted. But our true acceptance is based on Christ, our way to God. If we could only see that neither the good, the bad nor the ugly determine our value in our Father's sight. We stand accepted in the One who never changes, who is always perfect and without spot or wrinkle.

My sins trouble me, but they are covered with the blood of Jesus, and I am accepted by the Righteous One. I wrestle with temptation, but I am accepted by Him who has already overcome the powers of evil. I may have bondage in my life, but I am accepted by The Deliverer who has broken every chain.

Today as we focus on our acceptance in Him, let's honor our Savior and rejoice that as a believers we are "accepted in the beloved."

Heavenly Father, thank You for choosing to accept me. Lord Jesus, thank You for the finished work of the Cross. I ask for Your help to understand the permanence of Your acceptance. I desire to remain secure in Your acceptance. I now surrender the distractions in my life that hinder me from the truth that in Christ I am totally accepted. In Jesus' name, Amen.

Nelson Martin serves on the Apostolic Council of D.O.V.E. Christian Fellowship International. He and his wife, Sue, also serve on the Elder Team of Elanco D.O.V.E. Fellowship, Terre Hill where they lead a home cell group.

September 14

A Narrow Gate

"Enter through the narrow gate. For wide is the gate and broad is the road that leads to destruction, and many enter through it. But small is the gate and narrow the road that leads to life, and only a few find it." Matthew 7:13–14

When I first became a Christian in my early twenties, I "knew" what this narrow gate was. I understood that there were many rules that defined and narrowed the gate and that I must follow them to enter that gate. The rules included the Ten Commandments but encompassed so much more. I mustn't smoke or drink. I needed to always wear dresses that were modest and frugal. I needed to give to the church, the poor, and missions. I needed to watch my language. I needed to not watch TV. I needed to work hard and not be lazy. The list could go on and on.

As I matured in my faith, I became more aware of Christian liberty. I also knew that works do not save me. Still I was troubled by the story of the rich young ruler that appears three times in the gospels. The rich young ruler didn't do something right and therefore lost the kingdom of God.

Driving down the road recently, the truth dropped into my heart. The gate *is* narrow, but Jesus is the gate. He even says so in John 10:9. I miss the gate whenever I look to anything for salvation but Jesus. When we think of the rich young ruler, we think about his refusal to sell his possessions. But the most important part of Jesus' word to the young ruler was "…then come, follow me… (Luke 18:22)."

Lord, thank You for showing me the gate. Forgive me for trying to work things out on my own. You alone are the way, the truth, and the light. I want to follow You in all I do. Amen.

Karen Boyd is a member of the Pennsylvania Homeschoolers Accreditation Agency Board and the WITF Educational Advisory Board.

September 15

Make Disciples Of All Men (And Women!)

for Lancaster County

"Therefore go and make disciples of all nations, baptizing them in the name of the Father and of the Son and of the Holy Spirit, and teaching them to obey everything I have commanded you...." *Matthew 28: 19–20*

"Then we will no longer be infants, tossed back and forth by the waves, and blown here and there by every wind of teaching and by the cunning and craftiness of men in their deceitful scheming. Instead, speaking the truth in love, we will in all things grow up into him who is the Head, that is, Christ." *Ephesians 4:14–15*

The "Great Commission" not only calls us to bring salvation to the lost, but to teach new converts how to grow and mature in Christ. There is a great need for godly men and women to be raised up to train those who are younger in the faith how to obey His commands. May we in our region be the kind of disciples who reproduce reproducers for the glory of the Kingdom.

Lord, help me encourage younger believers in their relationship with You. May I be willing to walk alongside them in their spiritual journey and train them in the things You have taught me.

Today's devotional was edited from the 2003–2004 *Throne Of Grace Prayer Guide*, a weekly guide of Lancaster County prayer concerns gathered from regional intercessors and area prayer groups.

One

September 16

Unanswered Prayers

"… The Lord is my portion; therefore I will wait for him."
Lamentations 3:24

Have you been praying for something for years without seeing an answer? Are you wondering when breakthrough will come? Earlier in Lamentations 3, the author of reflects, "Even when I call out or cry for help, he shuts out my prayer. He has barred my way with blocks of stone… My splendor is gone and all that I had hoped from the Lord (Lamentations 3:8-9, 18)." In the natural, things looked hopeless. Answers eluded him. Yet, in the midst of brokenness, despair, and unanswered prayers, he began to offer a sacrifice of worship to God. Finally he could say, "The Lord is my portion; therefore I will wait for him. (Lamentations 3:24)"

God wants to draw us into a singleness of hope and passion where HE HIMSELF is our portion—not the things we get from him. Times of waiting for answers to prayer have a way of refining us and stripping away everything else until all that remains is to put our hope in God alone. (Psalm 39:7)

Entering that depth of intimacy with God, where He Himself is our portion, can be an excruciatingly painful process. Many times we are quick to echo Paul's words, "I want to know Christ and the power of his resurrection," but are not as enthused about finishing that verse: "…and the fellowship of sharing in His sufferings, becoming like Him in His death…(Philippians 3:10)." We want answers, promises, and resurrection power, but forget that death always precedes resurrection. Unanswered prayers can be the "crucifixion" that God allows to bring us to that place of knowing Him alone as our portion.

God, I don't understand why some prayers go unanswered, but I choose to offer a sacrifice of worship. Form within me that singleness of hope and passion where You alone are my portion. In Jesus' name. Amen.

Dwane Reitz is the prayer coordinator at Global Disciples in Lancaster, serves as an elder at Petra Christian Fellowship, New Holland.

September 17
Christ's Ambassadors
"… And he has committed to us the message of reconciliation.
We are therefore Christ's ambassadors…"
2 Corinthians 5:19-20

What is an ambassador? Webster defines it as "an authorized representative of his government for a special diplomatic assignment." So we are authorized by God for a specific assignment and that assignment is one of reconciling people back to God. Wow! Now that's a special assignment!

Second Corinthians 5:14 points out the ingredient for the motivation for this assignment. Christ's love compels us—I say again, Christ's love compels us! We need to internalize that.

What has Christ done for me? Having grown up in an unchurched home and having been involved in many immoral and destructive, fleshly behaviors, God's deliverance was a very welcome work. But we do not have to experience deliverance from this kind of bondage to know that Christ loves us. A key verse is Luke 7:47. Those who are forgiven much love much. From what have you been forgiven? Romans 3:23 clearly states that all have sinned and have fallen short. Recognizing our sin is very important to experiencing God's full forgiveness, and it sets us free for Christ's love to compel us to be His ambassadors. 2 Corinthians 5:18–20 gives us the blueprint.

For the past 15 years, I've worked with unchurched youth. I realized very early in this ministry that judging people's sin WOULD NOT draw them to God. If we want to be authorized for this special assignment, we must do it God's way. God's way was not counting men's sin against them (verse 19). I believe if we are to reach men and women, we must love the person regardless of their choices and life-style and hate the sin. This is what God has committed to us, and He is making His appeal through us.

Lord Jesus, give me the grace to be Your ambassador, to love as You loved and to not judge by outward appearance or sinfulness.

Bruce Fasnacht is the director of The Bridge Youth Center in Ephrata.

September 18

Wash My Feet

"No," said Peter, "you shall never wash my feet." Jesus answered, "Unless I wash you, you have no part with me."
John 13:8

L ike many traditions, we worship the Lord with a foot-washing service. It is not as hard to wash feet as it is to let your feet be washed. One year, I wrote this poem:

I said to many men, "May I serve you?"

But to a man, who because of pride is my adversary,

I would say, "Will you be served by me?"

I have asked the man to let me be the one in control and power.

Jesus stops by me.

I AM says to me, "Will you be served by me?"

I say "No."

He says: "Then you may have no part in me."

Thinking I have Jesus' point,

I turn to this man and say: "I will be served by you."

But Jesus just patiently looks at me with love.

Eventually, I say to the man: "You may serve me."

I realize that being in genuine community with other believers forces us to let others serve us in many ways. We live in community as Christians, and we are all one. Someday, persecution may happen; if it does, we will not ask each other specific questions about our traditions. No, we will hold each other's hands and face the wall together.

Lord God, today, teach me the humility I need to realize that I am not self-sufficient. I need You, and I need other believers around me who can pray, help and bless me.

Phil Reynolds is the pastor of the Mohler Church of the Brethren in Ephrata. His passion is evangelism and justice

Stand In The Gap

"I am appealing to you for my child, Onesimus, whose father I have become during my imprisonment...I am sending him back to you, sending my very heart...Perhaps that is why he was parted from you for a while, that you might have him back forever, no longer as a slave but more than a slave, as a beloved brother...both in the flesh and in the Lord."
Philemon 10,12,15–16 (Revised Standard Version)

When Abraham Lincoln worked as an attorney, a wealthy client once insisted on suing a poor man who owed him two dollars and fifty cents. Lincoln tried to discourage him, but the man was adamant. So Lincoln agreed to represent him for a legal fee of ten dollars. After Lincoln received the money, he promptly gave five dollars to the poor man, who willingly confessed and paid the two fifty he owed! Restitution was made through a third party.

Paul passionately appeals to Philemon: "Don't only receive Onesimus as a brother—also free him from slavery!" Paul loves Onesimus and wants his friend to stay. But Onesimus must be returned to Philemon. Paul reminds Philemon of his apostolic authority—while refusing to use that authority to command Philemon like a slave. Likewise, Paul implies, Philemon should think carefully before he issues commands to the slave who has become his brother.

Like Paul, Philemon and Onesimus, we Christians are bound together in chains of love. But living in love's reality will require a radical change in us. It will require us to embrace all Christians as our brothers and sisters, and to become Christ's slaves, serving the least of these.

Lord Jesus give me courage and love to be a third party who stands in the gap, bringing reconciliation to broken relationships. May my relationship with You change every relationship in my life today. Amen.

Jo Ann Kunz serves as senior pastor at Hosanna Christian Fellowship, a non-denominational church in Lititz. She is also a spiritual director and staff member at Oasis Ministries, Camp Hill.

September 20

Living Stones

"You also, like living stones, are being built into a spiritual
house…" *1 Peter 2:5*

Today almost everyone in our country is affiliated with a church,
a synagogue, a mosque or some other form of worship. Coming
together on Saturday or Sunday, people will show up and give
"praise" to their God only to return home to their weekly routine. If the
appearance of all worship seems the same, what separates the born
again Christian from other religions?

The answer can be found in 1 Peter 2:2–7. As stones, we are called
to be cemented together into a spiritual house. This means that we are
stones with a purpose chosen by God. In Acts 5:12–16 the early Christians, the foundation of the spiritual temple, met in Solomon's portico,
part of the Jewish temple. Since the foundation of the new temple was
laid through Jesus and the apostles, God saw fit to allow the Romans to
destroy the Jewish temple in 70 AD (Matthew 24:1–2). Now God wants
to establish his glory in *us*. But if we choose to become stones on heaps
of rubbish (Nehemiah 4:2–3) how can God fulfill His purpose?

It is not enough to go to church if we allow the rubbish of our sins
to separate us from the true fellowship. If we allow disunity and sin to
come between us we are only fulfilling the desire of the Tobiahs of the
world (Nehemiah 13:8). It is through our unity of worship that God's
glory will be revealed. This can only be done through living stones,
stones cemented together to create a spiritual house for God's glory to
fill. The question that you will have to ask yourself is: "Do I just go to
church or am I going to be part of God's new temple?" Also ask yourself this question: "Am I a stone properly placed in the temple or am I
a rock by the roadside?"

Lord, make us living stones cemented together with a purpose.

Bill Willis is a layman at New Covenant Christian Church.

September 21

The Suddenlies Of God

"And suddenly there came from heaven a noise like a violent rushing wind, and it filled the whole house where they were sitting." *Acts 2:2 (American Standard Bible)*

Pentecost was an occurrence that I call a "suddenly of God". A "suddenly" is a moment when God surprisingly breaks into time and space with an intervention of the Kingdom. The Greek word translated "suddenly" here means "without warning or unforeseen". It was used for the suddenness of a lightening bolt. Pentecost was a spiritual explosion – like a flash from heaven. Repeatedly in the Bible and throughout church history God has intervened with suddenlies.

While our lives are not a constant stream of suddenlies, neither are our lives filled with only natural events. God still steps into our lives and suddenly changes. Notice that although this was suddenly given by God, the believers were waiting for Him with "one accord" prayer.

There are other "suddenlies" in the Bible that changed the course of earthly events. In Acts 12:7 "an angel of the Lord suddenly appeared" to Peter while he was in prison. This suddenly was preceded by prayer, as the church prayed for his release. In Acts 16:25 "about midnight Paul and Silas were praying and singing hymns of praise to God… and suddenly there came a great earthquake." This suddenly was preceded by prayer and praise. Praise is a weapon that will bring God into any situation.

Sometimes God sends a suddenly into our lives to get our attention like He did when He struck Saul on the road to Damascus in Acts 22. These are a few extraordinary suddenlies, but we have many small ones which are also interventions of God into our lives. Look for God to intervene suddenly today and over the next few weeks. Pray and expect God to show up in situations you encounter.

Father I expect You to intervene suddenly in my life, and I ask You to give me eyes to see You at work.

Barry Wissler is the senior pastor of Ephrata Community Church and leads HarvestNet, a resource ministry linking churches and ministries as partners in Harvest.

September 22

Community Transformation

"If my people, who are called by my name, will humble themselves and pray and seek my face and turn from their wicked ways, then will I hear from heaven and will forgive their sin and will heal their land." *2 Chronicles 7:14*

Pray! for Lancaster County

"I urge, then, first of all, that requests, prayers, intercession and thanksgiving be made for everyone....This is good, and pleases God our Savior, who wants all men to be saved and to come to a knowledge of the truth." *1 Timothy 2:1–4*

In both the Old Testament and the New we find a call on the people of God to intercede for their land. We are the salt and the light of our community. It is through our prayers that God moves to bring spiritual and social transformation. The Church is the one appointed to pray for more conversions, for increase in congregations, and deepened commitments to Christ. The Church is to intercede for a decline in crime rates, divorce rates, domestic violence, racism and poverty. Let us today be about the work assigned to us; let us humble ourselves and pray.

Father, thank You for the transformation of Lancaster County. May we find increased favor in our community as You forgive our sin and heal our land.

Today's devotional was edited from the 2003–2004 *Throne Of Grace Prayer Guide*, a weekly guide of Lancaster County prayer concerns gathered from regional intercessors and area prayer groups.

September 23

Past The Surface

"…The Lord does not look at the things man looks at. Man looks at the outward appearance, but the LORD looks at the heart." 1 Samuel 16:7

It is a characteristic of God to have the ability to look past the outward appearance of a person, whether it be impressive or offensive, and look directly into their heart. That characteristic was later manifested in the life of Jesus Christ. Jesus could look past those things that others found offensive—leprosy, sickness, being a social outcast, even the sinful reputation of someone like Matthew—and look directly into the heart and know the "key" to bringing those persons into a relationship with God.

In the same way, Jesus was not impressed by the trappings of this world and was therefore not influenced by a person's wealth or social stature. Jesus looked past the impressive clothing and entourage of those such as the rich young ruler in Luke 18, and the social status of the Pharisees and Sadducees, look directly at the heart.

We can all recognize that it is our human tendency to look at a person's outward appearance. Their social status, cultural differences and life-style can often become a barrier that prevents us from ministering to the true needs of the heart. The good news is that God desires to form His character in us, including the ability to look past the outward appearance of people and see the heart.

Dear Lord, enable me to see people as You see them. I thank You for Your perfect example of looking past the outward appearance of those You encountered, so that You could truly minister to their hearts. Lord, I want to be like You. Develop this characteristic in me, that I might see people as You do. In Christ, Amen.

Kevin Eshleman is the executive pastor of Ephrata Community Church and serves Lancaster County through the ministry of the Lancaster Youth Network of Churches.

September 24

The Word Of Testimony

"Therefore, King Agrippa, I was not disobedient to the heavenly vision, but declared ... that they should repent, turn to God, and do works befitting repentance. For these reasons the Jews seized me in the temple and tried to kill me." *Acts 26:19-21 (New King James Version)*

Paul was preaching the Good News everywhere and this upset the Jewish leaders. So Paul was brought before King Agrippa regarding the accusations against him. Rather than preaching, he shared his personal testimony, hoping his listeners would respond. Our testimony carries enormous power in opening a way for us to speak to those who initially oppose us. Another incident in scripture is in John 9, when Jesus healed the blind man on the Sabbath. This put the Pharisees in an uproar and they questioned him and his parents. After they questioned him over and over again, he said something like, "Look, all I know is, I was blind, and now I see."

The religious rulers did not want to recognize that Jesus was sent from God. Today we also have those who choose not to believe in Jesus. We live in a society that often contradicts Christian values. They have been blinded and their eyes need to be opened to the truth of Jesus Christ. Many times our testimony will catch their attention. People can dispute what we believe, but when they hear what Jesus has done in our lives, they cannot deny it. Revelation 12:11 says, "and they overcame him by the blood of the lamb, and the word of their testimony." Let's see ourselves empowered to share Christ, to be bold and take every opportunity to share the good news of Jesus.

Father in Jesus' name, I come to You. I desire to take a hold of every opportunity you put before me to share Your love and salvation. I thank You that I am an able minister of reconciliation.

Sam Smucker is the senior pastor of The Worship Center and serves on the Executive Team of the Regional Church of Lancaster County.

September 25

Bringing In The Harvest

"Do you not say, 'Four months more and then the harvest'? I tell you, open your eyes and look at the fields! They are ripe for harvest." *John 4:35*

Recently a brother was scheduled to meet with me about a matter. As the time drew nearer, I received an email from him saying that he could not meet because he needed to get his corn crop in before the rains came. As I pondered that matter, the Lord brought several ideas to my mind.

My friend was intense about getting the crop in, since that was his responsibility. If he did not get the crop in, he would lose God's gift. He had tilled the ground, he had planted the seed. God had watered the crop, made it grow, and now it was the time to reap the harvest. Jesus said "the harvest is ripe, now".

The other thing that came to me was my friend was *going after* the crop. The harvest was not coming into the barn on its own for him to arrange after it arrived. He was going out after the crop.

My final thought was that my friend knew exactly what to do to get his crop. Many say, "I do not know what to say or what to do to gather in the crop." My friend knew what to do and how to do it. He could have stayed in the barn and prayed that it would come in on its own or that someone else would bring it in. My friend realized his personal responsibility.

If the crop was not brought in now, it would perish and be lost. He would need to wait for another year and hope for another time and another crop.

Father, please give me and the church of today the intensity and desire to bring in the harvest ASAP. Please help me realize my responsibility in bringing in the "crop".

Dick Landis is the pastor of Living Hope Community Church.

September 26

Possessing His Peace

"Thou dost keep him in perfect peace, whose mind is stayed on thee, because he trusts on thee." *Isaiah 26:3 (Revised Standard Version)*

It is often difficult to possess peace of mind especially when facing difficulties which have an uncertain end. We want to experience peace in the midst of problems, but all too often it seems to escape us. One means of coping is telling ourselves that "everything will be okay once this current crisis is over and things return to normal." This way of thinking may bring temporary comfort, yet result in future disappointments and rob us of the very peace that God desires for us to experience. Life is filled with unexpected twists and turns, and to think that peace is experienced only when we aren't faced with challenges is shortsighted. The Lord's desire is not that we just cope; He makes it possible for us to experience peace—a lasting, perfect peace no matter what comes our way.

Perfect peace comes as we center our thoughts upon Him who is the Prince of Prince, whose Kingdom is filled with peace, who promises to keep in perfect peace all whose thoughts are focused upon Him. Train your mind in whatever you are facing to concentrate upon who He is and ask that His peace reign in your entire being—body, mind, soul and spirit.

Isaiah 26:3 in the New Living Translation says, "You will keep in perfect peace all who trust in You, whose thoughts are *fixed* on You." Don't delay in possessing for yourself the deep peace of God which is perfect no matter the severity or extent of the storm you face.

Lord, please help me to keep my thoughts fixed upon You and live my life today fully aware of Your sovereignty and awesome power. Whatever challenge I am facing will pass, but Your love, grace and peace are forever constant. Peace is mine today and everyday because of You.

Reyna Britton, RN, is the quality standards coordinator for Lancaster General Hospital and is the wife of Duane Britton, senior pastor of D.O.V.E. Christian Fellowship Westgate Celebration.

A Full-Bore Attack

"We demolish arguments and every pretension that sets itself up against the knowledge of God, and we take captive every thought to make it obedient to Christ." *2 Corinthians 10:5*

D o wandering minds ever end up in good places? Our culture saturates our minds with lust-inducing temptation and horror-filled images that some call entertainment. But we're also bombarded by more subtle messages that seep in to encourage an "I deserve it" mentality or thoughts that would define dependency on God as being weak. Worse yet are thoughts that stem from the Enemy: they may start as tiny seeds, but can fully blossom into paralyzing (and typically unfounded) fear, recurring shame from things that have been confessed and fully covered by Christ's mercy, or untrue "justification" for holding onto unforgiveness.

Are we too willing to simply pray for God's help with our thoughts...and then go right on thinking them? Paul exhorts the Corinthians to "take every thought captive." That won't be accomplished with a dainty approach—it's a war!

The brain is a muscle that needs conditioning and regular flexing. When our strengthening is fueled by the Holy Spirit's power, thoughts can be taken captive and permanently held at bay. Be ruthless in dealing with ungodly thoughts —quickly recognize them for what they are, pray for the Spirit's help, and forcefully replace the thoughts with God-honoring images or Scriptures that counter them. Fight! Strike back! A passive approach will not lead to victory. Only a full-bore attack will take—and hold—them captive. "The mind of sinful man is death, but the mind controlled by the Spirit is life and peace (Romans 8:6)."

Holy Spirit, give us Your insight to recognize all types of ungodly thoughts. Strengthen us as we war against thoughts that would drive us away from Christ. And give us the power to condition our minds for the ongoing battle.

Diane Moore, a Lancaster United for Life board member, is active in politics, and plays keyboard for the music ministry at New Covenant Christian Church.

September 28

Called To Reconcile

"Therefore, if you are offering your gift at the altar and there remember that your brother has something against you, leave your gift there in front of the altar. First go and be reconciled to your brother; then come and offer your gift." *Matthew 5:23,24*

God is very interested in the quality of our relationships with other believers. Knowing an offended believer will more easily withdraw, he calls the offender to reconcile. If we have offended, we are to bring healing. Jesus didn't limit the scope of this command to one local church or denomination. It applies to the entire body of Christ. In this context, who is my offended brother? Is he Amish? Is he charismatic? Fundamentalist? Methodist or Presbyterian? Catholic or Mennonite? Assemblies of God? We tend to worship with those of like doctrine and passion, forgetting that Jesus has "broken down the dividing wall" between all Christians (Ephesians 2:14). We agree with other groups who share our faith but we aren't necessarily interested in developing unity beyond those with whom we are comfortable.

We are called to reach out. Have we dismissed certain groups as too conservative, too radical, worldly, dead, formal? Have we offended other groups by ignoring them or judging them? What if we began a process of healing through changing our minds (the real meaning of reconciliation) about another denomination? What if we purposed to fellowship with those who are "offended", in a manner that honors their heritage? What if we began to pray together, eat together, worship together? I suspect if we did, we would win our brother's heart. And afterwards, our gift at the altar would be one of the best presents we have ever offered our Father.

God, give us a heart to reach out to others in Your body across this region. Make us reconcilers where we have offended and replace our arrogance and fear with Your love. Thank you, Jesus.

Janet Richards, author, intercessor, actor, is currently called to regional intercession and to reconciliation of the Anabaptists with the Swiss Reformed church.

September 29

Who's Your Daddy?

"But as many as received Him, to them He gave the right to become children of God, to those who believe in His name."
John 1:12 (New King James Version)

At a local hardware store an elderly gentleman said "I should know you; who's your daddy?" After I told him, he said, "You look just like your dad." People have often thought that I was my dad, calling me by his name. In a similar way, since we are children of God, we will reveal His nature and image. I think it's fascinating to watch children imitating their parents. We should imitate our Father, God. Ephesians 5:1 tells us, *"Therefore be imitators of God, as beloved children."*

The way to live the life that Jesus lived is spending time with the Father. When I was a child, I got to go places with my dad where I couldn't have gone on my own. Well, Christian, you can also go places with God, your Father, where you couldn't go on your own. When I was with my dad I felt "big" and confident. You, too, can go forward with confidence, approaching life with God right there with you.

When I answered the telephone, people would often say "You sound right like your dad." As Christians, our words should reflect God's voice. God's words reveal God himself and we should sound like Him. We deeply need to experience God as Father. I believe that the key to knowing God is for us to understand His Father's heart. J.I. Packer, a prominent theologian, says that the best judge of a person's Christianity is their understanding of God as their Father. It's important!

I am thankful that I am Your child. I want to really know Your Father's heart and experience the impartation of Your nature. Fill me with Your presence and conform me into Your image so that I represent well as your son or daughter.

Barry Wissler is the senior pastor of Ephrata Community Church and leads HarvestNet, a resource ministry linking churches and ministries as partners in Harvest.

September 30

Second Chance God

"Then the word of the Lord came to Jonah a second time..."
Jonah 3:1

A s one prone to sin each day, I am grateful that God is not a "three strikes and you're out" kind of God. I would have been disqualified from the team long ago if that were the case. Instead, our Creator is a God of grace and compassion; slow to anger and rich in love (Psalm 145:8).

This truth must have comforted Jonah, the runaway prophet. God commissioned him to preach against the Ninevites' sin. Fearing these violent and oppressive enemies, Jonah sought to flee the call of God upon his life by running the other way. In the process, he was disobedient and rebellious, fell deeper in to sin, and soon placed other people in harm's way. Eventually he found himself in a pit of deep despair-inside the belly of a great fish-pondering his foolishness. God rescued him, and He recommissioned Jonah to go and preach to Nineveh. The results this time were astounding!

How often have I missed a blessing in my life because I was not obedient when God's call on my life was evident? How often have I failed to appreciate that God didn't let me wallow in my sin, but restored me to a right relationship with Him? Our God is a God of the second chance. He wants us to succeed! We should never allow ourselves to feel that any sin is so great that He will not take us back and allow us to try again.

Dear God, thank You that Your anger burns slowly while Your grace and mercy are available moment by moment. Guard my life against foolish living and let not my sinful ways lead me into pits of despair. Restore me. Help me to be all that You desire so that You may be glorified and the world will hear of Your saving love. Amen.

Brad Hoopes is the director of development at Dayspring Christian Academy and has served as a pastor here in Lancaster County.

October

Supporting families in Lancaster County

October 1

Obedience

"Does the Lord delight in burnt offerings and sacrifices as much as in obeying the voice of the Lord? To obey is better than sacrifice, and to heed is better than the fat of rams." *1 Samuel 15:22*

for Lancaster County

"Why do you call me, 'Lord, Lord,' and do not do what I say? I will show you what he is like who comes to me and hears my words and puts them into practice. He is like a man building a house, who dug down deep and laid the foundation on rock. When a flood came, the torrent struck that house but could not shake it, because it was well built." *Luke 6:46–48*

Living a life of full obedience means hearing the words of God and *putting them into practice.* No matter how hard we may try to circumvent with sacrifices of our own making, nothing takes the place of obedience. Failing to obey His voice, as the Scripture points out, is like building without a foundation. Only works done in obedience will be able to withstand the torrents of life. May we individually and collectively seek to hear God's will and put it into practice.

Jesus, let me not be as those who call you 'Lord' but don't do what You say. Speak to me today, and help me obey every word.

Today's devotional was edited from the 2003–2004 *Throne Of Grace Prayer Guide*, a weekly guide of Lancaster County prayer concerns gathered from regional intercessors and area prayer groups.

October 2

Quotas Or Relationships

"For I tell you that unless your righteousness surpasses that of the Pharisees and the teachers of the law, you will certainly not enter the kingdom of heaven." *Matthew 5:20*

During the year 2000, my wife and I served as missionaries in Rome, Italy. Part of our assignment was to help visiting teams from American churches learn how to evangelize in a foreign culture. We quickly discovered that before they left the States, many of these teams had asked the Lord for a certain number of souls to be saved. They had unconsciously developed "quotas" for the people they wanted to convert.

We watched with dismay as most of their attempts to convert people ended in frustration. What may have worked in America was often unsuccessful in Italy. They could recite the four spiritual laws and explain the plan of salvation, but it was often with a view toward eliciting a predetermined response rather than establishing a genuine person to person relationship. This left many Europeans with the feeling that they were being sold something. The quota of saving souls had become more important than the person to whom salvation was being offered.

I often reflect on this when I try to share my faith: am I really interested in the one who is before me, or am I just trying to fulfill some perceived religious duty? I think back to my own turning point. Jesus didn't have a program to sell: He freely gave what was truly needed. He spoke the Truth. He loved me. And when He touched my heart, I said "Yes!"

Lord, thank You for eternal life and for the joy of being Your child. Please give me a heart like Yours that can truly love another. Amen.

Rusty Richards is a regional worship leader and intercessor and is involved in Anabaptist Reconciliation initiatives. He and his wife Janet live in Ronks and attend Petra Christian Fellowship in New Holland.

October 3

My Father's House

"'Why were you searching for me?' he asked. 'Didn't you know I had to be in my Father's house?'" *Luke 2:49*

This one statement from Jesus shows the depth of understanding he had of the very essence and purpose of his life. As a 12-year-old boy, Jesus understood that his life was inextricably bound to that of his Father's, and where his Father was, that was where he had to be. Jesus did not need to be at his family's house, he had to be at his Father's house.

The significance of the word translated as "had" can be easily overlooked. The word in the Greek language carries with it the idea of intense need, absolute necessity, of that which is compelled. Jesus was saying that he had an intense inward need to be where his Father was.

This type of intense inward need is elsewhere expressed by the Psalmist who wrote, "How lovely is your dwelling place, O LORD Almighty, my soul yearns, even faints for the courts of the LORD… Psalm 84:1–2."

Why this intense longing? Why this need? The answer is found in Psalm 36:7–9, where David says, "How priceless is Your unfailing love! Both high and low among men find refuge in the shadow of Your wings. They feast on the abundance of Your house; You give them drink from Your river of delights, for with You is the fountain of life; in Your light we see light."

Only where the Father is can one find unfailing love, perfect refuge, endless provisions and delights and the fountain of life itself! Is it any wonder that Jesus knew he needed to be with his Father?

Lord, in You is found all that satisfies, all that refreshes, all that gives life. Lord, let all other objects and relationships take second place to You. I need You more than anyone or anything else. Lord, hear the cry of my heart!

Brett R. Miller is a guidance counselor at Warwick Middle School and serve with his wife Jennifer on the worship team of New Covenant Christian Church.

October 4

Covenant People

"'The remnant that are left of the captivity…are in great affliction and reproach; the wall of Jerusalem also is broken down,
and the gates thereof are burned with fire.'…I sat down and
wept, and mourned certain days and fasted, and prayed before
the God of heaven." *Nehemiah 1:3–4 (King James Version)*

Nehemiah saw the devastation of his people and decided to do
something about it. As a cupbearer to the king, he heard of
great affliction and reproach among his people and the condition of the wall of Jerusalem. He was so sad and moved with compassion that it compelled him to fasting and prayer. Here was a nation of
people that God had made a covenant with, who were set apart to be
above all other nations. They had been abundantly blessed and now
they were in a state of reproach, of shame. They did not follow God's
commandments and were defeated in battle. Nehemiah sought God for
a solution and God showed him what to do.

The body of Christ today has been given this same covenant of
blessings and victory. I want to be like Nehemiah, moved with compassion and mercy. Those in captivity, reproach, or shame need to receive God's covenant. We have been set apart for this time, for this
community, for our area of influence. We have the answer and the ability and power of the Holy Spirit in us. God will give us solutions to
meet every need. Let's be driven to seek God like Nehemiah, to be
moved by compassion and bring reconciliation, restoration and healing to broken lives.

*Father, In Jesus' name, I thank You that You have given me the ability
to minister to those You are sending me. I thank You for Your compassion and mercy as I minister to those You have placed in my area of
influence.*

Sam Smucker is the senior pastor of The Worship Center and serves
on the executive team of the Regional Church of Lancaster County.

October 5
Too Difficult?

"Is anything too hard for the Lord?" Genesis 18:14

For Sarah, the suggestion that she would have a child seemed so ridiculous that she laughed. The Lord then asked Sarah a question, "Is anything too hard for the Lord?"

How often do we laugh at God? The Lord rarely gives us simple things to do. To the Lord they may be simple, but to our own natural perspective and outlook, they appear difficult and impossible. I laugh and then miss God's opportunities in my life. I get what I look for. When I look for only the simple, I miss the opportunities to partner with God in His work.

During a recent time of worship we were singing, "Try me now and see. See if I can be completely yours." And God said, "Do you realize what you just sang?"

I responded, "Shh! Not so loud God! This is church. I am worshiping You."

God asked, "Do you really want me to try you to see if you can be completely Mine?"

And I replied, "Sure God—as long as it's not too difficult."

And God said, "How quickly you forget! Stop making your decisions based on whether it is difficult—whether you can do it. Remember, nothing, absolutely nothing is too difficult for me! There are times in life when the road ahead feels way too difficult. It is those times when God says, "That's exactly where I want you. If it weren't too difficult, you would run ahead of Me and try to do it on your own. But always remember, nothing is too hard for the Lord!"

Dear Lord, replace my fears and anxieties with Your love and peace. Give me eyes to see what You are doing today. Give me courage to join You in Your work today even if it seems risky and uncomfortable. For Your glory and honor! Amen.

Ron Zook serves as the pastor of New Holland Mennonite Church.

Who Am I?

"Then God said 'Let Us make man in Our own image, according to Our likeness; and let them rule over the fish of the sea and the birds of the sky and over the cattle and over all the earth, and over every creeping thing that creeps on the earth.' God created man in His own image, in the image of God He created him; male and female He created them ."
Genesis 1:26–27 (New American Standard Bible)

Day to day life can make it difficult to remember who I am and what I am to be doing. The world, my flesh, and the children of men have distorted views of who I am supposed to be. If I listen to those demands too seriously, I forget that I have been made in His image. I forget that He sent His Image, His Son, for me to know, love, and serve while I live and move and have my being. When I remember His love for me, and seek Him in His word by His Spirit and prayer, I am renewed in the image of His love. Then I am again free to be about my Father's business: the doing of His will! I can be just like our Older Brother who did His will and has gone before us.

Lord Jesus, I thank You for creating and redeeming me to be like You, so that I can serve You and others as a priest in Your kingdom.

Robert M. Howse Jr., MD. trains family physicians at Penn State University Good Samaritan Hospital Family and Community Residency Program. He resides in Lititz.

October 7

Subtle Intruders

"Now a man named Ananias, together with his wife Sapphira, also sold a piece of property. With his wife's full knowledge he kept back part of the money for himself, but brought the rest and put it at the apostles' feet." Acts 5:1–2

Suppose when you get home this evening an intruder meets you. What will you do? Will you lash out in anger, will you flee the scene and call 911, or will you reach out saying, "Welcome to my home"? I hope it will not be the latter. You know, we Christians are not always as wise. We allow subtle intruders, like sin, into our lives and often welcome them.

In Acts 5 we see that sin intruded into the home of Ananias and Sapphira and they opened the door and welcomed it. The rest of the story, though sad, is no surprise. Peter asked, "What made you think of doing such a thing? You have not lied to man, but to God. When Ananias heard this, he fell down and died."

A little later Peter questioned Sapphira. "Tell me, is this the price you and Ananias got for the land"? "Yes," she said, "that is the price." Peter said to her, "How could you agree to test the Spirit of the Lord? Look! The feet of the men who buried your husband are at the door, and they will carry you out also." Ananias and Sapphira both died at the hands of the same intruder.

Has some sin recently intruded your life? If so, let me advise you to get rid of it before it gets rid of you.

Dear Father, help me to take a strong stand against those sinful thoughts, attitudes and habits that would try to intrude into my life and destroy my relationship with You.

Bob Kern is the associate pastor at Grace Brethren Church at Willow Valley and chaplain at Willow Valley Conference and Resort Center. Heard regularly on Christian Radio Station WDAC with "Bits of Truth".

October 8

Lancaster City:
Our County Seat

Pray!

for Lancaster
County

"All the believers were together and had
everything in common." *Acts 2:44*

In the Church, there should be no barriers between brothers and sisters. Sadly, we are sometimes guilty of stereotyping one another and perpetuating divisions due to different life-styles. Today, we want to confess any such mindsets that might hinder our unity. May those who live in the County tear down any stereotypes they might have of those living in the City. And may those in the City tear down any stereotypes they might have of those living in the County. As we allow the Holy Spirit to unearth any hidden prejudices and accept those different from ourselves, we will tap into the richest blessings of our Father.

Father God, as we confess our weaknesses regarding how we view those different from ourselves, forgive us. We who are in the County pray a blessing on those in the City. We in the City pray a blessing on those in the County. We ask that You would truly make us one, and that the world would know You because of us.

Today's devotional was edited from the 2003–2004 *Throne Of Grace Prayer Guide*, a weekly guide of Lancaster County prayer concerns gathered from regional intercessors and area prayer groups.

October 9

A Spiritual "Foreigner"

"So Boaz said to Ruth, 'My daughter, listen to me. Don't go
and glean in another field and don't go away from here. Stay
here with my servant girls. I have told the men not to touch
you. And whenever you are thirsty, go and get a drink from the
water jars.'" *Ruth 2:8–9*

You probably know Ruth well. She was the Moabitess "foreigner" who left her own people, turned from their gods, and followed her mother-in-law, Naomi. Boaz is the Israelite "kinsman-redeemer" who eventually married Ruth.

Some of us can identify with Ruth as a loyal follower. We have also left all to follow Christ: we chose the unpopular way and left friends and family who aren't interested in our faith. Sometimes we feel like a spiritual "foreigner", pursuing God when others won't.

Like Boaz, God responds to those who have left all with, *"don't go away from here. Stay here glean in my fields."* Boaz had heard about Ruth's loyalty. Like Boaz, God's heart is richly blessed by our loyalty to Him. He responds with a promise to protect and defend us, just as Boaz promised protection to Ruth. God gives us Living Water, just as Boaz invited Ruth to drink water whenever she was thirsty. God is so very pleased that we have chosen Him. Yes, He chose us first, but we have responded and His heart is enraptured with our devotion.

As Boaz said to Ruth, Jesus says to us, "I will repay you. I will richly reward you: I, the God of Israel, under whose wings you have come to take refuge (Ruth 2:12)." Our Kinsman-Redeemer loves us deeply, and delights that we have followed Him.

Thank You, God, for loving me. Thank You that I am the "apple of Your eye (Psalm 17:8)." Draw me to Yourself more and more, and let me love You with my whole heart. Amen.

Janet Richards, author, intercessor, actor, is currently called to regional intercession and reconciliation work. She is married to Rusty Richards and lives in Ronks.

October 10

Christopher Columbus' Birthday

"Therefore go and make disciples of all nations, baptizing them in the name of the Father and of the Son and of the Holy Spirit, and teaching them to obey everything I have commanded you..." *Matthew 28:19,20*

Christopher Columbus, Christ-Bearer, would carry Christ across the sea to peoples who had never heard of Christ. Columbus's heart cry was to take the gospel to lands that never heard the gospel of Christ. " The fact that the gospel must still be preached to so many lands in such a short time, this is what convinces me. It was the Lord who put it into my mind, I could feel His hand upon me, the fact that it was possible to sail to the Indies...For the execution of the journey to the Indies I did not make use of intelligence, mathematics or maps... no one should fear to undertake any task in the name of our Savior. It is simply the fulfillment of what Isaiah had prophesied."

Do our lives reflect the Christ-Bearer heart with in us that cries out for the lost? Are you willing to allow the Holy Spirit to impart to you the same love for the lost as our Lord Jesus?

Father, forgive me of not loving those who do not know You, soften my heart for the lost, and love them as You do. Open my eyes to see those around me who know do not know You, incline my ears to hear what You are saying about the lost. For Your house Lord Jesus. Amen.

Jeff Burkholder is chairman of the Board of Supervisors, Elizabeth Township.

October 11

Secret Place

"I will not give sleep to my eyes or slumber to my eyelids, until I find a place for the Lord, a dwelling place for the Mighty One of Jacob." *Psalm 132:4,5 (New King James Version)*

In our desperate search for the Lord, we have learned that there is a "Secret Place" where we can meet Him face to face. There is such a place for each stage of our spiritual journey that we need to build for Him.

There is no "pre-packaged" place for His presence; we have to build that "Secret Place" so that we can begin the intimate journey that our hearts cry out for.

First, we need to gather the materials for the building. The blue print is developed out of desire, love for His presence, and a willingness to search for intimacy. The foundation itself is built from worship, which creates a strong and solid base for intimacy. The building materials for the "Secret Place" are a pure heart, repentance, testing of our faith, humility, and the Corner Stone who determines where the walls will be built.

We are workmen in our own "Secret Places". Each worker needs to be a skillful, trustworthy, honest, carrier of the Truth and not a seeker after his/her own good, but willing to sacrifice all.

Now, we, if we have the components together from the above checklist, are ready to build. How desperate are you? If you are like me and want to see Him face to face above all else, then "Arise and begin working, and the Lord be with you (1 Chronicles 22:19)."

Dear Father, my desire above all else is to see You face to face and to have the unspeakable privilege of being in Your presence. Let me not rest until I have built a "Secret Place" where You and I can meet, so that I may in turn be fully equipped by Your presence to fulfill Your purpose in my life. In Jesus' Name, Amen.

Rosemary Chambers is the director of Kingdom Women Ministries.

October 12

Humble Pie

"...before honor comes humility." Proverbs 15:33 (New American Standard Bible)

At work a while ago my department was being recognized at a meeting and in another meeting, a project team I was working with was mentioned. In both cases my name was missing. A few months later, a team I was on was highlighted. Again I was missing. In each of these cases I was very angry. I was being humbled. And I wasn't listening.

Many other people went through things where they were "humbled". Jesus wasn't recognized as the Messiah, the early church wasn't recognized as speaking the truth, David wasn't recognized as king, and many more. A good example of how to deal with this is David.

In 1 Samuel 16 David was anointed as king of Israel. Before taking the throne he served his father, he served Saul even when Saul had tried to kill him (1 Samuel 18–19). Then Saul declared war on him! All through this time David could have stood up and said, "I am God's anointed king!" In fact he did the opposite, and as a result he was honored for hundreds of years after he died (2 Kings 20:6). Before honor came humility.

I've now learned to serve the leaders over me. It doesn't matter if I get noticed in any way, only that their goals are accomplished. God will use me in whatever way suits Him best, and I will not question His decisions. Interestingly since I've made that decision I've been honored many times.

Jesus, please help me to seek Your will for my life and not my own. Help me to be humble in all cases and not to seek the praise of others, only the praise of You. Thank You for the times You have humbled me. Amen.

Jim Michaels is the youth music team leader and a home group leader at New Covenant Christian Church.

October 13
Whose Life Is It Anyway?

"...You are not your own; for you were bought at a price; therefore glorify God in your body and in your spirit, which are God's." *1 Corinthians 6:19–20 (New King James Version)*

Twenty years later, I can still remember the exact location where I was driving on the Fruitville Pike when God spoke to my heart. I was traveling from one medical specialist to another, trying to get to the bottom of a serious health condition. In my car, I scanned the results of an ultrasound test and read scary words describing an even scarier condition. And worst of all, the doctor's handwritten words scrawled across the bottom of the report—"Conception for Lisa will be highly unlikely."

Tears stung my eyes and I heard myself say internally, for the umpteenth time in the previous weeks, "My life, my life, what's happening to my life?" I'd lifted the words from a video our ministry used, where a post-abortive woman cried out, "My life, my life, what's happening to my life?" It seemed odd to me that I was parroting this woman's words in my heart, so I asked the Lord why. His clear response was, "You're saying, 'My life, my life' because you think it's *your* life. But it's not. It's Mine. You've been bought with a price—the precious blood of Jesus Christ. You belong to Me. Lay your life down."

Hot tears flooded my cheeks as I realized He was right. I did belong to Him. Jesus did purchase me. What right did I have to claim ownership of my life? Right there in the car, traveling south on the Fruitville Pike at the route 30 overpass, I surrendered everything to Him—my life, my health, my childbearing capabilities.

And twenty years later, there are no regrets—just the peace of belonging to my Father who owns me.

Father, thank You for purchasing me. Thank You that I belong to You. Thank You for the sweet peace of surrender.

Lisa Hosler is president of Susquehanna Valley Pregnancy Services

October 14

Incredible!

"Love never dies. Inspired speech will be over some day; praying in tongues will end; understanding will reach its limit. We know only a portion of the truth, and what we say about God is always incomplete. But when the Complete arrives, our incompletes will be canceled." *1 Corinthians 13:8–10 (The Message)*

Thanks to weddings, 1 Corinthians 13:1–7 are some of the best-known verses in the Bible, but this chapter goes far beyond marital love. That's the point of verses 8–10, quoted above from Peterson's *The Message*. We really do not and cannot understand the fullness, the complete-ness of God's love. We pen our praise and sing our joy. We seek in wordless prayer, but it all falls short. The most inspiring sermons, the most glorious sacred music, the most fervent prayers for understanding: all are incomplete.

But we are told to hope unswervingly (1 Corinthians 13:13). We are to trust steadily that when the Complete arrives, and "...He hands over His kingdom to God the Father" all our incompletes will be canceled (1 Corinthians 15:23). We are to love extravagantly. (I guess that means seemingly beyond our means). What a comfort! What a thrill! I cannot understand how on earth God will clean up this mess we humans have made. I cannot understand how Christ will look at the ways I have disappointed Him, with errors both of commission and omission, and say, "You are forgiven. Come home. You are complete. All the incomplete grades you earned in life are canceled." Incredible!

It is not for me to understand. All I can do is hope, trust and love—extravagantly.

Dear God, keep me from falling into the trap of trusting the way the world judges our lives, of expecting the Complete here on earth. Remind me every day that Your Fullness will indeed be revealed—in Your time, not mine.

Bill Adams is a community volunteer in Lancaster and at First Presbyterian on Orange Street. He was formerly chairman and president of Armstrong World Industries.

October 15

Blessing Christian Leaders

Pray!

"Now we ask you, brothers, to respect those who work hard among you, who are over you in the Lord and who admonish you. Hold them in the highest regard in love because of their work...."
1 Thessalonians 5:12–13

There is a clear call as to how we are to regard those in ministry. *Because of their work* we should honor them and show them the utmost respect. Let's make it a part of our day to pray that pastors and ministry leaders will abide in the presence of Jesus as a way of life and leadership. Let's ask God to grant those who are over us in the Lord to have increased vision and discernment, and to walk in integrity and humility.

Father, we thank You for those you have placed in positions of spiritual authority. Thank you for giving them Your heart for Your people. May we respond to them not as burdens, but as blessings by offering them up to You in our prayers. We ask You to strengthen and sustain them, protect them from discouragement that often accompanies ministry, and help them to rely on You rather than themselves in all things.

Today's devotional was edited from the 2003–2004 *Throne Of Grace Prayer Guide*, a weekly guide of Lancaster County prayer concerns gathered from regional intercessors and area prayer groups.

October 16

Esteemed By God

"...This is the one I esteem: he who is humble and contrite in spirit, and trembles at my word." *Isaiah 66:2*

There is probably not a person alive who does not, to some extent, care what others think about them. Even now, as an adult, I am desirous of pleasing or even impressing my dad. When he comes to town I try and make certain that the grass has been recently mowed, the cars washed, and things put away. I desire to please him. I want him to be proud of me.

But the judgment of my father is nothing to be compared with the judgment of our heavenly Father. How can I please Him? How can I impress Him?

Isaiah gives us a glimpse into what God is looking for. It has nothing to do with human accomplishments or even places of power. It centers not on what kind of name we have made for ourselves or how well we are known. It centers upon this alone: am I man after God's own heart? And here, in this single verse, Isaiah lets us in on that heart. Here is what God is looking for. This is what God esteems: humility, contrition of spirit, and a trembling at His word.

Are you humble? Do you understand, under God, your proper place in life (see 1 Corinthians 1:26–31)? Are you contrite in spirit? Have you been crushed? Do you understand that without God you are nothing? And do you tremble at His word? Do you OBEY His word? If so, you may be a man (or woman) that God, in a very particular way, esteems. He may have His eye on you! His plan may be to do especially great things through you.

Lord, I desire to please You. But You have suggested that there are certain kinds of people You are looking for, and Lord, I desire to be that kind of person. Teach me Your ways, in Jesus' name.

Doug Winne is senior pastor of Lancaster Evangelical Free Church in Lititz.

October 17

Our Trust In Jesus

"But how then would the Scriptures be fulfilled that say it must happen in this way?" *Matthew 26:54*

Jesus knew He would be arrested long before it happened. He knew about Judas, the close friend that betrayed Him. He knew Peter would deny Him three times before the night was finished. He knew all the disciples were about to bolt in fear. He knew it all. Jesus was calm despite knowledge of that night's details. He resigned Himself to the will of the Father. This point is a challenge to us as His people.

We can often be caught off guard because we do not know what a day, a month, or a year hold in store. Peter was caught off guard, as most of us would have been in his position. He reacted with his first instinct to a mob with swords and clubs. We too have natural instincts, and our instincts, like Peter's, get us into trouble. Some pass off their frequent human shortcomings to being only human. They point out that we are not like Jesus, with perfect knowledge and responses. Unfortunately, excuses keep us from turning to the one that can change us.

Knowledge of what will take place is in itself not a calming factor in life. God is kind to keep from us insight that would paralyze our lives. What does bring us into a deep sense of trust? Our eyes must be fixed upon Jesus. We trust that He knows what is about to take place in our lives. His words were proven true concerning his arrest, trial, crucifixion, burial, and resurrection. His words can be trusted to transform lives today.

Lord, help me today to keep my faith and trust in You. I pray this because I do not understand world events. In the confusion and struggles I face today, and the reactions with which I am tempted to respond, speak to me.

Bruce Heckman serves on the leadership team of Immerge, preparing people for cross-cultural ministries.

October 18
A Waiting Creation
"The creation waits in eager expectation for the sons of God to be revealed." *Romans 8:19*

Have you ever said these words? "I am so frustrated. I am getting so angry. I am frustrated with…everything!" "Everything" can include major world issues like injustice and hatred to simple but very real personal situations like the failure to find the time to communicate with your family. Frustration is a growing emotional state in our society. It is manifested by ever-increasing fits of anger. Two examples are road rage and fistfights at Little League games.

Rage, real rage…the smoldering ember of emotion waiting for the right blend of circumstances to be ignited by the spark of frustration, is becoming an inferno. A few short years ago terrorists' bombings and kids shooting classmates were scenes from horror movies, not evening news stories. Today is different. The world's on edge!

In the midst of this volatile setting, the words of the apostle are more poignant than ever. "The creation waits in eager expectation for the sons of God to be revealed." Reading the balance of the passage it seems that creation is subject to frustration in the hope that it will be LIBERATED from the bondage of decay and brought into the glorious freedom . We Christians, the sons of God, are the hope of the world. We have the key to overcome frustrations; we have the peace that passes all understanding. We are "more than conquerors."

The world is waiting for you. Don't just conquer frustration, overcome it with good. As you do, bondage is broken and others see the freedom of being a Christian. We display the victory over past behaviors as new creations living new lives. What joy…being free from past sins! No wonder the world so eagerly waits.

Lord, today make me more than a conqueror. Let me meet today's divine appointment, knowing I can reveal your triumphant mercy to an eagerly waiting world.

Scott Boyd is a representative in the Pennsylvania General Assembly and served as an elder at New Covenant Christian Church.

One

October 19

The God Who Is

"...for he that comes to God must believe that HE IS, and that He is a rewarder of those who diligently seek him."
Hebrews 11:6 (New King James Version)

People struggle with the reality of God. How hopeless are those who don't believe in God! And how tragic that many of our pews are filled with born-again men and women who are slaves to unbelief. So many of us have knowledge of God; so few of us experience, or even hope for, the presence of God in our lives.

The mere knowledge that Jesus healed two thousand years ago, or even ten years ago, or last year, cannot fill the soul or satisfy the need of the present moment. Teaching will do little good unless God is present. We must long to see the goodness of God in the land of the living. We must contend for that goodness, live in that goodness, manifest that goodness and pour out that goodness upon others. Then people will see the reality of God, and they will enter a relationship with the God WHO IS, the God who rewards all who diligently seek him. Like Jesus, we must desire the manifestation of the Father's power and love. With Jesus, we must be able to say, "If you don't believe me, believe the works that I do!"

Thank God that Jesus Christ is the same, yesterday, today and forever! Let's come to God, believe in God, and watch Him work His mighty works in our midst and in the world around us.

Father, we declare that YOU ARE. We declare that You reward all who seek You with whole hearts. Help me to seek Your face always. I am "blessed-blessed," because You are so good to me! May I pour out Your goodness upon others, so they may know the One WHO IS. In the name of Jesus, Amen.

Phil Hernandez lives and pastors in Lancaster City. His church, In The Light Ministries, is "A Place Where God is Changing Lives."

October 20
Connecting To God Through Worship

"Rise up, . . . and go, worship the LORD…" *Exodus 12:31 (New American Standard Bible)*

The cry of God to Pharaoh was "Let my People Go." Pharaoh would not let God's people go worship, so God had to convince him. Only after ten confrontations was Israel allowed freedom to go worship. We too must confront whatever taskmaster keeps us from worshiping God—things like apathy or lukewarmness.

Praise causes dry times to end, refreshing to come, and our path to open. In Numbers 20, Edom refused to let the people of Israel pass by. Again in Numbers 21, Israel got to a place where they couldn't move forward. They were thirsty, without water, just like we are at times. But God commanded Moses to do one thing: gather Israel to sing! "'Assemble the people, that I may give them water.' Then Israel sang … 'Spring up, O well! Sing to it!'"

A person who will stop and praise will always advance. When we praise even if we don't feel like it, God will refresh us, and we'll be able to advance. Habbakuk said: "Though the fig tree should not blossom and there be no fruit on the vines . . . yet I will exult in the LORD, I will rejoice in the God of my salvation."

The Hebrew words for "worship" are actually words for body posture. A large percentage of our communication is non-verbal. We are exhorted in Psalm 134:2, "Lift up your hands...and praise the LORD." Psalm 47:1 says, "Clap your hands, all you people; shout to God with cries of joy." Psalm 33 says, "Sing to him a new song; play skillfully..." Psalm 95 tells us, "Come, let us bow down in worship, let us kneel..." We are even told in Psalms 149: "…praise his name with dancing."

Father I want to confront anything that keeps me from freely worshiping You.

Barry Wissler is senior pastor of Ephrata Community Church and leads HarvestNet, a resource ministry linking churches and ministries as partners in Harvest.

October 21

The Prayer Match

"Your name will no longer be Jacob, but Israel, because you have struggled with God and with man and have overcome."
Genesis 32:28

Jacob wrestled with God in a physical way and he overcame and was blessed. I don't know anyone who has wrestled with God literally (He is not in *my* weight class!), but many of us have wrestled with God in a figurative way. Sometimes we might struggle because we don't understand why something bad has happened to our loved ones, or us or perhaps we are looking for an answer from God and it just doesn't come. Other times, just to pray is a chore. If we are willing to make the effort, and grapple with God in our times with Him, we, like Jacob, can find God's blessing.

Prayer is something that Christians take for granted. How hard can it be to pray anyway? For me, it is often a struggle to pray, I fall asleep, my thoughts drift off to other things, or some other distraction takes me away. I give up the match far too easily rather than continuing to fight through to quality time with God.

If we recognize that prayer can be a battle, not only with God, but also with the evil one who wants to keep us from praying, we are more likely to succeed and find that blessing! Often times the best strategy is to pray with others to keep the concentration up and to be able to overcome. ("Where two or more are gathered in My name, there I am in the midst of them..."). May we fight to spend time with the Lord, may we overcome and then God's blessing will come.

Dear Father, help me to be an overcomer in prayer, may I not be afraid to honestly struggle with You in prayer, and may You give me strength to defeat the attempts of Satan to interfere with my prayer life.

Chip Mershon is a family physician at Cornerstone Family Health Associates in Lititz, is the chairman of the Water Street Rescue Mission Medical Clinic board and is an active member at the Lancaster Evangelical Free Church.

October 22

Relationship
With Jesus

"You diligently study the Scriptures because you think that by them you possess eternal life. These are the Scriptures that testify about me, yet you refuse to come to me to have life."
John 5:39–40

"Come to Me all you who are weary and burdened, and I will give you rest. Take My yoke upon you and learn from Me, for I am gentle and humble in heart, and you will find rest for your souls. For My yoke is easy and My burden is light."
Matthew 11:28–30

As individuals and as communities, it is easy for us to perpetuate traditions and habits that have long lost their meaning. Because we are still operating in the structure, we may find it hard to recognize that the *life* has diminished. How necessary it is, then, for us to examine ourselves to make sure we remain in contact with the Living Word, not just the "letter of the law." If there are unhealthy or unbiblical traditions or religious habits that hinder the work of God's Spirit, we must repent and ask God to restore us to a vibrant, living relationship with the One to whom the Scriptures testify.

Father, we ask Your forgiveness for where we have refused to come, and have relied on our own ways. Help us come today and lay down our weary burdens and take up Your yoke. We confess that Your blood is sufficient for our sins. Restore us to a vital relationship with You and give us rest, as well as an infectious joy in serving You.

Today's devotional was edited from the 2003–2004 *Throne Of Grace Prayer Guide*, a weekly guide of Lancaster County prayer concerns gathered from regional intercessors and area prayer groups.

One

The Faith To Fly

"...If you have faith as a grain of mustard seed, you will say to this mountain, 'Move from here to there,' and it will move; and nothing will be impossible to you." *Matthew 17:20 (Revised Standard Version)*

Jesus said, "All things are possible to him who believes (Mark 9:23)." When I was young, I believed those words with the faith of a child. And my "all things" was flying—like Superman! Phooey on the law of gravity—I had faith! Jesus walked on water, didn't he? Healed blind eyes? Rose from the grave? I tried hard to fly!

As I grew, I realized I'd need a real good reason to fly. I couldn't tempt God (Jesus didn't swoop down from the temple roof just because Satan dared him to). I couldn't open my attic window and jump, but I would've bet my best comic book that when that holy opportunity for flying came, I would fly!

When Paul said, "I can do all things through Christ who strengthens me (Philippians 4:13)," he meant it. But "all things" doesn't mean just anything. It means all things that God calls us to and leads us through. All things that meet us as we rise each day to face the world and to undertake the work at hand. It means we can love all people, even our enemies. It means submitting to God, resisting the devil and watching him flee—and having done all, finding ourselves still standing in the grace of God. There will be miracles—but the greatest miracle is that no matter what comes, our faith can face it. "This is the victory that overcomes the world: our faith (1 John 5:4)."

P.S. I married a gal who spent a good deal of her childhood trying out her mustard seed of faith on a tree in her back yard. Today, her prayers move mountains. But when she wants a tree moved, I borrow our neighbor's chainsaw.

Father in heaven, thank You for the blood of Your Son, the Spirit of truth, and the faith of a child! Amen.

Mark Ammerman serves on the leadership team of In The Light Ministries in Lancaster. He is the communications director of the Regional Church of Lancaster County.

On Being Biscuit

"And I pray that Christ will be more and more at home in your hearts as you trust in him." *Ephesians 3:17 (New Living Translation)*

My dog Biscuit loves to play Scuffle, which is when she bites me playfully as she tries to prevent my grabbing her writhing little body and wrapping my arms around her until she lies quietly—belly-up—on my stomach. When she finally gets to this position, she relaxes and enjoys a belly rub, almost sleeping as she's curled up in my arms.

Recently, I was pondering how one surrenders to God. It was difficult for me to envision surrender to a God who seems at times out of my personal reach. Does He care that I am giving Him something I've been holding dear? Will He take advantage of my now surrendered heart? As I would hear admonitions to lay it all down and surrender all, it was hard for me to imagine God as a loving parent.

One evening, I tried to divert my troubled mind by playing Scuffle with Biscuit. I chased her down, grabbed her round the belly and quickly got her into a submissive position on my lap. We just sat there for a while—I, rubbing her pink little belly and she, enjoying a quiet moment with her favorite person. As we sat in quietness, God spoke.

That was when I knew what He wanted surrender to be. To submit to God didn't mean blindly giving my life away to a God in the unreachable cosmos. It meant (being Biscuit) giving in because I know I will be lying in my Father's arms, not a bad place to be— in fact, the best place in the world to be with my favorite Person, allowing Him to gently chase me down and hold me tenderly, massaging gently the places that hurt.

Lord, help me to know Your true character that I might surrender to Your tender embrace. Amen.

Ranita Hurst and her husband Brian are worship directors at Living Hope Community Church.

Sycamore Tree

"So he ran ahead and climbed a sycamore-fig tree to see him,
since Jesus was coming that way. When Jesus reached the
spot, he looked up and said to him, 'Zacchaeus, come down
immediately. I must stay at your house today.'" *Luke 19:4–5*

Our church needed actors to play a role in a significant production. First we considered the question, "Who is this story in
Luke 19:3–5 about?" It is tempting to say it is about Zacchaeus,
but it's not. Sure Zacchaeus plays a role—he is lost, friendless, a sinner, certainly curious, financially well off, and small in stature. Many
people in today's society could play this part.

The crowd also plays a significant role in this story; the crowd in
my life can be the media, parents, peers, and church—things that keep
me from seeing Jesus. The crowd is fickle, loud, pushy, judgmental,
elitist and good at keeping the less fortunate away.

There is Jesus, too. It might be hard to find someone to play His
role…maybe we should just let the Son of God be the Savior of the
Lost. This story is not about seeking a tax collector but about seeking a
Savior.

There is one more character needed for our play, the role of the
sycamore tree—that advantage which allows our seeker to see Jesus, to
make eye contact with the One who longs for reconciliation. The true
sycamore tree is strong and high enough to allow a seeker to see a full
view of Jesus Christ.

*Lord, help me to become like the sycamore tree, firmly planted on the
truth and willing to let sinners use me to improve their view of Christ.
Help me to be faithful, trustworthy, strong, well-rooted, and pruned of
dead branches that cannot support the weight of the lost. Amen.*

Tim Brouse husband to Julie and youth pastor at Hosanna Christian
Fellowship and a sycamore seedling.

October 26

One Heart, One Mind

"The goal is for all of them to become one heart and mind –
just as you, Father, are in me and I in you, So they might be
one heart and mind with us. Then the world might believe that
you, in fact, sent me." *John 17:21 (The Message)*

The word used here for "all" is the same word used in Acts 2:1.
It suggests our need for relational revelation. My interpretation
of Acts 2:1 goes this way, "They were absolutely all together in
close association in the same place with fiery passion." Who showed
up while they were waiting? It was the Holy Spirit of God in a powerful demonstration of God's presence!

What causes God to show up? What were the disciples doing in
that upper room? Look back at Acts 1:14, for there we find the answer:
"They all joined together constantly in prayer." The wisdom that resulted was to elect Matthias by drawing straws to replace Judas. How
often have we opened a meeting with prayer and asked God to bless
our wisdom at the end? Are we willing to hold out for God to show up?
To stop what we are doing until we hear direct orders?

True unity in Christ comes by impartation. Waiting together with
one mind and heart seems to be an irresistible invitation for God to be
present among us. How many of us, like Thomas, are willing to believe
it when we see it? We should not seek a better program, greater atten-
dance in services, more excellent music, or more effective strategies to
reach the lost. We seek a *groom*. Everything else is preparation or it
becomes distraction. When Jesus shows up all will notice and many
will believe.

*Jesus, may our desire be for You alone. Please appear so we might
rejoice in your presence. Amen.*

Jeff Snyder is senior pastor of Columbia United Methodist Church.

October 27

Rest

"Nevertheless, I tell you the truth. It is to your advantage that I go away; for if I do not go away, the Helper will not come to you; but if I depart, I will send Him to you." *John 16: 7 (New King James Version)*

We have all experienced feelings of confusion and uncertainty as we walk through our daily life. My own observation reinforces the expression that "change is always lurking around the next corner or over the next hill." No matter how hard we try to create our own safe haven, life has a way of barging in and disrupting our well thought-out plans. Whether it's the children, parents, work, church, sickness, or a myriad of other possibilities, the truth is that life is full of uncertainties.

There are times we want to be alone and other times we wish we had someone close who understood us. Our emotions and sense of well-being are under constant attack from the circumstances of life. Our own limitations and shortcomings are apparent to us and we find ourselves wanting to cry out "Help!"

The God who created us is not caught off guard when we express our human frailties, nor is he perplexed at the complexities of life's uncertainties. His response was to shed His blood, that he could then go to the Father and send to us His Holy Spirit "the Comforter". In the Christian believer, the Holy Spirit resides to guide us through the mine fields of life. He has promised never to leave or forsake us, to be closer than a brother.

There is no news, circumstance or uncertainty that is going to catch Jesus by surprise today. In that truth we can rest.

Dear Jesus, I trust You with my life today. Thank You Holy Spirit for Your comfort and guidance today. I rest in Your Lordship over my life and its circumstances. Amen.

Wayne Kaufman pastors at Gates of Praise Ministries, Gates of Praise House Church Network, and is a board member of Harvest Net, The Regional Church of Lancaster County and the Lancaster House of Prayer.

October 28

Love's Kingdom And Love's Work

"And now these three remain: faith, hope and love. But the greatest of these is love." *1 Corinthians 13:13*

The Beatles weren't that far off the mark when they sang "all you need is love, love—love is all you need."

Through faith in Jesus we find the very thing we hope for, love. How cool is that!? God is love! What could be greater than finding and knowing the love of God in Jesus?

At times, I find it helpful to use the word "Love" in the place of God's name. For example, in Matthew 6:33, Jesus says, "The thing you should want most is God's kingdom and doing what God wants." When I insert Love, it reads like this: "The thing you should want most is Love's kingdom and doing what Love wants," I suddenly find an immediacy in this statement. Is "Love's kingdom and Love's work" the thing I want most?

In Matthew 22:37–40 Jesus drives the point of "doing love's work" when he said, "Love the Lord your God with all your heart, all your soul, and all your mind. This is the first and most important command. And the second command is like the first: Love your neighbor as you love yourself."

Even the world recognizes our need for Love. OK, let's sing the Beatles tune again with a slight twist. "all you need is God, God—God is all you need...He loves you yeah, yeah, yeah, He loves you yeah, yeah, yeah!"

Heavenly Father, Lord Jesus, Holy Spirit, fill me with love, strengthen my faith, increase my hope in You. Let me live this day walking in the greatest thing of all, You alone, the very essence of LOVE. Amen.

Steven Courtney, award winning performing songwriter, performs family friendly concerts for schools, churches and community events.

October 29

Let There Be Light

"For with you is the fountain of life; in your light, we see light." *Psalm 36:9*

"This is the message we have heard from him and declare to you: God is light; in him there is no darkness at all." *1 John 1:5*

for Lancaster County

Although no one would refer to the age in which we live as the *Dark Ages,* those with spiritual eyes know we are surrounded by with darkness. There seems at times to be an overwhelming suppression of the truth. But the same God who said, "Let there be light" is the same One who declares that He Himself is the light, and that the darkness will not overcome it. As we receive the truth and take it to our surroundings, we literally shed light in the darkness. We have been commissioned to let our light shine before men, and as we do, it will infiltrate every area of society and the darkness will be expelled.

Lord, thank You that in Your light we see light. May that light shine through me today at home, in my family, my place of work, my neighborhood. May the darkness be replaced with truth. May death be defeated by life.

Today's devotional was edited from the 2003–2004 *Throne Of Grace Prayer Guide*, a weekly guide of Lancaster County prayer concerns gathered from regional intercessors and area prayer groups.

October 30
The God Transformation

"For as the rain comes down, and the snow from heaven, and do not return there, but water the earth and make it bring forth and bud, that it may give seed to the sower and bread to the eater..." *Isaiah 55:10* (New King James Version)

We so often quote the verse that follows: "God's word will not return void or empty." But look at what God is saying to us as He gives us a spiritual "life lesson" through nature. He is saying 'Look at the rain, look at the snow...and learn My ways from them, which are not your ways, which are higher than your ways."

What is He saying to me? Rain and snow come down from heaven as elements, water. They are wet, frozen. These do not hit the earth and bounce back up to heaven in the same form. What takes place is the God transformation of watering the earth, allowing the seed sown there to bud and bring forth fruit, and more seed as well, for on-going increase.

When we take His precious promises into our heart, we can trust that He will allow that "seed" within to be watered and nurtured to bring forth the harvest of His provision (not necessarily looking in the end like what we thought it would.) Seed and bread certainly don't look like rain and snow, but one is the direct result of the other.

Father, Your ways ARE higher than mine and Your thoughts as well. Help me to see with Your eyes so that when Your promises bring forth answers, I will recognize the miraculous, though it looks very different from what I expected. Thank You for teaching me Your ways through nature, in Jesus' name.

Diana Oliphant is a small group minister, missionary and servant/leader from The Worship Center.

October 31

Whose Power?

"And seeing them straining at the oars, for the wind was against them, at about the fourth watch of the night, He came to them, walking on the sea; and He intended to pass by them." *Mark 6:48 (New American Standard Bible)*

The day was long, as the days often were when the disciples were with Jesus. Just when they thought it was time for a break, Jesus assigned the impossible task of feeding dinner to the multitudes, five thousand men, plus women and children. Twelve baskets later, He told the disciples to cross the Sea of Galilee ahead of Him by boat.

Obediently, they started out and ran into fierce winds. They persevered and strained against the wind until Jesus finally came to them walking on the water between three and six in the morning. Amazingly, "He intended to pass by them." Why would the Lord intend to leave them facing such a struggle, especially when they were there because they had obeyed Him?

The answer is found four verses later: *"for they had not gained any insight from the incident of the loaves, but their heart was hardened."* The miracle of the loaves and fishes demonstrated that God's power and resources are far greater than man's.

The disciples could not make progress against the wind because they relied upon their *own* strength and experience. Once they received their assignment, they hurried to complete it—in their own power, even after witnessing Jesus' power over the wind and waves (Mark 4).

How many times have I exhausted myself straining to row against the wind? Too often I remember His power and authority only after mine is gone. How much better it would be if I would keep my heart soft and remember that apart from Him, I can do nothing!

Lord, keep my heart soft before You. Help me to grow in insight and remember each day to carry out the assignments You give me only in Your strength and authority. Amen!

Don Riker serves congregational, ministry, and business leaders as part of Teaching The Word Ministries in Leola.

November

Godliness In Government

Pray!
for Lancaster County

"I urge, then, first of all, that requests, prayers, intercession and thanksgiving be made for everyone—for kings and all those in authority, that we may live peaceful and quiet lives in all godliness and holiness. This is good, and pleases God our Savior, who wants all men to be saved and come to a knowledge of the truth." *1 Timothy 2:1–4*

It is interesting that the Scripture tells us that one of the ways we can please God is to intercede for our government leaders. Not only do the people benefit from leaders who make righteous decisions, but the leaders themselves need to come to a knowledge of the truth. So it behooves us all to pray for godliness to prevail in our government. We should pray for our leaders to have wisdom, grace, protection and godly counselors. We should intercede for them to have courage to stand for righteousness based on the truth of God's word.

Father, we thank You for governing authorities from the President to the Governor to our local officials. We uphold them to You and ask You to lead them in the many decisions they will be making this day. Help them to walk with integrity and honesty. May they choose godly principles that promote the acquisition of peaceful, quiet lives.

Today's devotional was edited from the 2003–2004 *Throne Of Grace Prayer Guide*, a weekly guide of Lancaster County prayer concerns gathered from regional intercessors and area prayer groups.

November 2

My Talk

"Do not let any unwholesome talk come out of your mouths, but only what is helpful for building others up according to their needs, that it may benefit those who listen." *Ephesians 4:29*

As a parent, I have often wondered why it is so much easier to let my children know when they've done something wrong than it is to let them know when they've done something right. That same attitude can carry over into our marriages, our jobs, our schools, our churches and our neighborhoods. I am not against discipline. All of us need correction at times or need to know when we have hurt somebody. But, it sure seems easier to speak the "bad" about somebody or to somebody than it is to speak the "good" or words of encouragement.

This verse has been a challenge to me over the last ten years. In fact, it has been one of my three "life verses". I have failed more times in this area than I would like to admit, but I continue to challenge myself to obey Paul's admonition. What kind of talk comes out of my mouth? Is it wholesome or unwholesome? Do my words "build others up according to their needs?" Are my words a "benefit" to those who hear them?

I have heard Christian leaders say that if Christians obeyed just this one verse, seventy-five percent of our problems in the church would be solved. I have a hunch that same obedience might improve our witness in the world also!

Dear God, today may my talk be wholesome and may I speak words of encouragement to others that will build them up, and may what I say benefit those who hear me. Amen.

Jim Rhen is the founding pastor of East Cocalico Church of the Brethren, Reamstown and is currently the pastor of Mechanic Grove Church of the Brethren, Quarryville.

November 3

Bonsai Christians

"Blessed is the man who trusts in the LORD and whose trust is the LORD. For he will be like a tree planted by the water, that extends its roots by a stream and will not fear when the heat comes; but its leaves will be green, and it will not be anxious in a year of drought nor cease to yield fruit." *Jeremiah 17:7–8* (New American Standard Bible)

This promise makes it obvious that God wants us to flourish and live a fruitful life. In a year of drought it is easy to see which plants have a good supply of water, and harvest time reveals the difference as well. We are each God's plantings. As Isaiah 61 says, we "will be called oaks of righteousness, the planting of the LORD, that He may be glorified."

Bonsai is the art of stunting the growth of a tree. This process keeps it looking normal except it stays very tiny. The tree is forced to survive in a small shallow pot so it does not have a lot of room to stretch its roots out. Often it is purposefully planted in poor quality soil and its nutrients are limited. So, the tree survives and ages but stays tiny and unproductive.

Unfortunately, many Christians live like Bonsai trees. They are real trees, but they don't grow to their potential size. They were created to thrive, bear fruit, and give shade to others but they never do, because their growth has been stunted.

We need to put our roots down deep into Jesus and drink deeply of the river of life that flows from His presence. We need to feed on his words regularly and spend time communing with Him in prayer. Today, remember how much you need Him. Draw from Him throughout the day and talk to Him often.

Father, we know that You want us to stay strong and grow. I want to let the roots of my inner being grow deeply into Your love and the truth of Your word.

Barry Wissler is senior pastor of Ephrata Community Church and leads HarvestNet, a resource ministry linking churches and ministries as partners in Harvest.

November 4

To Be United

"When Jesus came into the region of Caesarea Philippi, He asked His disciples, saying, 'Who do men say that I the Son of Man, am?'" *Matthew 16:13 (New King James Version)*

We, the people of Lancaster County, are privileged to live in an area that is rich in spiritual diversity. We have ever-increasing opportunities to worship together, to pray together, to plan community outreaches together, and to simply share our faith with each other. It is amazing to me that in this diversity of culture and spiritual heritage—whether we believe in pre-tribulation or post tribulation, gifts of the Spirit, or signs and wonders—there is clearly one common truth that binds us all together. Jesus asked Simon Peter, "Who do YOU say that I am?" Peter's response then was as it should be now in our region: "You are the Christ, the Son of the living God." We are a region whose heart's cry is to be united. Our response to this question is foundational to our becoming one with our Lord and with one another.

Jesus, I thank You that we can pray in agreement with You. Make us one, just as You and the Father are One. Thank You for revealing to each of us that You are the Christ and upon this truth the foundation for unity is laid.

Pastor Ruby Jones, founder of Perish No More Ministries, provides daily encouragement through small groups in our communities.

November 5

Be Content

"… for I have learned, in whatsoever state I am, therewith to be content. I know both how to be abased, and I know how to abound: every where and in all things I am instructed both to be full and to be hungry, both to abound and to suffer need. I can do all things through Christ which strengtheneth me."
Philippians 4:11–13 (New American Standard Bible)

The verses leading up to this passage, and those following, depict the writer (the Apostle Paul) as bearing up under all the challenges that were thrown at him. How often during difficult times and challenging struggles do we perceive our situation as "unfair"? Our reaction is too often, "Why me?"

Paul is exhorting us to look at situations, both good and bad, as occasions for us to grow and to learn patience. The Lord allows trials and tribulations. Our response to them may or may not help us in our walk towards Him.

I may not like what's happening to me. I may wonder why. I may not be happy with my circumstances. But as the Apostle Paul exhorts us, "be content". Verse 13 provides hope: "I can do all things through Christ who strengthens me." That promise is the source of my contentment and my hope. It is the path for me to walk upon to help me handle the tough times.

Dear God, help me to grow in dependence upon You in tough times. May I see these tough times as opportunities to develop an even greater trust in You. I thank You for delivering me through these current situations. In Christ's name, Amen.

Allan Thrush is an administrator in the Elizabethtown Area School District.

November 6

Getting Ready!

"...For the wedding of the Lamb has come, and his bride has made herself ready. Fine linen, bright and clean, was given her to wear. (Fine linen stands for the righteous acts of the saints.)"
Revelation 19:7-8

I have helped with some weddings—friends, sisters, roommates—the list gets pretty long. I never realized just how much work a wedding really was until recently when I was the bride and the one making the plans! I had a long list of things that needed to be done before our BIG day.

Being the bride wasn't easy. Family and friends who help you plan sometimes have different opinions. You can just get plain tired of focusing so much time on THE DAY. It's tempting to want to push it aside and forget it. One of my bridal guides from my mountain of wedding books and magazines put it well, "The bride may find out the easiest part about the wedding is saying 'yes' to the proposal."

During a time of prayer recently, I was impressed by an amazing truth! If the church is the Bride of Christ, why am I expecting life to be a carefree, dreamy time? There is a lot of work to be done between now and the marriage supper of the Lamb. Don't get me wrong! Our Groom, Jesus, doesn't want us to be stressed out, crying over little details. It truly is a wonderful time.

It is important to prioritize our time and be resourceful with the task at hand. It really is a task to be accomplished. Whatever your call within the body of Christ is—evangelist, teacher or youth worker—know you are an important part of preparing the bride for the big day. Planning yet another event or sitting through one more meeting can be a significant part of preparing the spotless bride.

Lord, help me to prioritize and guard my heart. I know I am doing it all for my Groom, Jesus. The ultimate BIG day is right around the corner! Even so. Lord Jesus, come!

Sarah Sauder is the director of House to House Publications.

November 7

Don't Be A Picky Eater

"Then he said to me, 'Son of man, eat this scroll I am giving you and fill your stomach with it.' So I ate it, and it tasted as sweet as honey in my mouth." *Ezekiel 3:3*

The genesis of Ezekiel's story gives me the chills, like watching an episode of *Fear Factor*. He is given this grand vision and then called to take a scroll with unappealing words and add it to his diet. Then I'm struck with the revelation of this act. God's spokesmen were never intended to speak His truth with their own opinions sharing the same airwaves. Instead the message is intended to be *our appetizer* before we serve God's people their meal. It's like the difference between a balloon filled with water and one filled with air. The first balloon has a life giving substance to contribute while the other is just filled with… well, you get the point.

Chances are we have the same response to the lessons God is teaching us as I have towards unfamiliar foods. I'm a reluctant risk taker when it comes to my digestive system. There is a risk involved when the Lord calls us to action, but we would do well to remind ourselves of the vision. The surprise Ezekiel received in the form of a vision gave him the impression of a privileged calling, which took some of the sting out of the aftershock of what the Lord was asking him to do. He was to apply the word inwardly before proclaiming it outwardly. It is in our best interest to understand and be obedient to the process. Let us be encouraged that although what God gives us might seem hard to swallow at first, in the end, it may taste "as sweet as honey."

Father, forgive me for my opposition towards the "hard to swallow" process. Renew in me the courage and determination to be obedient despite the cost.

Jamie Centeno is the field director of Lancaster Teen Haven and serves as an elder, multi-media ministry and young adult leader at In the Light Ministries.

November 8

Compassion

"Then the King will say to those on His
right, 'Come, you who are blessed by my
Father; take your inheritance, the kingdom
prepared for you since the creation of the
world. For I was hungry and you gave me something to eat, I was thirsty and you gave me something to drink, I was a stranger and you invited me in, I needed clothes and you clothed me, I was sick and you looked after me, I was in prison and you came to visit me....whatever you did for one of the least of these brothers of mine, you did it for Me.'" *Matthew 25:34–40*

Pray!
for Lancaster County

If we are to be truly effective in ministering to the world, it is necessary that we be filled with the compassion of God. Only His love can give us the proper perspective to see the hurting around us. Only His love can soften our hearts to the point that we recognize the eyes of Jesus looking back at us when we reach out to those in need. Whether feeding the hungry or housing the homeless— in the natural or the spiritual—may we remember that what we are doing for others, we are doing for Him.

Lord Jesus, help us this day, this week, to look for the needs You have called us to meet. Either individually or corporately, may we not neglect "the least."

Today's devotional was edited from the 2003–2004 *Throne Of Grace Prayer Guide*, a weekly guide of Lancaster County prayer concerns gathered from regional intercessors and area prayer groups.

No Ordinary Life

"Then Enoch walked with God three hundred years after he became the father of Methuselah.... And Enoch walked with God; and he was not, for God took him." *Genesis 5:22,24 (New American Standard Version)*

In a frustrating world filled with pain and death, where can we find the invigorating life we crave? Jesus claimed to offer an overflowing life in contrast to death and destruction (John 10:10)! The problem is that many claim to know Jesus, but don't enjoy that kind of life!

Enoch lived in a time in which everyone was dying. Genesis 4 presents a downward spiral of false worship, selfish anger, jealousy, deception, murder, lying and rebellion. Genesis 5 recounts the resulting broken record of every man living for a while, and then dying, yet Enoch was different. He had no ordinary life; he walked with God! He also did not experience death; he "was not!" Genesis presents Enoch as an example of hope for the rest of us that we don't have to be stuck in the dead end rut of existing in pain and frustration until death. Instead we can enjoy life in relationship with God.

The picture of walking with God is graphic. It reminds us that we must focus on God and stay in step with him! We cannot go our own way, expecting that He will come along! Am I staying with Him in honest and consistent attention to His way and step? As we see with Abraham, this walk starts by grace through faith (Genesis 15:6) and it continues by grace through faith (Genesis 17:1). When we stray, we can and must return quickly to the path of life. God graciously forgives, and when I am with Him, I need fear no evil.

Dear God, help me to understand what Your path is and be willing to follow completely in Your ways. Help me to see where my path strays from Yours and return quickly to the path of life. Amen.

John Soden is the associate professor of Bible at Lancaster Bible College.

November 10

God's Updraft

"Those who wait on the Lord shall renew their strength; they shall mount up with wings like eagles...." *Isaiah 40:31 (New King James Version)*

You're a young eagle—in "flight" school. Your mother seems to be changing your nest each time you have a flying lesson. Your brothers and sister eaglets are starting to say the same thing. "The nest seems to be shrinking, maybe Mom and Dad are about to rebuild up."

Dad is flying in higher circles now. Finally after a week of the kick, drop, flap, catch and mounting back to the nest, we see a pattern—and just as we get back to the old nest, it's not there! Did the movers come while we were at flight school?

This story has a happy ending. All the participants pass flight school and learn to fly on their own. We patiently wait for the air beneath us to heat up and become a mighty updraft. As the upsurging air rises almost violently, we begin to flap strong wings. Wings that were strengthened by training from mother kicking us out of the nest which she tore apart, are ready to soar. We are ready to mount up and fly away to lands and continents we couldn't imagine, to a higher place in God.

Lord there are times when I feel like You are tearing apart my safe little nest and forcing me to train diligently on behalf of an upcoming move in God, an updraft of the Spirit of God. Help me not to reject Your discipline as You work in me the desire and ability to mount up like eagles.

Dave & Renee Queen reside in Mt Joy. They served on staff with Campus Crusade for Christ for five years and with the Josh McDowell Ministry and Global Hope Network. They currently serve with the Joseph Project.

One

November 11

Tribute To Our Veterans

"These things that were written in the scriptures so long ago are to teach us patience and to encourage us, so that we will look expectantly to the time when God will conquer sin and death." *Romans 15:4 (Living Bible)*

The Christian's greatest hope is when we sit under the eternal government of God in Heaven where we will no longer have to deal with sin and death. But for now, God has instituted earthly governments to deal with sin, however imperfectly, even as Romans 13 indicates.

We are especially grateful on Veteran's Day for our government and the men and women who are willing to give of themselves and even lay down their lives for the greater good to prevail. Saying "thank you" just does not seem like enough. If we have veterans willing to die for a cause, some who are not even motivated by Christian principles, can we do anything less than to tell God we are willing to lay down our lives for the sake of the cross?

Jesus died for our sins, and many veterans died for our freedom. It is time to express our gratitude to both by giving our all for the good of others. "Be glad for all God is planning for you. Be patient in trouble, and be prayerful always (Romans 12:12, Living Bible)."

Dear Heavenly Father, You have given us so many blessings. We have been blessed with freedom and protection as a result of the sacrifices of these faithful ones in uniform. Now we commit our lives to Your service whatever the cost. May we not be motivated by a "works mentality," but rather by true love for You. In Romans 12:9, You tell us not to pretend that we love others, but to really love them. Jesus, our rally cry is to serve You by loving others. In Your Holy Name, Amen.

LaMarr Sensenig serves as an intercessor with his wife, Naomi, at D.O.V.E. Christian Fellowship Westgate Celebration.

A Man After God's Heart

"But now your kingdom shall not continue. The Lord has sought for Himself a man after His own heart, and the Lord has commanded him to be commander over His people, because you have not kept what the Lord commanded you."
1 Samuel 13:14 (New King James Version)

The prophet Samuel was rebuking Saul because he did not do what the Lord had commanded him to do. Samuel told Saul what was going to happen regarding his successor, the next king. Samuel said that the next king will be one who has a heart after God. When it came time to seek a king, the Lord told Samuel to go to the house of Jesse. "Fill your horn with oil, and go; I am sending you to Jesse, the Bethlehemite. For I have provided Myself a king among his sons (1 Samuel 16:1)." Jesse brought seven sons before Samuel but none of them were chosen. The youngest, David, was in the fields tending the sheep and Samuel commanded them to bring him in. God told Samuel that David was the one and he was anointed that day.

God spoke to Samuel that he was not to look at appearance or physical stature, for the Lord does not see as man sees. Man looks at the outward appearance, but the Lord looks on the heart. The shepherd boy did not go unnoticed. David had a heart after God. We can observe his heart as we read the many Psalms he wrote. What does God see as He looks in our hearts? Does He see the hunger and a thirst for Him that He saw in David? Do we have a desire to be more like our Father each day? Or are we going day by day, doing the activities that keep us buzzing through life? Do we pursue His wisdom in making important life decisions? These are some questions we need to ask ourselves if we want to please God and have His heart.

Father, I come to You and I worship and praise You. I desire to be diligent in seeking out your wisdom and guidance for every part of my life. Just like David, I too want to have a heart after You.

Sherlyn Smucker serves as Administrative Assistant with her husband, Pastor Sam, at The Worship Center in Lancaster.

November 13

Stand In The Gap

"So I sought for a man among them, that should build up the wall, and stand in the gap before me for the land, that I should not destroy it, but I found none." *Ezekiel 22:30 (American Standard Version)*

Take some time and read the context of the verse printed above, from verse 23 through verse 31. It is obvious things were not going well for Israel: "You are a land that is not cleansed", "priests have violated My law and profaned My holy things," among other things. There was plenty going on at that time to offend God. He would have had every right to simply destroy the people, after all—they deserved it!

But let me point out first of all the heart of God in verse 22; it is as if He is saying, "Even though things are really bad and the people offend me, my desire is for mercy and not judgment. If only there would be someone to ask me for mercy on behalf of the land."

As I notice the heart of God, I also must notice the neglect of man. How sad to see God's desire to bestow mercy on His people, yet He could not find one who would stand in the gap on behalf of the people to ask Him for that mercy.

May that not be true of our day and our time! God's heart is not changed. Even though there are people around who live life-styles that are offensive to God, it is still His desire to bestow His mercy on them. But may it not be said that God is looking for people to stand in the gap but finding none.

As God looks for those who will stand in the gap for our lost neighbors, co-workers, family members and fellow students, may He find us willing to stand there and pray for mercy for those in need.

Father, I thank You for Your heart of mercy. I pray that by Your grace, You would enable me to be diligent in standing in the gap in prayer for those around me in need of Your mercy. In Jesus' Name, Amen.

Kevin Eshleman serves as executive pastor of Ephrata Community Church.

November 14

Daring To Believe

"You have made known to me the path of life; you will fill me with joy in your presence, with eternal pleasures at your right hand." *Psalm 16:11*

Soon after leaving home to attend college, I began to question the Christian beliefs I had been taught throughout my childhood. Along with the doubting, I began to dabble in unwholesome activities. My life was going nowhere fast. A Godly professor cornered me one afternoon and quizzed me about what was going on in my life.

I told him just a little bit and he responded, "Do you know what your root problem is?"

I was intrigued, wondering how he had psychoanalyzed me so quickly. "Sure," I answered.

He looked me in the eye and said with firmness, "Your main problem is that you don't believe God is who He says He is...because if you truly believed, you wouldn't be messing around! And, you would dare to trust God with your future!"

I didn't like his words, and they nagged me constantly. After more weeks of continuing down a sinful, self-centered path, I knew I had to find out for myself if God was God! Was He truly interested in me?

I decided I would begin acting as though I believed *everything* in the Bible... and wait to see what happened!

Thirty-five years later I can testify from consistent experience that God has proved Himself to be exactly who He claims to be in the Bible. When I trusted Him with my future, He did "immeasurably more" than I could have asked for or imagined... just as He promised!

Today, if you dare to live as though you truly believe Him, He will do precisely the same for you!

Lord, I purpose to live as though I really believe You. I joyfully entrust this new day into Your hands, and each of my tomorrows as well.

Sharon Charles assists her husband John as they direct Abundant Living, a family counseling ministry in Lititz, PA.

November 15

A Blameless Walk With God

Pray!

"But now He has reconciled you by Christ's physical body through death to present you holy in His sight, without blemish and free from accusation—if you continue in your faith, established and firm, not moved from the hope held out in the gospel...." *Colossians 1:22–23*

"May God Himself, the God of peace, sanctify you through and through. May your whole spirit, soul and body be kept blameless at the coming of our Lord Jesus Christ. The One who calls you is faithful and He will do it." *1 Thessalonians 5:23–24*

God is after a pure bride, one that is blameless and free of spiritual compromise. He will do the sanctifying work, but we must cooperate with Him. It is essential that we repent and renounce any involvement in acts that are detestable to Him. Deuteronomy 18 lists a number of such practices. As we examine ourselves, we are free to declare the blood of Jesus and His Lordship over every area of our lives, past and present. He is faithful to do what He says He will do—sanctify us through and through.

Father God, thank You for promising to make us pure, blameless and holy. Thank You that You bring us to the place where we are without blemish and free from every accusation, no matter what our lives have been in the past. We ask You to show us now if we are involved in any evil thing which dishonors You. We renounce it today and receive Your forgiveness.

Today's devotional was edited from the 2003–2004 *Throne Of Grace Prayer Guide*, a weekly guide of Lancaster County prayer concerns gathered from regional intercessors and area prayer groups.

The Harvest

"Then He said to His disciples, 'The harvest truly is plentiful, but the laborers are few. Therefore pray the Lord of the harvest to send out laborers into His harvest.'" *Matthew 9:37–38 (New King James Version)*

The Lord is raising up a generation of harvest laborers that will be led by the Spirit to see the plentiful harvest of souls gathered. Growing up on a farm in Lancaster County, harvest was one of my favorite times of the year. There was an abundance of grain to be harvested and I knew there also was an abundance of work to be done. After high school, I joined a crew that traveled through the Midwest and harvested grain. At times we would gather grain with five combines in one field. Hundreds of thousands of bushels of grain could be gathered in a short time with the modern technology of the harvesters.

There is a massive harvest coming and we are being prepared to work together to bring it in. The Lord is calling the body of Christ to fulfill the Great Commission. Many are being called to the marketplace to minister to those who would not normally come into a local congregation. Our prayers will release them. We must believe that we are living in the greatest days of the harvest. We must resist the lies that people are not interested in our Jesus or that they already are good people. *"Do you not say, 'There are still four months and then comes the harvest'? Behold, I say to you, lift up your eyes and look at the fields, for they are already white for harvest (John 4:35)!"*

Lord, Many are desperate to have a revelation of the King of Kings and Lord of Lords. May we burn with a love for people so that many would come to know Him.

Eric and Regina Martin live in Lancaster City. They are members of HarvestNet and involved with Lancaster House of Prayer. Eric is serving the Lord in the marketplace as a carpenter for BrentMore construction.

November 17

Don't Give Up

"But if we hope for what we do not see, then we eagerly wait for it with perseverance." Romans 8:25 (New King James Version)

One day Jesus told His disciples a story to illustrate their need for constant prayer and to show them that they must keep praying until the answer comes. I love this widow described in Luke 18. She frequently appealed for justice against a man who had harmed her. The judge ignored her for a while, but eventually she got on his nerves and he decided to give her justice because she was wearing him down with her constant pleas.

This lady did not give up. She was persistent. She modeled perseverance for us. She was determined to pursue the justice due her. I smile when I imagine the response of the godless judge as he saw her standing in his courtroom yet another time. He probably rolled his eyes and muttered, "Oh, no. Not her again—Pul-leeze! Give me a break!" But no such luck. This lady would not be denied.

Do we have this kind of tenacity, this ability to dig in for the long haul, this confidence that if we "...keep on asking...[we] will keep on getting; keep on looking and [we] will keep on finding; knock and the door will be opened (Luke 11:9–10, Living Bible)"?

What is it that we are asking God for? What is the deepest cry of our hearts? Are we asking God to change our ministries, our marriages, our families? Are we trusting God for the salvation of a loved one? Do we or a loved one need healing? Is there a prodigal in our family?

Don't give up. I want to be like the persistent widow. I plan to dig in and pound heaven with prayer.

Lord, I have great hope that You will hear me and answer me. Help me to persevere and eagerly await your answer.

Mary Prokopchak is a registered nurse and serves with her husband, Steve, on D.C.F.I.'s Apostolic Council.

November 18

Are Any Of Us Anxious?

"Do not be anxious about anything, but in everything, by prayer and petition, with thanksgiving, present your requests to God."
Philippians 4:6

It seems silly to ask if any of us are anxious. After all, there are all kinds of things that raise our anxiety levels: war, terrorism, economic uncertainty, crime, marriage and family problems, and even conflict in the church. Yet when the Apostle Paul wrote his letter to the Philippians, he did so from a prison cell. In this situation of adversity he said, "do not be *anxious* about anything."

In Philippians 4:12, Paul testified, "I have learned the secret of being content in any and every situation." Careful study of this letter reveals that overcoming anxiousness began with the Apostle's *attitude.* He said, "rejoice in the Lord *always.* ...." But how is that possible in our pressure cooker world? Paul responds, "The Lord is near." Maybe we need the reminder that the Lord is close at hand.

Paul's antidote for anxiety also included right action. Our text verse underscores the importance of prayer to God with a spirit of thankfulness. Paul reminds us that we can do this because God's *peace,* which transcends our understanding, will guard our hearts and minds.

So, what should be our focus? Paul recommended that we think on the things that are true, noble, right, pure, lovely, admirable, excellent and praise worthy (Philippians 4:8). You and I cannot stop the storms of life from swirling around us. But like the tranquil eye of a hurricane, we can have the peace of God within us, when we practice what Paul preached.

Dear God, take away my anxiousness and help me to trust You. May I have the assurance that You are near, that Your peace stands guard over my heart and mind, and that You go with me. Amen.

Fred Moury is conference minister for the Susquehanna Region of the Evangelical Congregational Church. A resident of Lititz, Dr. Moury is a supervisory resource consultant and pastor to the pastors of the 27 Evangelical Congregational Churches in Lancaster County.

November 19

Speak To A Friend

"So the Lord spoke to Moses face to face, as a man speaks to his friend. And he would return to the camp, but his servant Joshua the son of Nun, a young man, did not depart from the tabernacle." *Exodus 33:11 (New King James Version)*

In this chapter, Moses was talking to God about some details. It was really important to Moses to go with God's presence and to have the reassurance that he and the people had found grace in God's sight. God assured him in verse 14, "My Presence will go with you, and I will give you rest."

God is the same today as He was in Moses' and Joshua's time. We can talk to God as a friend talks to a friend and enjoy His presence any time. Ephesians1:4 says we have been made holy and without blame before Him in love and we are accepted by Him. We, too, have found grace and favor in His sight. We can go to Him regarding anything, huge or small, and He will answer us.

I remember praying to God as a child. I was taught that God was there for me in any time of trouble and I took it to heart. It could have been a prayer that I would not be afraid of the dark or asking Him to help me with something at school. When we make a practice of regularly talking to God and being still enough to hear Him, we can more easily recognize His voice when He speaks. God is our friend and loving Father. Let's enjoy His presence and the relationship we have with Him.

Father, I thank You that You are always there for me like a friend. I thank You that You do not keep silent when I bring my challenges to You, but You always have an answer and a solution. My desire is to stay in Your presence for in Your presence is fullness of joy and peace.

Sherlyn Smucker serves as an administrative assistant with her husband, Pastor Sam at The Worship Center, Lancaster.

November 20
Thank You, Lord!
"In everything give thanks: for this is the will of God in Christ Jesus concerning you." *1 Thessalonians 5:18 (King James Version)*

Thanksgiving is like an ignition key. Just as turning the key starts up a car engine, thanksgiving fires up our faith. It is one thing to say that we are trusting God to do such and such. It is another to start thanking Him for the result, before we see it with our natural eyes.

The other day, I misplaced my glasses... something I seem to do more frequently now that I have reached those wonderful senior years! I looked high and low with no success, when suddenly I remembered that simple verse that has helped me so much throughout my life.

"Thank You Lord. I believe You are going to help me find my glasses!" I relaxed and turned my attention to something else. Just a moment later, I spotted them!

I haven't always received such rapid answers to my prayers. But I've found that, even when it appears my prayers aren't being answered just as I've wanted, I'm still a lot happier living with a thankful attitude.

Notice that the verse says, "*in* everything give thanks." It doesn't say we should thank God *for* everything. The wife whose husband is having an extra-marital affair doesn't thank God for the sin. But she can thank God that, in the midst of one of life's most difficult situations, He is with her and is helping her. It's this attitude of thanksgiving that transforms every day into a day of joyful contentment!

Lord, I purpose today to thank You, even before I see the answers to my prayers!

Betty Charles, along with her husband, Norm Charles, founded Abundant Living Ministries, a Christian counseling ministry in Lititz, PA.

November 21

No Fear

"They do not fear bad news; they confidently trust the Lord to care for them. They are confident and fearless ...."
Psalm 112:7–8 (New Living Translation)

Many experience a mixture of emotions when the doctor mentions the word "cancer." When I personally faced that unwelcome news it was as if a truck had run over me. What do you do when your world suddenly falls apart? A dear friend, Christian brother and partner in ministry came alongside my wife and me with the comforting words from Psalm 112. No one is exempt from tough times. A loved one dies, the job ends, tragedy strikes, fire or storms cause damage, terrorists strike. God neither takes us out of the world nor does He exempt us from life's ordinary disasters. What He does is allow us to rest our hearts on Him. We may not be able to praise Him FOR what happens, but we can praise Him IN what happens. Bad news need not shake us; God is still on the throne.

What are you facing today? Through your disappointment, struggle and tears, you can "praise the God and Father of our Lord Jesus Christ, the Father of compassion and the God of all comfort, who comforts us in all our troubles . . .(2 Corinthians 1:3–4)." Through His Spirit-energized Word, He will replace the fear with a confident trust that He will care for you and hold you in His eternal grip.

O God of all comfort, may You receive the highest glory through my confident trust in You today—even when facing bad news. Remove the fear and replace it with a stronger faith in You, so that others may see Jesus in me. Amen.

David D. Allen, Jr. is the associate pastor at Calvary Church. He also serves on the leadership council of the Regional Church of Lancaster County.

November 22

Thankfulness

"So then, just as you received Christ Jesus as Lord, continue to live in Him, rooted and built up in Him, strengthened in the faith as you were taught, and overflowing with thankfulness." *Colossians 2:6–7*

for Lancaster County

"Be joyful always; pray continually; give thanks in all circumstances, for this is God's will for you in Christ Jesus." *1 Thessalonians 5:16–18*

There is always reason to be thankful, but not just thankful when things go well. The Church can be *overflowing* with thankfulness no matter what situations we face. As we come into His presence with thanksgiving and His courts with praise, we learn how to be thankful in all circumstances. As we take the time to recount His many blessings, our roots grow deeper, our foundation is built stronger, and our faith is strengthened. May not only our personal lives be filled with greater expressions of gratitude, but may our corporate gatherings be characterized by outpourings of thankfulness. May we have such grateful hearts to God for who He is and for all He has done, that we can't even begin to contain our praise.

Lord Jesus, thank You, thank You, thank You. You have given us so much. Today we return hearts that are filled to overflowing with gratitude and thankfulness.

Today's devotional was edited from the 2003–2004 *Throne Of Grace Prayer Guide*, a weekly guide of Lancaster County prayer concerns gathered from regional intercessors and area prayer groups.

November 23

Living Gratefully

"In everything give thanks; for this is the will of God in Christ Jesus for you." *1 Thessalonians 5:18 (New King James Version)*

L ike a mother who trains her child to say "Thank you" when receiving a gift, even so our Heavenly Father trains His children to give thanks in everything. Why?

Giving thanks keeps us aware of Father's nature as the Great Giver. He gave His best to us, His Son Jesus Christ, to be the Savior of the world. Whether what is happening in our life seems good or bad, we can always be thankful for what we are and have through Jesus Christ.

When we seek to know God's will or how we shall respond to circumstances, giving thanks opens the door to discovering creative responses and helps to frame a positive outlook for hard situations.

To give thanks in everything requires us to think positively in each situation—appreciating the good rather than dwelling on the negative. A positive attitude is good for our health and relationships. Showing appreciation enriches the one we thank and refreshes our soul as well.

In the American workplace, more than half of the workers receive no appreciation for their work. I am thankful that the Lord has formed in me the discipline of showing gratitude to the associates in the organizations where I have served. It is now my delight to live by this motto: *thank everyone for everything.*

Over the years I have proven that the law of sowing and reaping applies to thank you notes, as well. How encouraging it is to give and receive notes of thankfulness for the presence, character, and service of one another in our daily lives.

Heavenly Father, form in me a grateful spirit. Cultivate in me the ability to see how to be thankful in each situation. Show me today whom You would have me to bless through expressing gratitude. Thank you for the indescribable gift of Jesus Christ!

Keith Yoder is the executive director of Teaching The Word Ministries, and a member of the Regional Council of the Regional Church of Lancaster County.

November 24

An Attitude Of Gratitude

"…You are precious to Me. You are honored, and I love you…"
Isaiah 43:4 (New Living Translation)

God deserves our thanks. God's love is deeply personal and all encompassing. He walks among ordinary people and sits among kings in high places. He has compassion and tenderness towards those who are needy. He is always faithful.

Don Jacobs recalls a true story of the blessings of harvest-time in a Kenyan church. A large basket was placed in the front of the sanctuary to receive offerings of praise and gratitude to the Lord for His goodness throughout the year. During the annual celebration service, people presented gifts. Soon the basket was filled with food. It was a day of returning thanks to God. Each gift was applauded as they sang songs of praise. "It is good to praise the Lord and make music to Your name, O Most High, to proclaim Your love in the morning and Your faithfulness at night (Psalm 92:1–2)."

When the music ended, the pastor asked once more, "Does anyone else desire to give something to God?" After a moment of silence, footsteps were heard coming from the back of the church. A barefoot teenager walked slowly toward the basket. Her hands were empty. What did she have to give? Stopping in front of the basket, she quietly prayed, then smiling, she rearranged a few items and crawled into the basket. The people of the congregation could hardly believe their eyes. The young girl gave all she had. She gave herself to God.

Thank you, God, for Your faithfulness as we enter into Your gates with thanksgiving and Your courts with praise. We praise Your holy name. For You, Lord, are good and Your mercy endures forever. Your faithfulness continues through all generations (Psalm 100:4–5). May each day we live be a day of Thanksgiving! Amen.

Dona L. Fisher is a chairperson for the Lancaster County National Day of Prayer Task Force and vice-president of Friendship Foundation, Inc.

Is A Crumb Enough?

"And she said, 'Yes, Lord, yet even the little dogs eat the crumbs which fall from their master's table.'" *Matthew 15:27 (New King James Version)*

Long did I ponder this, for in a wounded portion of my heart I mused, "If Jesus spoke such a word to me, I'd go off whimpering like a puppy!" But He spoke to her, "O woman, great is your faith. Let it be as you desire".

I asked for His explanation as to why He would speak thus to her, and also what she had within that kept her there unwavering.

The Lord gave a clear answer: "She knew that a crumb from My table was enough, and that crumb was sufficient to meet her need!"

No longer do I focus on the "lack" or insufficiency, regardless of the situation. Grace flows and I am becoming thankful for everything. He in turn, proves Himself faithful, time and time again.

There were places in my life where I was grumbling and complaining because the answer/portion received seemed small. When He began to open my eyes, the light of revelation illuminated situations and circumstances. Places and times often appearing as insurmountable mountains now become opportunities to rejoice and stand in unwavering faith. Grace is abundant for I now know and understand that a crumb from the Master's table is totally sufficient to meet every need.

Lord, I thank You that the portion of Your answered prayer is always just what we need. Thank You for teaching us not to compare our situations to others, but to trust Your wisdom and plan for us implicitly. Continue to open the eyes of our hearts, revealing opportunities for thanksgiving and joy as You daily work small miracles in our lives. In Jesus' name, Amen.

Diana Oliphant is a small group minister, missionary and servant/leader from The Worship Center.

To Seek And To Save

"And Jesus said to him, "Today salvation has come to this house…for the Son of Man has come to seek and to save that which was lost." *Luke 19:9–10*

W hile Jesus was walking through Jericho, a man of short stature wanted to see Him. The man ran ahead and climbed a tree so he could see Jesus when He passed. Jesus saw the man and said, "Zacchaeus, come down quickly for I must come to your house today." Of course this caused quite a stir among the people. They could not get over the fact that Jesus was actually coming to Zacchaeus, the tax collector's house. The effect on Zacchaeus was that he told Jesus he would return fourfold anything he had taken from anyone and give half of his goods to the poor. Jesus then said, *"Today salvation has come to this house, because he also is a son of Abraham; for the Son of Man has come to seek and to save that which was lost."*

Jesus' purpose was to come to earth to seek out the lost so they could be saved. Zacchaeus sought out Jesus and Jesus met him right where he was. Many in the world today need unconditional love and acceptance, the kind that Jesus showed Zacchaeus. The complaining crowd didn't stop Jesus from ministering. Let's make a decision to seek out those who are lost without Christ. It says in Jude 1:22–23, "And on some have compassion, making a distinction; but others save with fear, pulling them out of the fire, hating even the garment defiled by the flesh." This scripture hits us with the urgency to do what God has entrusted to us.

Father, I thank You that You have come to seek and save that which is lost. Lord, I decide to be open to Your direction in leading me to the ones who need Your saving grace. Lord help me to be obedient to Your voice.

Sherlyn Smucker serves as the administrative assistant with her husband, Pastor Sam at The Worship Center, Lancaster.

November 27

Mercy Triumphs Over Judgment

"Flee the evil desires of youth, and pursue righteousness, faith, love and peace, along with those who call on the Lord out of a pure heart. Don't have anything to do with foolish and stupid arguments, because you know they produce quarrels, and the Lord's servant must not quarrel; instead he must be kind to everyone..." *2 Timothy 2:22–23*

Leaders of all kinds are called to be peacemakers and to bring reconciliation between those who have a broken relationship with others, and above all, those who have a broken relationship with God. Our goal is not to prove who is right or who is wrong, but to bring peace and restoration.

We must look at the people whom we are giving leadership to—our family, our business, our youth group, our small group, our church of a few people, or a large church—as those whom He has entrusted to us. The biblical passage that always keeps me humble is Acts 20:28, "Keep watch over yourselves and all the flock of which the Holy Spirit has made you overseers. Be shepherds of the church of God, which he bought with his own blood." No matter how individuals look, act or how they have sinned, remember Jesus died for them just as He did for you and me.

Above all, remember James 2:13 when making decisions, "...Mercy triumphs over judgment!"

Lord, help me to make decisions today that reflect Your mercy and love toward others. Help me to be a peacemaker, in Jesus' name. Amen.

Carl Good is a member of D.O.V.E. Christian Fellowship's Apostolic Council.

November 28
Humility

"The fear of the Lord teaches a man wisdom, and humility comes before honor." *Proverbs 15:33*

While he was president of Tuskegee Institute in Alabama, a woman saw Booker T. Washington walking down the street. Not recognizing him, she yelled with blatant racist condescension, "Hey, you, come in and chop some wood!" Washington cheerfully chopped the wood and left without identifying himself.

When the woman discovered what she had done, she was horrified and went to apologize. "It's all right," Washington replied, "I delight to do favors for my friends." The wealthy woman was so moved that she eventually became one of the college's strongest supporters. Booker T. Washington understood the Biblical mystery that humility precedes honor. In quiet confidence he overcame racist indignities and won the day.

Humility is no refuge for the spineless, whining person of self-pity. Humility requires the courage of a redwood tree to remain elegant during suffering and hopeful during adversity. A humble parent can say, "Son, I was wrong." Humility can acknowledge the brilliant accomplishment of a co-worker. Only the humbled strong can nudge others to the front of the victory procession.

A humble attitude is the launch pad of prayer and worship. All across our county, people participate in worship to acknowledge our human weakness and Almighty God's wholeness. And our relationship with God goes beyond our Lancaster County houses of worship. At the crack of dawn over coffee, or in marketplace office, or during quiet leisure time, God recreates us as we humble ourselves before him.

Lord, by Your grace I face another day. Through your gifts. I labor with confidence. By Your strength, I can be dependable. Help me befriend my enemies, enable me to see and exalt the successes of Your grace in others' lives today.

Dave Witmer is a husband, father, church planter, pastor, writer and musician living in Lancaster City.

November 29

Acing Impossible Tests

"Therefore Jesus lifting up His eyes and seeing that a large crowd was coming to Him, said to Philip, 'Where are we to buy bread, that these may eat?' This He was saying to test him, for He Himself knew what He was intending to do."
John 6:5,6 (New American Standard)

How do you respond when the Lord clearly spot lights a problem that is well beyond your ability to solve and asks you what you plan to do? I can identify times when I responded as Philip and Andrew did as they recognized their limitations and the overwhelming, impossible size of the task.

Disciples of Jesus will often find themselves placed in the midst of a situation that is truly beyond their resources. Rather than be surprised, we should come to expect it. After all, a true disciple desires to be about their Father's business. If it truly is God's enterprise, it will always be God-sized. How should a mature disciple respond?

First, remember: God *always* knows what *He* is intending to do. He has a plan and He is more than able to carry out that plan. He sees the solution in advance of every problem we will ever face. We can rest in that truth and wait upon Him for direction.

Second, obey the simple steps the Lord does give. "Bring the lunch here. Have the people sit down. Distribute the bread and fish." (See John 6:9–14.) Suddenly, ordinary things are touched by the supernatural, and a miracle happens. The need is met, the problem is solved, and God alone gets the glory.

Finally, keep your heart soft and be sure to learn the lessons God has for us in each test. Those lessons will be foundational for future tests.

What is Jesus intending to do in and through your life?

Lord, help me rest in Your plans and Your power for the impossibilities I will face as I follow You.

Don Riker serves congregational, ministry, and business leaders as part of Teaching The Word Ministries in Leola.

Reality Of God's Grace

"For it is by grace you have been saved, through faith—and this not from yourselves, it is the gift of God—not by works, so that no one can boast." *Ephesians 2:8-9*

The day had come for the final exam in the Youth Issues class and everyone was doing some last minute studying. The professor came in and said he would review some of the material a bit before the test. That was great, but some of the review material was never gone over in class. When questioned about it, he said the material was in the book and that the students were responsible for everything in the book. No one could really argue with that.

Finally it was time to take the test. "Leave the test face down on your desk until everyone has one and I will tell you when to start," the professor instructed.

When the class turned the test over, every answer on the test was filled in! The bottom of the last page said the following: "This is the end of the final exam. All the answers on your test are correct. You will receive an "A" on the final exam. The reason you passed this test is because the creator of the test took the test for you. All the work you did in preparation for this test did not help you get the A. You have just experienced…grAce."

The professor then went around the room and asked each student, "What is your grade? Do you deserve the grade you are receiving? Did all your studying for this exam help you achieve your final grade?"

What a picture of God's grace! The professor said he had never given a test like that before and probably never would again. But he thought these students needed to experience the reality of grace.

Do you know the reality of God's grace toward you?

Father, I thank You that it is by grace that we are saved. By the power of the Holy Spirit, I ask You to give a fresh revelation of Your grace. Help me to know it, and share it with others. In Jesus' name, Amen.

Kevin Eshleman serves as executive pastor of Ephrata Community Church.

December

I bring you *good news*
that will be for
all the people
...a *Savior* has been born to you;
he is *Christ* the *Lord*
Luke 2:10,11

December 1

Fruitfulness

"I am the vine; you are the branches. If a man remains in Me and I in him, he will bear much fruit; apart from Me you can do nothing." *John 15:5*

for Lancaster County

"But the fruit of the Spirit is love, joy, peace, patience, kindness, goodness, faithfulness, gentleness and self-control. Against such things there is no law." *Galatians 5:22–23*

As we enter this Advent season, we are presented with a great opportunity to abide in the Vine. Rather than getting lost in the hustle and bustle, we can draw near to Jesus. Through our ongoing, obedient relationship to Him and our love for one another, we will bear much fruit to the Father's glory. The Scripture is clear: we can't do anything unless we remain connected to the Vine; we will dry up quickly if left to ourselves. Let's commit ourselves this season not to be distracted, but to strengthen our connection with the source. Let's allow His love, joy and peace to be revealed in us and through us across our region.

Lord Jesus, by Your grace, draw us near. Help us to spend more, not less, time with You in the midst of this busy season. Let us produce much fruit and bring great glory to the Father.

Today's devotional was edited from the 2003–2004 *Throne Of Grace Prayer Guide*, a weekly guide of Lancaster County prayer concerns gathered from regional intercessors and area prayer groups.

December 2

What On Earth Am I Here For?

"For we are God's workmanship, created in Christ Jesus to do good works, which God prepared in advance for us to do."
Ephesians 2:10

In the beginning God brought man into being (Genesis 1: 26). In the act referred to in the opening text, God brought our spiritual life into being. God alone created, producing something from nothing. When there was no human on earth, God called Adam into existence. When there was no life in me, nothing but spiritual death, God brought into existence a spiritual life within me, as I believed in Him. This creative work took place in union with Jesus Christ. What a freeing message! I am God's workmanship. I have worth and I am loved.

In Christ, the good works I do have been prepared in advance. There is no limit to these works, no matter how old I am.

In our society a person is handicapped by age but there is no "retirement" for one who is in Christ. Our father is glorified that we bear much fruit (John 15:8).

After retirement, we need not puzzle about what we may do to please God. He has long ago mapped out our entire course. My husband has moderate dementia. Some friends pity us, since this changes our focus. We served many years on the mission field and they see this dementia as a big, bad thing. But really, it is a blessing in disguise. We are discovering the good works God has planned in advance for us. What a blessed joy when, with unveiled faces, we all reflect the Lord's glory. We are being transformed into His likeness from glory to glory (2 Corinthians 3:18).

Thank you, Lord for Your grace which chose us in Him before the foundation of the world that we should walk in Your good works. Remind us as, we walk with our brothers and sisters, that we are mingling with your Glory. Keep us faithful in carrying out Your eternal plan, until Jesus comes.

Blanche Mohler Horst is a retired teacher and active member of Ephrata Mennonite Church.

December 3

House Cleaning I

"The priests went into the sanctuary of the LORD to purify it. They brought out to the courtyard of the LORD's temple everything unclean that they found in the temple of the LORD..."
2 Chronicles 29:16

If you have you ever gone into an old house and begun to clean it out, you've probably discovered dust and dirt all over everything. Often there are items left behind: broken down furniture, old magazines and books, clothes from another era, and bags or boxes of trash. There may be boarded up doors and windows. It's not a real pleasant place to be. For some of you, that may describe *your room*.

In the Bible, we read of someone that set in motion the task of cleaning out a very big and old house. His name was Hezekiah and the house he wanted to clean belonged to God. It was the temple in Jerusalem. Hezekiah gave the task of cleaning this temple to the priests and the Levites. He instructed them to remove everything that didn't belong in the temple.

Over the years there were many items brought into the temple that did not belong there: idols, shrines to other gods, and furniture that was used for worship ceremonies to those idols. The temple was no longer a place to glorify God. Those entering the temple did not wash in the laver. The lamps in the temple were not lit. The table of showbread was not kept in order. It was a disgraceful reminder of the neglect by the people of the worship of the Lord.

As soon as Hezekiah had the temple cleaned out, he returned all the correct furniture to its place. But he did not stop there; he started all the services of worship. The temple was once again serving the purpose for which it was built. It was bringing glory to God!

Pray and ask God to show you the areas of His temple that He desires cleaned.

David Tressler is the pastor of Family Ministry at Mount Joy Church of God.

December 4

House Cleaning II

"Do you not know that your body is a temple of the Holy Spirit, who is in you, whom you have received from God? You are not your own; you were bought at a price. Therefore honor God with your body." *1 Corinthians 6:19–20*

P aul, in the New Testament, talks about another temple that often needs cleaning out. In 1 Corinthians 6:19, we read that our bodies are the temple of the Holy Spirit. God lives within us. We are His temple. Sometimes we allow things that are not honoring to Him into that temple: greed, envy, hatred, jealousy, backbiting, and wrong attitudes. All of these furnishings do nothing to bring glory to God. Rather they are set up to worship our own selfish idols.

Colossians 3:5–10 tells us that we are to rid our temple of those furnishings and replace them with furnishings that bring glory to God. That is the purpose of our bodies: to bring glory to God! So we furnish the temple with the fruit of the Spirit: "love, joy, peace, patience, kindness, goodness, faithfulness, gentleness and self-control (Galatians 5:22–23)."

Paul told the Corinthian believers to "...glorify God with your body (1 Corinthians 6:20)." And so must we. In order to do a little house cleaning, reflect on your own life and ask yourself, is there anything in my life that needs to be removed? Is there anything that is not bringing glory to God? Are there furnishings missing in my life that would bring glory to God?

Pray and ask God to show you the areas of His temple that He desires cleaned. Take time to read the Word and ask God to use it to sweep clean all the corners of the temple.

David Tressler is the pastor of Family Ministry at Mount Joy Church of God.

December 5

The Kingdom

"This is what the kingdom of God is like. A man scatters seed on the ground. Night and day whether he sleeps or gets up, the seed sprouts and grows, though he does not know how…As soon as the grain is ripe, he puts the sickle to it, because the harvest has come." *Mark 4:26–29*

These verses have been both a constant reminder and conviction to me. Knowing that bearing fruit is a prevalent theme throughout the scriptures, it is easy to begin basing our "self esteem" on how much fruit we see ourselves bearing in our ministry. When we are in a season where things don't seem to be working too well we begin to doubt ourselves and God's feelings about us. In turn, when we go through times where we are seeing great things happening in our ministry, we think too highly of ourselves. In this way, we are often tempted to base our disposition on our perceived productivity.

These verses have been the bullhorn calling out to me in the midst of my pride or despair over ministry. They remind me that bearing fruit is not only beyond my control, it is even beyond my understanding. As a matter of fact, it is likely that success, as I define it, may not be success from God's eternal perspective. Jesus reminds his disciples of this in Luke 10 when they returned from a mission. They were excited over the fact that their ministry seemed to be a blazing success. Jesus exhorts them: "Do not rejoice that the spirits submit to you, but rejoice that your names are written in heaven."

Lord, no matter how successful my efforts appear to me today, help me find complete joy in the simple fact that You see me as your wonderful child. Please use my thoughts of eternity with You to guide me to a joyful desire to be obedient and faithful in what IS my call…spreading the seed and reaping the ripened fruit.

Tim Doering, pastor of discipleship ministries, Ephrata Church of the Brethren.

Pray Without Ceasing

"Pray without ceasing." "Pray continually." "Never stop praying." "Be unceasing in prayer." *1 Thessalonians 5:17 (Various Translations)*

When I was a child this verse was confusing to me. I wondered how anyone could pray without stopping. As an adult this verse has become a lifeline for me. Every day as I read the newspaper and listen to the news, I become aware of events in the world that affect people adversely. I hear about situations and needs from people that I love and care about. I am tempted to allow these needs to rob my joy and peace as I take on the weight of the world. What should I do with all the needs around me? Obviously it is impossible to spend every day on my knees with my eyes closed, praying.

But, I do believe it is possible to live with a prayerful attitude 24/7. This attitude is built upon our acknowledgment of our dependence on our Heavenly Father. He is attentive to His children and pleased when we come to Him in prayer. I am learning to take these situations to God as soon as I hear about them and as often as they come to my attention. If there is something more God wants me to do, He will let me know. Prayer allows me to be involved in seeing God's solutions released. I benefit by releasing the burden I feel and by knowing I am making a difference in people's lives. I have heard it said that God limits Himself to the prayers of His children. Let's make a difference in our world as we usher in the kingdom of God by praying without ceasing.

Dear God, thank You for the privilege of praying without ceasing. Thanks for the freedom that comes as we pray continually. We receive Your grace to be unceasing in prayer and to never stop praying.

Sue Martin serves with her husband, Nelson, on the Apostolic Council for D.O.V.E. Christian Fellowship International. She also serves as an elder of ELANCO D.O.V.E. Fellowship, Terre Hill.

December 7
Just Do It!
*"And remember, it is a message to obey, not just to listen to.
So don't fool yourselves." James 1:22 (Living Bible)*

My husband and I are at the leading edge of the "baby boomers". From time to time, I have felt a need to confront my declining physical abilities. To that end, we have purchased an Airdyne stationary bicycle, a treadmill, and a QVC Ab Builder "thing-a-ma-gig". Our bookshelves contain fine books detailing ways to stay active and healthy. I have become very knowledgeable about which foods supply the maximum nutritional values and what vitamins and minerals are needed by people my age.

Sadly, having all the correct equipment and learning everything I can about healthy living does not mean I am now more physically fit. I have to actually get on the bike, walk on the treadmill, eat the right foods, and take the supplements before my body can experience renewal.

Is it possible that we do the same thing with our spiritual lives? Do we read excellent Christian books, listen to inspired sermons, attend helpful teaching seminars? Do the majority of our CD's feature talented Christian musicians?

Having all the right resources means nothing. We must act on our knowledge, and obediently do what the Holy Spirit teaches us. We can not experience renewed spiritual strength unless we begin to flex our spiritual muscles.

Lord forgive me for being spiritually lazy. Teach me Your discipline. I want to be a doer of the Word.

Andrea Bomberger, wife of Henry Bomberger, president of Bomberger's Store Inc.

December 8

Generosity

"Remember this: Whoever sows sparingly will also reap sparingly, and whoever
sows generously will also reap generously.
Each man should give what he has decided in
his heart to give, not reluctantly or under compulsion, for God loves a cheerful giver. And God is
able to make all grace abound to you, so that in all things at all
times, having all that you need, you will abound in every good
work....You will be made rich in every way so that you can be
generous on every occasion, and through us your generosity
will result in thanksgiving to God."
2 Corinthians 9:6–11

Pray!
for Lancaster
County

We are blessed to be living in a region that is marked with generosity. May we continue to lay up treasures in heaven, where nothing can steal our investment. May we show the world that even in uncertain times, our God provides all our needs through His riches. Let us continue to sow into the Kingdom gener- ously and without reluctance. And we will reap a harvest of righteous- ness.

Dear God, grant me a glad and willing heart to give. I will be faithful in tithes and offerings, and seek to be generous on every occasion. I pray that my increased generosity will result in increased thanksgiving and honor to You.

Today's devotional was edited from the 2003–2004 *Throne Of Grace Prayer Guide*, a weekly guide of Lancaster County prayer concerns gathered from regional intercessors and area prayer groups.

December 9
Biblical Conjunctions
"...but God..." *Genesis 50:20*

CONJUNCTION (noun)...3) a combination of events or circumstances; 4) (Grammar) any member of a small class of words functioning as connectors between words, phrases, clauses or sentences." (*Random House College Dictionary*)

As I read the Bible I'm often struck by this "small class of words" that makes a big difference in my perspective. Sometimes those single words bring hope and elation; sometimes they bring a deflation of spirit.

For example, Psalm 34:19 reads "Many are the afflictions of the righteous..." Stopping at that point we might agree wholeheartedly. "Man, that's right. For the last four months my family has experienced nothing but struggles." Then we come to a three-letter conjunction: "...BUT the Lord delivers them out of them all." Struggle turns to hope. The small conjunction is a huge bridge between two very different perspectives.

In 1 Corinthians 16:8, we see another of God's conjunctions. As Paul pens his concluding remarks, he tells the Corinthians he is staying in Ephesus until Pentecost, "for a wide door for effective service has opened to me..." Sounds great doesn't it? Many opportunities for ministry. Who wouldn't stay in such a place?

Then we come to another conjunction: "...AND there are many adversaries." Again, that small word serves as a big bridge between two perspectives. The correct response is not to choose one statement or the other, but to hold both in dynamic tension.

The point is that opportunities rarely come without adversity; wide doors often coexist with circumstances which could slam the door in our face. Effective service frequently takes place in the context of opposition. For Paul to write anything different would be dishonest.

Lord, when I am in a tough place, show me Your perspective from the "right" side of the conjunction. Show me the wide door for effective service, the huge door of opportunity.

Dan Hoellwarth is pastor of ACTS Covenant Fellowship, Lancaster.

Trust In The Lord

"Trust in the Lord with all your heart, and lean not unto your own understanding; In all your ways acknowledge Him, and He shall direct your paths." *Proverbs 3:5–6 (New King James Version)*

Trust is a fundamental need for all of us. To be able to fully trust someone is to know that what someone says he will do, will be done. It's holding your heart fully open, dependent, and vulnerable to someone. Trust knows that your best interest is in good hands.

Just as a small child completely trusts and is completely dependant, so we are to be towards Father God. We need to know that nothing can separate us from His love. This includes death, trial, tribulation, sorrow and sickness. Through all these things, we are more than conquerors through Him who loves us. To trust is to take someone at their word and know we can depend upon them. Who better to trust than Father God who is fully dependable, trustworthy and faithful. He just asks us to trust and obey and He will direct our paths.

If someone close to you dies, will you trust God? If life seems dark and you cannot see in front of you, will you trust? If you do not understand what is happening around you, will you trust God? If He asks you to give up something very dear, will you trust Him? If you have something taken from you—loved ones, material blessings and health— will you trust Him? Job did, and God restored to him more blessings than he previously had. God is trustworthy and we can thank Him for that.

Father, forgive me for being reluctant to trust You. You are more trustworthy than anyone. Teach me how to lean on You instead of my own understanding. Today I chose to acknowledge You while you guide me through this day. Amen.

Cheryl Wissler is a counselor and office manager for Breath of Life Ministries. She and her husband Barry have two children and live in Ephrata.

December 11

Come Clean!

"But you were washed, but you were sanctified, but you were justified in the name of the Lord Jesus Christ...."
1 Corinthians 6:11 (New King James Version)

In my job as a tree trimmer, I get sawdust in my hair, eyes, nose, ears and even pockets! Fumes from my chainsaw permeate my hair and clothing. I collect the pungent smells of some trees from sliding around on them all day. The dust from dead trees covers my sweaty face. Some days, I sweat profusely. I often bleed because my hands and arms bear the brunt of unforgiving logs. Often, I walk through poison ivy. Ticks have found me to be tasty. I've had spiders in my pockets. Still, when I come home, my lovely wife will greet me at the door and kiss me on the lips!

We all must walk upon this earth and work. The world may get into our pockets. We may have curses spit upon us. Our ears may be seared with speech unbecoming children of God. Our eyes see so much before we can turn away. Fear, doubt, confusion, hurt, temptation and guilt will hang with us until shaken off.

Just as my wife greets me with love, so the church should greet the brethren warmly, overlooking the faults accumulated that week. We must be ready to lavish prayer and ministry on those who need help. As my wife welcomes me, she doesn't expect me to stay in that state. She has purchased the soap and prepared the shower. She has laundered the clothing that I will change into and prepared the meal to replenish my strength. I must use these things to my benefit. I must step into the shower. I must raise the fork to my mouth.

Lord, thank You that my sins have been pardoned, and I am accepted as righteous, because of the merits of the Lord Jesus Christ. Thanks for providing the Word to wash me clean. Help me to read it and listen and believe as I allow it to permeate my mind and life.

Carl Harper is the owner of Harper's Tree Service.

One

December 12

God With Us

"...God has come to help his people." *Luke 7:16*

A few years ago we received a calendar from some missionary friends living in France. The December scripture was taken from this passage in Luke 17: "...Dieu a visite son peuple (God has visited His people)." I remember thinking how much that verse captured the essence of Christmas (I kept repeating it in faulty French)! God came to visit His people, and He never left. The gospel of Matthew begins and ends with the declaration that He is here: "...they will call His name Immanuel, which means God with us (1:23);" "And surely I am with you always, to the very end of the age (28:20)."

Christmas, then, is a season of hope, hope that Someone is there. One of the basic needs of man is to know that he is not alone in the universe. The incarnation lets us see that in the midst of a world increasingly characterized by broken relationships and isolation, there remains a God who is both sovereign and near.

But the message of Christmas goes further. The tidings that Someone is able to bring incalculable good out of the most unlikely circumstances. Who would have thought that the Creator of the universe would have come to earth as a baby? Not only a baby, but a poor baby. I like what Brennan Manning says: Christmas is the promise that...in the end everything will be all right. Nothing can harm you permanently, no suffering is irrevocable, no loss is lasting, no defeat is more than transitory, no disappointment is conclusive. Jesus has come as the Redeemer to buy back the brokenness of our lives and put them back together. My favorite Christmas carol is:

Come Thou long expected Jesus, Born to set Thy people free
From our fears and sins release us, Let us find our rest in Thee.

We can celebrate today because, indeed, He has come.

Lord Jesus, thank You for coming and staying, for bringing us hope and help.

Becky Toews leads the women's ministry at New Covenant Christian Church.

December 13

The Lone Ranger Rides Again

"Render...honor to whom honor is due." *Romans 13:7 (Amplified Bible)*

The church has given the Lone Ranger a bad rap. "There can be no Lone Rangers in the Kingdom of God," we've declared, quoting Hebrews 10:25 to justify our words. The principle is biblical, but the rap ain't right! The Lone Ranger wasn't a lone ranger.

It's true that he alone survived the ambush that slaughtered his troop of Texas Rangers. In this, he was the "lone" Ranger, but even here he wasn't alone because a compassionate Indian named Tonto rescued him from death, nursed him to health and became his trusted partner in a lifelong calling to defend their far-flung neighbors against every evil and injustice of the Wild West.

In many ways, the Lone Ranger's life is worthy of Christian emulation. He was committed to cross-cultural, inter-racial relationships. He networked with law officials across the West. He was accountable to the law, trusting himself to a circle of close friends who knew who he really was. He upheld righteousness, was a champion of the poor and weak, and was totally committed to the good of others—even at the risk of laying down his own life. He wasn't vengeful, shooting only to wound and not to kill. He didn't drink, smoke, swear or covet. He had a spotless reputation with those inside and outside the law. According to a creed he wrote, he believed "that all things change but truth." Like Paul the apostle, he was a "tent maker", owning a silver mine which supported him so that he could serve others. He molded his silver, symbolizing purity, into bullets which became his trademark. His creed declares that he believed "in my Creator, my country, my fellow man."

No Lone Rangers in the Kingdom of God? Hey, get a white hat!

Father in heaven, give me a horse and let me ride! Amen.

Mark Ammerman serves on the leadership team of In The Light Ministries in Lancaster City. He is the communications director of the Regional Church of Lancaster County.

December 14

Ragtime Love

"While we were still sinners, Christ died for us." *Romans 5:8*

I marvel at God's unconditional love. He didn't wait to love us until we were loveable. He loved us when we were living in sin, in our own self-willed deception. For some of us, we were relying on our own religiosity, others on doing good. But in spite of those "filthy rags", He still loved us.

Since we have come to know Christ personally, He has placed His love within our hearts, and since we are to "love our neighbor as ourselves", He frees us to love as He loved. It's not a matter of gritting our teeth and loving another person because it's a Biblical command. His life within us enables us to love another person even in difficult and challenging circumstances. It may not be an artesian well experience, but just as God was able to love us so He enables us to love others.

God loved us while hating the sin we were involved in. God's love for us didn't cause God to be soft on sin. He loved us as a person and yet dealt with the hated sin.

In applying this to the marriage relationship, I don't believe that God expects us to love everything our spouse does. We can, however, have a godly love for our spouse while disliking some of his/her behaviors. It is no secret that men and women look at circumstances through different lenses. But in spite of that, each couple can experience a godly unity in marriage. Since the same love that God demonstrated "while we were still sinners" is now in our hearts as children of God, He enables us to love others in the same godly manner.

Thank you, Heavenly Father, for loving us in Your unconditional way. Help me to release that love to everyone I relate to today. In Jesus' name, Amen.

Pastor Titus Kauffman is the assistant pastor and counselor at Petra Christian Fellowship, New Holland.

Kindness

"Therefore, as God's chosen people, holy and dearly loved, clothe yourselves with compassion, kindness, humility, gentleness and patience." *Colossians 3:12*

for Lancaster County

W
e know that Christmas is a season when many are looking for kindness and compassion. We are well aware of heightened loneliness and depression that many experience in what is supposed to be a joyous time. The Church, God's chosen people, are equipped to meet those needs. As we clothe ourselves with love and acceptance for all those searching for the truth, as we embrace and welcome all those who come into our midst, we are engaging in the work that those who are *holy and dearly loved* are called to do.

We can experience a mighty harvest in our region this Christmas season as we exhibit the attributes of our Savior.

Lord Jesus, You are the God of all compassion and kindness. We thank You for Your humility, gentleness and patience with us. This Christmas season, please help us to reflect those characteristics to a hurting, searching world. Help us to reach out to family members, neighbors and friends in Your name.

Today's devotional was edited from the 2003–2004 *Throne Of Grace Prayer Guide*, a weekly guide of Lancaster County prayer concerns gathered from regional intercessors and area prayer groups.

December 16

The Father Heart Of God

"...He arose and came to his father. But when he was still a great way off, his father saw him and had compassion, and ran and fell on his neck and kissed him." Luke 15:20 (New King James Version)

I have heard it said that the message of the gospel is best summed up in Luke 15. The parables of the lost sheep, the lost coin and the lost son are all paths into the heart of God. I am often stirred most by the picture of the Father heart of God painted in the story of the prodigal son.

It may be the way I see my own journey in the story that so draws me to it. A son, eager for experience and to "grow up", scorns his father and seeks his own way in the world, only to find himself empty and alone. He decides to return home as a servant, knowing he has lost his place as a son.

The prodigal misunderstands the father's heart, just as we often misunderstand God. Instead of rejecting him, the father runs to embrace him, not just restoring him as a son, but blessing him with more than was his previously. Even though he misunderstood the way back, that one step toward home set the father running after him. And even though we so often misunderstand the ways of our Father, He is eager to embrace us again.

One weak glance heavenward can undo the heart of the uncreated God (Song of Solomon 4:9), just as one weak turning of a son restored him to his father's embrace.

Abba, allow us to know Your heart. You are our Heavenly Father and we embrace Your love as You have embraced us. Teach us Your ways and guide us into Your truth. Amen.

Jed Burkholder serves at Lancaster House of Prayer, a worship and prayer movement seeking to establish a place of 24 hour prayer in Lancaster County.

December 17

Spiritual Meat

"As newborn babes, desire the pure milk of the word, that you may grow thereby, if indeed you have tasted that the Lord is gracious." *1 Peter 2:2–3 (New King James Version)*

A newborn baby needs milk so that it can grow and develop until it is able to eat meat. So it is with our spiritual walk. When we are born again, we need to desire (crave, earnestly desire) the sincere (pure, spiritual) milk of the Word so that we can be nurtured and grow in the Lord. The rate of growth of our spirit man will be determined by how much we feed it the Word of God. We can stay in the baby stage all our lives, or we can continue to strengthen our inner man, becoming rooted and grounded and able to handle the strong meat of the Word.

In 1 Corinthians 3:1–2, Paul exhorted the Corinthians about their spiritual state. "And I, brethren, could not speak to you as to spiritual people, but as to carnal, as to babes in Christ. I have fed you with milk and not with solid food; for until now you were not able to receive it and even now you are still not able." Let's keep feeding on the Word of God. Let's keep hungering and thirsting after God and His righteousness, being strengthened with might through His Spirit. That we may be rooted and grounded in walking in love and that we may be filled with all the fullness of God.

Lord, I thank You for Your Word. I thank You that my inner man is continuing to be strengthened with might through Your Spirit. Lord, I ask You to create in me more of a hunger and thirst for Your Word. I commit myself to You today, and I make the decision to read, hear and be a doer of Your Word. Thank you, Lord, for You said that those who hunger and thirst after righteousness shall be filled.

Sherlyn Smucker serves as the administrative assistant with husband, Pastor Sam at The Worship Center, Lancaster.

December 18

His Special Pets!

"If you, then, though you are evil, know how to give good gifts to your children, how much more will your Father in heaven give good gifts to those who ask him!" *Matthew 7:11*

D o you ever think God has special pets... people like Billy Graham, James Dobson, or Elisabeth Elliot? Have you ever felt like a no-name Christian, not very special or important to the great God of the universe? Satan wants us to believe that we don't count much, but in reality our heavenly Father is always looking for ways to bless *all* His children!

When vacationing in New Jersey, Sharon and I drove through several residential neighborhoods looking at various styles of decorative Victorian-style fences. My boys and I were planning to construct a new patio, and I wanted to get some ideas. All of a sudden we spotted a beautiful fence... just the type we would like. And it appeared to have a very simple style of construction. I thought, "If only I had a tape measure, I could measure the fence and make notes that would help us later." We decided to circle the block one more time.

Imagine my surprise when I spotted something shiny in the center of the next intersection, directly underneath the traffic light. I stopped, then darted out on the street to pick up... a brand new tape measure! Some folks would say, "What a nice coincidence!" But I don't think so! God was demonstrating His extreme interest in even the small concerns of ordinary people like me!

God is always giving good gifts to all His children. Scripture tells us that every good gift we enjoy comes from Him. Perhaps we just need to open our eyes more often and look at what might be right in front of us!

Lord, help me today, to be alert to the many little (and big!) evidences of Your love and interest in me! And thank You for loving me, just as much as You love all Your children!

John Charles and his wife Sharon serve as directors of Abundant Living, a family counseling ministry in Lititz, PA.

December 19

Good News

"How beautiful are the feet of those who bring good news."
Romans 10:15; Read Romans 10:15–17

For the past 15 years God has done so many marvelous things in the prison where I am an assistant chaplain and church volunteer. One afternoon I had the privilege of passing through one of the cell blocks where men were very discouraged about their lives and mistakes they had made. One of the young men asked if I could be his spiritual advisor and counsel him. Being moved by his request, I said "Yes!".

We went into one of the counseling rooms, and I could tell all he wanted to hear from me was "Jesus". I began telling him about God's love and the kingdom of God. He told me that he was at church the previous Sunday and heard me singing, so he asked me if I could sing the song that I sang at that service. As I joyfully began singing, God's Spirit filled that small counseling room and the young man gave his life to Jesus.

The Gospel is simple; that's why it's called "good news". Jesus said in John 3:7, "Do not marvel that I said to you, 'you must be born again.'" Many people are caught by surprise at this statement, but God's heart is that all men taste and see the kingdom of God. The prisons across this nation are filled with people who are longing to hear good news because our world is filled with so much bad news. Let us be Jesus' feet and mouth wherever we go!

God, I ask you to help us to be your feet and mouth, that we would take the gospel into dark and discouraging places and speak the good news of Your gospel, so that people could see hope and be encouraged. Help us Lord to count others better than ourselves and be Your fresh aroma, in Jesus' name. Amen.

Marvin Lyons serves as assistant chaplain and church volunteer at the Lancaster County Prison.

December 20

Springs Of Life

"Watch over your heart with all diligence, for from it flow the springs of life." *Proverbs 4:23 (New American Standard Version)*

I usually think of the "springs of life" as something that benefits the individual. It wasn't until recently that I realized the greater potential of those springs flowing out *from* the individual. What flows from us always affects those around us. We don't always know when or where people will draw life from our hearts, but we can be certain that it will—over and over.

For most of my life I've held administrative, behind-the-scenes roles. But ever since I began working with Steven Courtney, I've encountered a completely different perspective on life. Standing in front of crowds from 25 to 1,000 with the sole purpose of giving each person, young or old, an encouraging experience, I have consistently been amazed at what God will do.

Recently a mom who attended one of our concerts emailed us the next day. She was thankful for the enjoyment we had brought to the children but was particularly thankful for something she saw between two adults. The two grown-ups lived close together and had a "disagreement" of some nature. While listening to one of the songs that spoke of the importance of loving your neighbor, they looked at each other and smiled. The simplest song that came from our hearts met those neighbors where they were and made a difference.

Every believer, whether they know it or not, will make an impact on those with whom they come in contact. What kind of impact, good or bad, is up to each of us. Watch over your heart. Guard what goes in, for whatever is in abundance there, will come out.

Lord, remind me daily of the great treasure You have implanted in my spirit. Guard it...yes, but may I always be ready to give from it to those who need.

Hank Rogers serves as drummer for the Steven Courtney Band.

December 21

Too Busy To Rest?

"Come to me, all you who are weary and burdened, and I will give you rest." *Matthew 11:28*

est? Now? How long will it take? I'm too busy to rest! We may chuckle at this, yet how often have we had this thought? Our schedule seems to have little time for the luxury of "rest". Especially now, during the Christmas season, rest seems to be something that eludes us.

Celebrating Christ's birth can be, well, *busy*! We have family gatherings, decorating the tree, shopping for gifts, extra church Christmas planning and programs to attend. Even the *thought* of rest can evaporate quickly.

What is rest? How can I fit it into my day?

First, the Lord promises rest to His beloved. That's us! We're His beloved. God desires to commune with us throughout the day. As we pray and worship the Lord, we will find rest and peace renewing our soul. Resting is not designed to fit into a time slot, but to be practiced throughout our day. The Lord's rest gives calm on even the most hectic of days, a rest that eases our burdens and fills us with joy.

This Christmas season make it a priority to spend time snuggling in your Father's arms. The busier your day, the more valuable and important resting in God's presence will be. As we take on an attitude of rest, we will resonate a sweet calm, even though our day may be filled.

Let us celebrate this joyful time of year with our spirit, soul and body renewed through practicing His presence.

Lord, as I look at the days ahead, I ask for Your rest and grace. May I take on and accomplish only that which is Your best. In the midst of the hustle and bustle of this holy season may I find and abide in Your rest. As my eyes rest on You may I be enveloped with rest.

Lucinda Dise is the wife of pastor/senior elder, Allen Dise, of D.O.V.E. Christian Fellowship Manheim.

December 22

Good News Of Great Joy For All People

Pray!

"For unto us a child is born, to us a son is given, and the government will be on His shoulders. And He will be called Wonderful Counselor, Mighty God, Everlasting Father, Prince of Peace." *Isaiah 9:6*

A Savior has been born: a Savior who is also a wonderful counselor; He has all the answers to our problems. A Savior has been born: a Savior who is also a mighty God; nothing can defeat Him.

A Savior has been born: a Savior who is also an everlasting Father; we are birthed by His love into a life that never ends.

A Savior has been born: a Savior who is also the author and the sovereign of peace; He resolves every conflict.

A Savior has been born: a Savior who is Christ the Lord!

Jesus, thank You for filling our incredible need for a Mighty Savior. You are the reason we celebrate this season. Today I will spread the good news by reminding others that You have come to bring the peace and love of God for all.

Today's devotional was edited from the 2003–2004 *Throne Of Grace Prayer Guide*, a weekly guide of Lancaster County prayer concerns gathered from regional intercessors and area prayer groups.

December 23

Unwrap The Gift!

"And Christ became a human being and lived here on earth among us and was full of loving forgiveness and truth."
John 1:14 (Living Bible)

The joys of the Christmas season are here! Festive sights, sounds, and smells fill the air. Gifts are a big part of the tradition we look forward to… well, at least some of us do. I keep my eyes open all year long for unique Christmas gifts. I love wrapping them and almost dread Christmas day because that means the wonderful season is over for another year.

The most important present this season doesn't get picked up at Park City shopping mall or delivered via UPS. It was given at the first Christmas—it came wrapped up in the Christ child. It's the gift of "God with us!"

This gift works the best when used everyday! Open the gift of God's presence today. Pray with your children, in an important meeting, or even in congested holiday traffic. Any time that a decision is unclear or tension is mounting is a great time to open the gift! You can talk to God either in your heart or invite others to join you. Ask His counsel. Leave your worries and concerns with Him. Ask Him for direction for your day.

I thank God for my mother who modeled for us the reality of answered prayer. God was part of our lives and real to me as a child because I saw Him at work. In our shrinking world, we experience many religions and religious people. What is the difference in our lives as Christians? We need to live the gift of "God with us."

Lord, we are thankful for the gift of Your Son this Christmas. During this joyful season may we keep You at the center.

Sarah Sauder is the director of House to House Publications.

December 24

Holy Call

"I am the Lord's servant, and I am willing to do whatever He wants. May everything you said come true." *Luke 1:38 (Living Bible)*

Every time I think about Jesus coming as a baby I am awed at the plan of God for my salvation. I am stilled at the way the angel announced to Mary her part in this wonderful plan. There is a certain appreciation and honor for the mother of Jesus, who humbly and joyfully accepted this important call of God for her life.

Having gone through seven pregnancies myself, I cannot imagine riding a donkey those last days before delivery! And I have wondered where she stashed all those "swaddling clothes", in her overnight bag? She was devoted to God and to her husband.

I have often vacillated between peace and anxiety around the Christmas season. One year our budget did not allow us to buy many gifts. I asked the Lord for creativity. I enjoy sewing, so I began to look through my fabric pieces, and I began to work. The week before Christmas I turned out six flannel shirts for my husband and five sons, and two blouses for my two daughters. I had fun with this project; it was an answer to prayer. I experienced joy, while I prepared clothing for my household. I enjoyed listening to Christmas music. I remembered Mary's swaddling clothes, which she wrapped around Jesus for the first time. Mary's response to the angel in Luke 1:38 (Living Bible) says: "I am the Lord's servant, and I am willing to do whatever He wants. May everything you said come true." And then the angel disappeared.

Heavenly Father, give us faith to give an enthusiastic 'Yes' to You when You call on us, because we never know the full extent of our obedience to You. Be honored and glorified in our celebrations of Your first coming and help us to be ready for Your second coming. Even so come, Lord Jesus. Amen.

Naomi Sensenig and her husband, LaMarr, serve with D.O.V.E. Christian Fellowship Westgate Celebration in intercession and spiritual parenting.

December 25

The Wonder Of Jesus!

"This Jesus has God raised up..." *Acts 2:32*

This was Peter's proclamation on the Day of Pentecost. It is still Christianity's most incredible fact. Christ's resurrection guarantees for the believer some major blessings:

We have a living Savior. Death had done all it could do to Jesus. And when that was finished, new resurrected life from God brought His dead body back to life. From this experience every believer in Jesus can anticipate their own resurrection someday (1 Corinthians 15:20). A few years ago, I stepped out from the Garden Tomb near Jerusalem and a fellow traveler said, "I don't know exactly what I was expecting, but there was nothing to see." Praise God!

We have a loving Savior. That is what brought Jesus into the world in the first place (John 3:16). He not only lived, He loves. It is a love-filled life. Over and over, the New Testament says that Jesus was "moved with compassion." It is what makes Jesus want to shuffle up and be close to us and sometimes take us by the hand or whisper in our ear or even carry us. His was a love big enough to die for us.

We have a lifting Savior. The song writer says, "Burdens are lifted at Calvary." Sometimes Jesus lifts the burdens of a debilitating sickness. He promises to lift the burdens of confessed sins (1 John 1:9). In Acts 4, a crippled man was only asking for and expecting to receive pennies. But Peter said, "In the name of Jesus Christ of Nazareth, rise and walk."

We have a leading Savior. Due to the resurrection power that brought Jesus out of the grave, we have a leader who stands head and shoulders above every other manufacturer of religion.

We follow Christ because He lives, He loves, He lifts and He leads.

Dear God, continue to grip us with the wonder of our resurrected Savior.

James Myer is one of the team ministers at the White Oak Church of the Brethren, Manheim.

The Other Christmas Account

Revelation 12

For most of us Christmas is full of tradition that has attached itself to the true meaning of the Christmas story. For some, Christmas is just a time to gather with family, party, give and receive gifts, then let life return to normal as the New Year dawns and the debts of the holiday come due.

Every year, those of us who follow Jesus face the challenge of keeping Christmas Christ-centered. How do we do so in a world that bombards us with commercial clutter and popular pagan icons such as Santa Claus? The anchor for us must be the Christmas story itself, carefully considered until our hearts are full of gratitude to the One who gave Himself as a gift.

Some years back I realized that scripture records a *third account of Christmas seldom read as a Christmas story and often missed at Christmas.* In Revelation 12 we see the true drama of the incarnation of Christ as the "woman clothed with the sun" gives "birth to a son, a male child, who will rule all nations with an iron scepter." This also is the story of the birth of Jesus.

It casts the Christmas story as a drama of the heavens in which the full host of evil is pitted against the Son of God. It graphically tells me that it is also about spiritual warfare, about conquering, and being on the side of the One who wins the ultimate battle. It is truly an epic event.

This Christmas, and in the ones yet to come, read the gospel accounts of Christmas, but also read the Revelation 12 account. Make room for the full story of Christmas including the drama of battle and victory in heavenly realms. Let the victory inspire and challenge you for…"now has come the salvation and the power and the kingdom of our God…(Revelation 12:10)."

Thank You, Jesus, for coming as the true gift as well as the conquering victor.

Glen Yoder serves as the senior elder at Ephrata D.O.V.E. Christian Fellowship and serves with D.O.V.E. Mission International.

December 27

Permanently Altered

"And he touched my mouth with it and said: "Behold this has touched your lips; Your iniquity is taken away, and your sin purged." *Isaiah 6:7 (New King James Version)*

O pen mouth, insert foot" was a good motto for the Apostle Peter. He always had an opinion and always something to say about everything. He was prone to boasting and making promises he could not keep. Remember his declaration to Jesus ("unlike the rest I will not stumble!") only to find himself weeping just a few hours later, having stumbled as much or more than the rest.

In the book of Acts we see a different Peter, one who is thoughtful, considerate and caring of others' needs. In fact, there was such a change that people would bring the sick and oppressed out in the streets in the hopes that Peter's shadow might pass over and heal them. What can change a man so fully that his character and personality are permanently altered?

In the upper room at Pentecost, Peter's personal encounter with the Holy Spirit forever changed him. The experience is described in Acts as "tongues of fire"—the effect on Peter's life was dramatic and measurable by the works he did and the life he lived.

We each must have a life-changing, ongoing experience with the Holy Spirit if our speech and actions are to be conformed to the image of Christ. We must have more of Him if the world is to see less of us. Isaiah's experience must be ours; our mouth and heart need to be touched by His burning coal, our sin purged, and our life empowered to do His will.

Jesus, touch my mouth with the burning coal of Your Holy Spirit. Cleanse me and use me to glorify you this day. Here I am, send me. Amen.

Wayne Kaufman pastors Gates of Praise Ministries, Gates of Praise House Church Network and a board member of Harvest Net, The Regional Church of Lancaster County and the Lancaster House of Prayer.

December 28

Simple Truths Of Life

"Guide me in Your truth and teach me..." *Psalm 25:5*

A famous theologian was asked, "What is the most profound thought that you know?" This is what he said: "Jesus loves me, this I know, for the Bible tells me so." Often times the most profound truths about God are the most simple. I would like to share several very simple yet profound truths that have helped me to rest in God both during the good times and tough times of my life.

- **I know I am designed and cherished by God.** "Before I formed you in the womb I knew you, before you were born I set you apart; I appointed you as a prophet to the nations (Jeremiah 1:5)." I'm not just a social security number to God. I am his child. I am loved unconditionally.

- **I know God is committed to me no matter what.** "...if we are faithless, He will remain faithful, for He cannot disown Himself (2 Timothy 2:13)." If God is for me who can be against me? It is impossible for anything to separate me from the love of Christ (Romans 8). God will only allow to come into my life that which fits His eternal purpose.

- **I know I can rest in God's unchanging character.** "He is the Rock, His works are perfect, and all His ways are just. A faithful God who does no wrong, upright and just is He (Deuteronomy 32:4)." He is always good. His ways are always right and perfect. He is always faithful. He doesn't make mistakes.

Elisabeth Elliot said the way she worked through the tragic death of her husband, killed by the Inca Indians, was to focus on who she knew God was. She had to look inward instead of outward.

Lord, today I choose to rest in Your love for me and Your unchanging character. You will work everything together for good in my life. I choose to trust You.

Lester Zimmerman is the senior pastor of Petra Christian Fellowship in New Holland.

December 29

With All Your Heart, Mind, Soul And Strength

Pray!
for Lancaster County

"'For I know the plans I have for you,' declares the Lord, 'plans to prosper you and not to harm you, plans to give you hope and a future...You will seek Me and find Me when you seek Me with all your heart.'" *Jeremiah 29:11–13*

"Therefore, I urge you, brothers, in view of God's mercy, to offer your bodies as living sacrifices, holy and pleasing to God—this is your spiritual act of worship." *Romans 12:1*

As we anticipate the New Year, let's ask God to give us a deeper revelation that our lives are His and not our own. Let's decide to remove the clutter from our minds and all that robs our devotion to Him. Let's prioritize our schedules according to His Word and desires. Let's believe for ourselves and for our region that He truly has plans to prosper us and not harm us, and that He has a hope and a future for Lancaster County. Let's tell God we want to be a part of His plan, and ask Him to consider us as living sacrifices for His glory.

Lord God, we have been bought with your blood, and we belong to You. Take over our schedules, our priorities, our desires and aspirations, and conform them to Your word. Help us today, and every day, to commit ourselves to Your commandments and the leading of Your Spirit.

Today's devotional was edited from the 2003–2004 *Throne Of Grace Prayer Guide*, a weekly guide of Lancaster County prayer concerns gathered from regional intercessors and area prayer groups.

December 30

Is It Worth It?

"Even though you have ten thousand guardians in Christ, you do not have many fathers, for in Christ Jesus I became your father through the gospel. Therefore I urge you to imitate me."
1 Corinthians 4:15-16

Paul and Timothy: what a perfect pair. Paul understood the importance of a term used these days: *spiritual parenting.* We can learn from this example in the Bible. Some may think of parenting biological children. Others may think of taking a person "under their wing" and discipling them. What about raising up and sending out the next generation? Passing on the wisdom the Lord has given you to someone who is younger? The generation younger than you is crying out for spiritual parents. Whether you are 90, 40, 20, or 10, as a Christian you are qualified and there is someone you can be pouring your life into.

The Lord placed this concept of spiritual parenting on my heart around the age of 15. I have been spiritually parenting young people along the journey of life ever since. Seeing the change in the lives of those that I take time for is what makes the sacrifices worth it.

Yes, pouring your life into someone will take time. Being willing to listen and pray with individuals is a sacrifice. You may have to choose to spend time with your spiritual son/daughter instead of going shopping or with friends to a movie. But, I personally know it is worth it!

Is there someone in your life you could begin parenting spiritually? Look around your church, school, workplace, or in your local community and ask God to show you how to begin this exciting journey.

Oh God, I pray You would open my eyes to those You are placing in my life to begin parenting spiritually. Help me to realize I am qualified and that it is worth the sacrifice of my own desires and time to be pouring into this next generation. I love You, Lord!

Lesley Johnson is the publications assistant for House to House Publications and the D.C.F.I. youth team communication coordinator.

December 31

Connecting With God

"And a woman who had a hemorrhage for twelve years, and could not be healed by anyone, came up behind Him and touched the fringe of His cloak, and immediately her hemorrhage stopped." *Luke 8:43 (New American Standard Bible)*

This woman made a connection with God that changed her life! The Bible tells us very little about this woman, except of her need for God. For 12 years, she was not only in pain but was considered unclean and untouchable. But this day she made a connection with the Almighty! She believed that she *could* connect with Him if she pressed into Him. In spite of her long-standing problem, she refused to accept a permanent "victim" mentality. She didn't just say "this is just how things are going to be with me." She was desperate to connect with Him. She could have felt that making the connection was going to be too hard or not worth the trouble.

This woman had to ignore the discouragement of others who told her there was nothing anyone could do. She even ignored all the religious notions that tried to disqualify her, saying "You are unclean, you can't connect with Him." As we connect with God, we need to persevere and keep pressing through.

So let me get personal with you, OK?—How's your connection with God? In this age of cell phones, we learn to watch our "connection" to maintain clear communication. If we lose our connection, we need to move to a different place. Someone once told me that God's telephone number is JER-333 (Jeremiah 33:3) "Call to me and I will answer you and tell you great and mighty things which you do not know." That's a promise.

Father, I want to maintain an open connection with You throughout this day. I believe that You are interested in my situation and that You will supply my needs as I bring them to You in prayer.

Barry Wissler is senior pastor of Ephrata Community Church and leads HarvestNet, a resource ministry linking churches and ministries as partners in Harvest.

What is the
Regional Church of Lancaster County?
A cooperative network of Christian leaders dedicated to relational partnership in the growth of the Kingdom of God in Lancaster County.

Jesus prayed "...for those who will believe in me...that they all may be one, as you Father are in me and I in you—that the world may believe that you sent me (John 17:20-21)."

The Regional Church of Lancaster County believes that the most powerful witness of God's love is the relational biblical unity of His people. If the manifest unity of God's people can actually cause the world to believe that the Father sent the Son, then our disunity must be a major factor in the unbelief that is so prevalent (in spite of our best evangelistic efforts) in society today. This should move us to repentance and a renewal of our commitment to love one another in purposefully relational ways.

This unity cannot, however, be mandated by mission statement or manufactured through concerted effort. The unity of all believers—paid for at Calvary (Ephesians 2:14-16)—can only be imparted to us by the Father through the Holy Spirit. What we CAN do is position ourselves to walk in it, proclaim it as the Father's will, live it out as best we can through loving relationships within the body of Christ, and pray (as Jesus did) for the Father to manifest it in our midst.

The Regional Church of Lancaster County, as an organization, was formed to impart a vision for Christian unity and create a living, relational context for furthering that unity. But when we speak of the "regional church" as it pertains to all Christians in Lancaster County, we are speaking of the Body of Christ in our region as seen from a "heaven's eye view". When God looks upon His Church in Lancaster, He sees more than our separate camps, communions, confessions and councils. He sees a "regional church", made up of believers in every community, church and walk of life. He honors our individual "wineskins", but He sees us in a much larger and more fully relational context. He sees His children—His family.

What is the vision?

- To encourage and help equip the whole church to grow and mature in Christ (Ephesians 4:1–16)
- To strategically work together to revive and revitalize the church in our region (Revelation 2:2–7)
- To serve together as a loving and united Christian witness to every resident of our county (Luke 10:25–37)
- To work and pray for the ultimate spiritual and social transformation of Lancaster County (2 Chronicles 7:14; 1 Timothy 2:1–4)

What is the mission?

Our mission is to help present the life-changing power of the gospel of Jesus Christ to every soul within our region—praying, planning, walking and working together to see the Kingdom of God established in every Lancaster home, community and marketplace—including the media and the worlds of commerce, education and government. "Thy Kingdom come, Thy will be done on earth as it is in heaven."

What are the mission strategies?

- To blanket the region with continual prayer and worship
- To saturate the region with the gospel witness of Jesus Christ
- To mobilize initiatives to transform our communities with God's love
- To guard the well-being of the church through reconciliation, relationship, accountability, intercession and spiritual discernment

No matter where God has placed you—whether in ministry service or in the marketplace—you have been called to embrace the vision of biblical unity and Kingdom transformation for our region. Please check out our website for current regional initiatives and ways to participate in the vision of the Regional Church of Lancaster County. Together let's embrace the life-changing power of the gospel of Christ. Let's devote ourselves to building relationships and cooperating in ways that position us for the answer to Christ's prayer that all God's people be ONE.

www.theregionalchurch.com
The Regional Church of Lancaster County
343 North Charlotte Street, Lancaster, PA 17603
Phone (717) 293-9287

One